W9-BVA-095

THE IWAKURA MISSION IN AMERICA AND EUROPE

Iwakura Tomomi flanked by the four vice ambassadors, from left to right, Kido Takayoshi, Yamaguchi Masuka, Itō Hirobumi and Ōkubo Toshimichi. COURTESY ISHIGURO KEISHŌ

In Honour of

Professor W.G. (Bill) Beasley

doyen of Meiji Studies in Britain

over five decades

The Iwakura Mission in America and Europe

A NEW ASSESSMENT

EDITED BY
Ian Nish

JAPAN LIBRARY

MEIJI JAPAN SERIES: 6

THE IWAKURA MISSION IN AMERICA AND EUROPE
A NEW ASSESSMENT

First published 1998 by
JAPAN LIBRARY

Japan Library is an imprint of Curzon Press Ltd
15 The Quadrant, Richmond, Surrey TW9 1BP

British Library Cataloguing in Publication Data
A CIP catalogue entry for this book is available from the British Library

ISBN 1-873410-84-0

Typeset in Garamond 11 on 12pt by Bookman, Hayes, Middlesex
Printed and bound in England by Bookcraft, Midsomer Norton, Avon

CONTENTS

FOREWORD

A HIGH-POWERED delegation led by Prince Iwakura Tomomi visited the United States and Britain in 1872 and the major countries of Europe in the first half of 1873. The findings of the mission had vast effects on the subsequent development of Japan as a nation-state. It seemed fitting therefore to commemorate the 125th anniversary of that visit which fell in 1997. Since the triennial conference of the European Association for Japanese Studies was held in Budapest, Hungary, in August 1997, it seemed appropriate to devote a session of the History, International Relations and Politics section to a discussion of the mission. Fortunately, papers were offered covering the activities of the mission in many of the countries visited, while the audience included a number of experts in this field who had not themselves offered papers.

The intention behind the session was not so much to duplicate the work that has been done, or is in progress, on Japanese sources for the mission. Rather it was primarily to ask what materials existed in American and European sources which would throw light on the mission and on the Western reaction to it. Thus, it was not the wide-eyed accounts chronicled by the Japanese that we were interested in so much as the wide-eyed accounts of their hosts, whether they were politicians, journalists or the general populace. This was not always easy to do. Understandably, this was a difficult task because in the nature of things the Iwakura mission was of more importance to Japan than it was to the countries visited. Some of the papers show up the lacunae in the sources and the scarcity of information on this point.

After the success of the session, attention turned to whether the results of these various research papers could be published. It was first necessary to redress the balance of the papers. Because the original conference session did not deal comprehensively with the countries to which the delegation travelled, it has been necessary to ask contributors to modify their papers in some cases. In the case of other countries, it has been necessary to recruit new contributors to the project. We are particularly grateful to them for taking part at short notice.

Bearing in mind the stern reserve which publishers normally apply to conference papers, we are doubly grateful for the enthusiasm with which Mr Paul Norbury has taken up our proposal. As editor, I have to thank my co-chairman of the History session, Dr Bert Edström of the University of Stockholm. I must also thank the contributors who have helped greatly by sending in their papers so punctually. For the general organization of the conference we are grateful to the Budapest College of Foreign Trade and to the office-bearers of the European Association for Japanese Studies without whose help this academic project would not have been realized.

We hope that the resulting volume will offer some new insights on the mission and raise doubts about some of the myths that have arisen around it. We had no agreed agenda: the authors wrote independently and no attempt has been made to prescribe the form that their essays should take. We cannot claim to have said the final word but trust that this collection may make some contribution to the many research projects which are being pursued in Japan and around the world on this important world event, the Iwakura mission.

IAN NISH
March 1998

EDITOR'S NOTE

Japanese Names
Japanese names have generally been rendered with the surname or family name preceding the personal name in accordance with normal Japanese practice.
Bibliography
There is no overall bibliography in this volume; but selected bibliographies appropriate to individual countries are to be found at the end of chapters 1, 2 and 7.
Beio Kairan Jikki
There are occasional variations in the romanized spelling of the Kume diaries.

LIST OF CONTRIBUTORS

ANDREW COBBING is the author of *The Japanese Discovery of Victorian Britain* (Japan Library, 1998). He currently holds a Japan Foundation research fellowship, 1998-9.

BERT EDSTRÖM is Senior Research Fellow at the Center for Pacific Asia Studies, University of Stockholm, Sweden. He is the author of *Japan's Quest for a Role in the World* (Stockholm, 1988) and editor (most recently) of *The United Nations, Japan and Sweden: Achievements and Challenges* (Stockholm, 1998).

OLAVI FÄLT is a professor of history at the University of Oulu, Finland. He is the author of several books on Japan in Finnish and has published studies on *The interpretation of the crisis years of 1930-41 in the Japanese English language press* (1985) and *The clash of interests: the transformation of Japan in 1861-81 in the eyes of the local Anglo-Saxon press* (1990).

FUMIKO ITO is the Curator, Kume Museum of Art, Tokyo.

SHIGEKAZU KONDO is an Associate Professor at the Historiographical Institute, University of Tokyo. His specialization is the role of documentation in the political structure of medieval Japan.

SILVANA DE MAIO is Lecturer in the Instituto Italiano per l'Africa e l'Oriente (IsIAO), Rome, and PhD candidate in the Graduate School of Decision Science and Technology, Tokyo Institute of Technology.

IAN NISH is Emeritus Professor of International History, London School of Economics and Political Science. He is the author of 'The Iwakura Mission in Britain: The issue of Treaty Revision' in *Proceedings of the Japan Society*, no. 133 (1983), pp. 52-64.

IAN RUXTON is Professor of English, Kyushu Institute of Technology, Kitakyushu, and author of the *Diaries and Letters of Sir Ernest Mason*

Satow (Edwin Mellon Press, forthcoming).

RICHARD SIMS has taught Japanese history at the School of Oriental and African Studies, University of London, since 1966 and is the author (among other studies) of *French Policy towards the Bakufu and Meiji Japan, 1854-95*. (Japan Library, 1998).

ALISTAIR SWALE is a lecturer in politics at the department of East Asian Studies, University of Waikato, Hamilton, New Zealand.

SEIJI TAKATA belongs to the Research Staff, Kume Museum of Art, Tokyo.

ULRICH WATTENBERG was a member of the Deutsche Gesellschaft fur Natur-und Volkerkunde Ostasiens, Tokyo (vice-chairman, 1988-92). Since 1997 he has been attached to GMD-Research Center for Information Technology and has lectured at the East Asian Department, Freie Universitat, Berlin.

WILLY VANDE WALLE is Professor and Director of the Department of Oriental Studies at the Katholieke Universiteit Leuven, Belgium.

INTRODUCTION

Ian Nish

IN NOVEMBER 1871 the representatives of the powers in Tokyo were informed that Japan was about to arrange for a special embassy to set off for the United States and Europe. As they reported to their governments they did not find it entirely surprising because Japan had already sent abroad two missions: the Takenouchi mission to Europe in 1862 'the first official government mission to Britain' and then the 1865-6 mission. It was 1866 when Fukuzawa Yukichi published his experiences of journeying abroad in the first volume of *Seiyo jijo* (Conditions in the West). So there was much awareness of Western progress and a desire that Japan should share in it. In practice, however, the preoccupation of Japan's leaders with the restoration of the Emperor Meiji, the civil war and the move of the capital to Edo (Tokyo) left little scope for the new 'reformed' government to take up the problem of its relations with the West. Surrounded by many divisive domestic problems, it is amazing that they were able to contemplate sending a major delegation around the world as early as the autumn of 1871. But, in spite of battles over the constitution of the delegation and the timing of its visit, the leadership was sufficiently assured to let senior figures join the mission.[1]

What was special about this mission when the details leaked out was the eminence of the participants. Prince Iwakura Tomomi, the *udaijin*, who was chosen to head it was among the most important members of the government. He proposed to take with him four vice-ambassadors: Okubo Toshimichi; Kido Koin (Takayoshi), Ito Hirobumi and Yamaguchi Naoyoshi. The first two were among the leaders of the day. Ito was still young and Yamaguchi the representative of the Foreign Ministry who was a specialist in international law was on the periphery of politics. But Iwakura assembled a large delegation with lots of promising specialists such as Tanaka Fujimaro of the Education Ministry with his entourage of inspectors. Moreover, there were linguists. In each port of call there were *ryugakusei* who had enough of the language to act as their interpreters. All in all, there were some fifty emissaries and about sixty *ryugakusei*.[2]

This was a master-stroke which for boldness and originality would put most governments to shame. Half the senior leaders of the new administration were sent abroad for an indefinite period which could not in the nature of things be short. In the end it was extended much beyond the original intention to twenty months. But was it seen at the time in Japan as being important? The treaty port press did not cover it in great detail. Occasional mention filtered through from press associates in Europe but there was only restrained coverage. And that was not necessarily accurate.[3]

The motives underlying the mission differed over time and according to the thinking of the participant concerned. The essayists will describe their perception of them as seen in each of the countries visited. When the delegation left Edo, a foreign observer described its motivation as follows:

> . . . a personal Mission to the European [sic] Courts, designed to represent in a becoming and dignified manner the aspirations of the Empire towards a fitting and acknowledged place in the comity of nations.[4]

Alistair Swale has dealt at length with the question of Treaty Revision over which the commissioners' views changed frequently. (chapter 1) At the point of departure it was not intended as a negotiating mission because Iwakura thought the revision of treaties could be deferred until the embassy returned from abroad in one year's time (then the expected duration of the mission). Equally important was the collection of information on how modern industrialized societies worked. Not less important was the projection of Japan's image as a modern state: Japan must impress foreign governments with the quality of Japan's modernization in the hands of the new, young ministers and convince them of the solidity of its foundations.

The Iwakura commissioners reached San Francisco on 15 January 1872 and Washington on 29 February. Persuaded that they might succeed in negotiating a new treaty with Secretary of State Hamilton Fish, they discovered that they did not possess acceptable plenipotentiary powers to sign a treaty. Okubo and Ito, therefore, returned to

Japan in order to obtain the appropriate Letters of Credence. Meanwhile, the Japanese put forward the proposal that a conference of treaty powers to revise the Japan treaties should be held somewhere in Europe, an idea that was anathema to Secretary Fish. By the time Okubo and Ito rejoined the mission, the 'negotiation' had been relegated to second place behind the needs of information-gathering.

Dr Swale has no doubt that the reception of the delegation by the Americans, whether it was the administration, the businessmen or the press, was warm and enthusiastic. The cordiality of the American welcome to the mission was such that those in Europe had difficulty in matching it.

Because of the protracted nature of the commissioners' stay in the United States, the schedule for their visit to Britain was greatly held up, much to the inconvenience of the London government. Eventually, the mission reached Liverpool on 17 August. The British government had been intrigued by the proposal the Japanese had put forward in America for a European conference which would have had the effect of putting the world spotlight on Japan. That the US had declined the idea did not automatically mean that Britain would follow suit. Indeed, Britain had watched the progress of the Japanese delegates through the US with vigilance and suspicion because since the civil war the Americans had been pursuing their interests unilaterally, not least in Japan. For their part, foreign representatives in Japan did not favour talks being conducted outside Japan and felt that the minutiae of the treaty question could not be understood by those far removed from Japan. London accepted their recommendation.[5]

The second half of August was for a host of reasons the worst time to launch an official visit to London. Parliament was in recess until the end of October, and cabinet ministers were frequently out of the capital. Queen Victoria had already gone to Scotland for her summer holiday on 15 August and, since the death of her consort, had not generally been available for audiences in London till the end of the year. Iwakura and his advisers took the view that they would not raise policy matters until they had had their audience with the sovereign. This left plenty time for the wide-ranging visits of inspection on which the mission had set its sights. These are fully covered in Ian Ruxton's and Andrew Cobbing's papers (Chapter 2).

Between September and early November members of the delegation had either individually or in groups visited twenty British cities and travelled over 2000 miles. In discussion with Foreign Secretary Lord Granville, they made clear that their ultimate objective was for certain modifications of the treaties to bring them into line with the altered situation of Japan since the Meiji restoration. But they were more anxious to hear Britain's views than they were to put forward specific proposals of their own; and Britain was no more anxious to be specific. Granville raised the dual issues of religious toleration and the foreigners' right of travel throughout Japan and greater facilities for European ships to visit Japanese ports, matters which were to crop up in their discussions elsewhere in Europe. Asked whether extraterritoriality could be ended quickly, Granville replied that it could be done as soon as Japan had a proper code of laws administered by tribunals which Britain could trust.

Two weeks after the official audience with the Queen at Windsor Castle on 5 December, the delegation left Victoria station. They were accompanied as far as Dover by their two escorts, General Alexander and W.G. Aston of the British Far East consular service as interpreter.

If their timing in Britain was not ideal, their timing in France over the Christmas New Year period was a strain on both sides. As Richard Sims points out (Chapter 3), the focus of their policy discussions was on treaty revision and on religious freedom for Christians. In the press and among the public, there appears to have been a subdued reaction.

They paid two of their shorter visits to Belgium (from 18 February 1873) and to Holland (from 24 February). Their experiences in Belgium (Chapter 4), a small but highly industrialized state, were very relevant to Japan and are fully recounted in Professor Vande Walle's account which contains a great deal of intricate press comment. Here, more forcefully than elsewhere on the continent, the Ultramontane party had unleashed a furious campaign against the Japanese ambassadors. Iwakura in particular was targeted on the grounds that he had (allegedly) issued the order which had resulted in the massacre of 2000 Christians in Edo. The complaints were probably erroneous.

On the mission's activities in Holland the writings of Dr Miyanaga throw much light. With the Dutch the Japanese had a special relationship because of their settlement at Deshima throughout the *sakoku* period.[7] The visitors were therefore taken special care of by persons with Japan connections. They were escorted by Polsbroek, the Dutch minister in Japan (1869-70) who had stayed there for 12 or 13 years. They also associated much with van der Tak, a Dutch merchant who had served under the Nederlandsche Handel Maatschappij at Deshima from 1859 and with Bauduin who had been a doctor and teacher in Japan. The ambassadors were interested in the Dutch monarchy and were hospitably received by members of the royal family. They went to many factories and covered most of the important cities in this important small country: the Hague, Rotterdam, Leyden, Delft, Amsterdam. If there was one object which excited their special curiosity it was the canal system of Amsterdam, on which a special investigation was launched.

From 7 March the mission allocated three weeks to Germany (Chapter 5) which was in triumphant mood after the achievement of her unification, her victory over France and the occupation of Paris. They were later to return in transit on two occasions, thus covering not just the centre, but also the northern ports and the southern cities. It was a skilfully arranged itinerary and ensured a more thorough coverage of the country than elsewhere on the continent. This is fully covered by Dr Ulrich Wattenberg. Their stay included influential interviews with Chancellor Bismarck, whose thinking was to have a considerable impact on some of the Meiji leaders.

Already the remote thunder of disputes in the beleaguered ministry in Japan was reaching them. At the end of his German stay, Iwakura received a positive order to send someone back to Japan. After some anguished discussion, it was agreed that Okubo, one of the deputy leaders, should return and he left the mission, travelling independently to Frankfurt-am-Main and on to Marseille to join his ship.

The rest of the party travelled on to Russia (Chapter 6) which was allocated only two weeks. While Russia was a vast country which was a potential threat to Japan in its northern outreaches, her problems (notably the emancipation of serfs inaugurated in 1861) were not relevant to Japan. The tsarist monarchy was a matter of intense fascination to the Japanese; and the imperial family was particularly hospitable to the visitors. They formed strong links of cordiality which were slightly out of line with the political uncertainties between the two countries.

KIDO'S PARTY

Further pressure was brought to bear on the delegation as its stay in Russia drew to a close. The result was that Kido, the other deputy leader, was required to go back to Japan post-haste. He detached himself from the main party but continued with a progress through Europe which can only be described as leisurely. He passed to Posen, Berlin (Ostbahnhof) on his way to Vienna.

During his time in Austria-Hungary, a country not covered at our conference, Kido was able to attend the opening ceremony of the Great Vienna Exposition on 1 May. Kido was taken to the grounds in a carriage escorted by Heinrich von Siebold who worked for the Austrian legation. The exposition was opened by the Emperor Franz-Josef in the presence of the Empress, and the Prince of Wales, later to become King Edward VII, in an altogether glittering occasion.

It was the first international exhibition at which the new Japanese state had exhibited (though Japanese goods assembled by Sir Rutherford Alcock and goods of the Satsuma clan had earlier been shown at the London Exhibition in 1862). In March 1872 the Japanese government had on the urging of M. Calice, the Austrian minister in Edo, decided to take part in the Vienna exhibition. Bearing in mind the expenditure likely to be incurred by the Iwakura mission, there were financial constraints on the government's decision but it finally opted to participate. This difficult decision was – perhaps surprisingly – supported by the treaty port press: 'It seems to us that in view of the fundamental idea which lies at the root of the action of the Government, the idea namely of making Japan the first of the Eastern nations, if not of drawing her abreast of the Western nations, she has done well in spending so much care, time, trouble and money upon that collection of her products which is to represent her at Vienna'.[8] Kido was not easily pleased. He had much discussion with the officials involved in what was an expensive venture, considering that it coincided with the equally expensive Iwakura mission itself. He was particularly concerned about her performance in the Japanese Pavilion. His diary comment is shrewd and perceptive:

> The people of our country are not yet able to distinguish between the purpose of an exposition and of a museum; therefore, they have tried to display a mountain of tiny and delicate Oriental objects without regard for the expense. This seems to invite contempt for the dignity of our country on the part of others.[9]

Kido also debated with the local Japanese representative about the 60 to 70 Japanese artisans and technicians who had been brought over at state expense to study crafts in Austria but only for a mere 5-6 months – a quite inadequate period for the purpose in Kido's view. Kido, like the other delegates, was subject to some degree of lobbying and special pleading during his sojourn in Europe.

The Kido party departed for Italy (Venice, Florence, Rome, Naples, Rome, Milan, Como). They then moved on to Switzerland en route to a trip down the Rhine valley (Strassburg, Mainz, Bingen, Cologne). Finally, they visited Chaumont, Paris, Lyon and Marseille where they joined their steamer. Their final view of Europe was when they called at Naples before undertaking the 45-day journey home.

MAIN PARTY

When the Kido party split off, the rest of the mission, led by Iwakura, went by way of North Prussia (Stettin, Mecklenburg, Lubeck, Hamburg and Kiel) to Denmark. The delegation spent a week of springtime in the environs of Copenhagen from 18 April. This has been studied in most detail by Dr Nagashima Yoichi who has written much-respected studies in Japanese, Danish and English on bakumatsu and related subjects. J.F. Sick, the Danish king's emissary to Japan in 1870, was the escort of the Iwakura group. He had devised an itinerary which contained a meeting with King Christian IX at his palace.[10]

The delegates spent the week 23 to 29 April in Sweden. Dr Edström's paper (chapter 7) uses newspaper and other sources to illustrate the pains which business, diplomatic and education leaders took to welcome the delegation. One group, leaving via Malmö, travelled back by way of Copenhagen. The others departed from Sweden by the Lübeck boat to Hamburg, where both parties joined up again. They then set off via Hanover, Frankfurt and Munich en route to Italy.

Silvana de Maio in one of her two papers in this volume covers the elaborate journeyings of the party in Italy from 8 May to 1 June (chapter 8). Here more than elsewhere they were conscious of, and revelled in, the historic past of Rome, Pompeii and Venice. Here, too, they experienced the feeling that they were visiting a new country, united as recently as 1861, with problems some of which resembled their own.

In June they visited the Dual Monarchy of Austria-Hungary. Vienna was in festive mood. On four separate occasions (6, 9, 14 and 17 June), the commissioners visited the Great International Exhibition which Kido had already visited. This showed the primacy in Japanese thinking of being represented on international occasions and being recognized on terms of equality with the world trading nations. The Vienna Exposition was the first occasion on which Japan had of her own volition exhibited. The great cost which she was prepared to bear was a sign that the new government was ready and anxious to establish itself as a player on the world stage, something that the bakufu had never really been in a position to do. The Vienna Exposition attracted much enthusiasm and served as a model of many later exhibitions in Japan.

In line with their actions in other countries, the ambassadors also had audiences with the Emperor and members of his court and discussions with Foreign Minister Andrassy. They observed the military manoeuvres, covering infantry, cavalry and artillery. Their plans included a visit to Pest, the capital of Hungary; but their hosts said that it would be inconvenient and they called it off.

From 19 June to 15 July – an inordinately long time in view of the size of the country – they visited the cantons of Switzerland. Among the minor powers visited, Switzerland was allocated four weeks, plus the period that Kido had earlier spent. More than elsewhere , time was spent on sightseeing and enjoying the beauty of the country, its lakes and mountains. But the Iwakura mission conducted a circuit of visits – Zurich, Thun, Interlaken, Lucerne, Bern, Lausanne, Geneva. They met the 'president', discussed with experts the Swiss experience of municipal government and met businessmen. This Swiss sojourn is a subject not covered in our collection of essays. One can only hazard the guess that they were recuperating from their exertions and lingering while they awaited their homeward-bound boat.

Finally, they snatched a few days in the south of France. They visited Lyon on 15 July and set sail from Marseille on the 20th. This brings the length of their stay in France into line with that for the US, Britain and Germany.

Their original plan had been to visit Portugal without calling on Spain. But requests for extension of their stay in order to follow in the footsteps of their predecessors in 1862 were refused by Tokyo which insisted on the entire delegation returning to the crisis at home. They returned to Yokohama on 13 September and were soon swept up in the problems of the day. Leaders of the delegation ran into violent political arguments over a possible attack on Korea which was only prevented when the peace party won the day. The experience in the West had cut deep and was influential in altering the outlook of the government.

It seemed appropriate to append to the main country-by-country papers a Supplement consisting of four special studies that impinged on and thus further illuminated the main theme. First, Silvana de Maio (chapter 9) deals with one of the important results of the mission: the decision that Japan's modernization and enlightenment depended on the recruitment of promising foreign teachers. Just as we find Mori Arinori in the United States recruiting Professor David Murray from Rutgers for general education, so in Britain we find Okubo recruiting Henry Dyer from Glasgow University to teach science and engineering in Japan.

In chapter 10 Professor Fält deals with the foreign community in the leading treaty port of Yokohama. It was possible for the commissioners to see their activities in perspective after visiting the countries from which the foreigners came.

Finally, we include two essays dealing with Kume Kunitake, the chronicler of the mission, officially the secretary to Prince Iwakura. We owe to Kume and his reports, which took some years to compile, much of what we know of the activities and thinking of the Iwakura mission. Professor Kondo (chapter 11) charts the later years of Kume's career, first as bureaucrat, then after 1879 as professor of history attached to the Shushikan (the Historiographical Institute) later to be absorbed in the Imperial University of Tokyo. There he published a sceptical essay which questioned the origins of the Japanese state as set out in the *Kojiki* and was finally dismissed. Next, Miss Ito, the librarian of the Kume Museum of Art in Meguro, Tokyo, gave the conference a paper on the resources of the Museum opened in Kume's name, dealing with the works published and the research being pursued. She has now revised it with the expert help of Dr Takada (Appendix I). It is hoped that it will encourage further studies of the Iwakura mission through the perceptive eyes of Kume.

We have not written about the procedures adopted by this overmanned deputation. A division of labour operated. Okubo, Kido and Ito were from time to time detached from the main body, the body associated with Iwakura himself. They were the senior members who were concerned with the 'Grosse Politik ' of their assignment. Then there was the educational mission which followed a more specialist path. Thus we have reports of the mission from a variety of sources. At each level they impressed their hosts. Iwakura, a man of 47, acquitted himself well with political leaders of greater age and experience. He was already popular in his home-country and enhanced his reputation by this trip:

> . . . a man who has won much regard and good-will, as well for his enlightenment as his amiable disposition and excellent character[11]

Meanwhile, the younger members were scurrying about enquiring into various aspects of Western life. There was in fact no shortage of young students overseas who were ready to carry out investigations on behalf of their leaders. In their eyes the latter were heroes of the Restoration and often their fellow-clansmen. The diaries of those in Europe are full of meetings where the seniors received the feedback from their juniors' researches and the late night conversations which resulted in hotels around Europe.

A mission of this sort which spent one year and ten months in making its circuit of the world could not be totally consistent in its dealings. It wobbled (as we see from the essays) in its attitude to treaty revision. Instructions from Tokyo were imprecise and communication was not easy.[12] The *Japan Weekly Mail* writes of 'the ample and constant correspondence maintained between the leading members of the Mission now in Europe and the heads of administration in Yedo'.[13] Certainly both managed by letter and by telegram to keep in touch. Both Tokyo and the delegation in Europe benefited from the availability of the telegraph; but it was an expensive instrument and was sparingly used. But there were so many big issues afoot in Japan that the ambassadors abroad had a considerable amount of discretion. To a large extent, they were making policy on the hoof in an environment which they were only gradually getting to know.

The Iwakura mission was important for Japan's entry on to the world stage. And it was regarded as important by politicians of the Victorian age who received the ambassadors with the courtesy appropriate to a newcomer in world politics but who also had a shrewd eye on the trading possibilities which that newcomer might present in the future.

1

AMERICA

15 JANUARY-6 AUGUST 1872

The First Stage in the Quest for Enlightenment

Alistair Swale

BARELY THREE YEARS after the Restoration in 1868, a group of high-ranking government officials and diplomats, the Iwakura mission, visited the United States. The mission, led by one of the prominent aristocrats in the Restoration, Iwakura Tomomi, was arguably Japan's first attempt at top-level and full-scale diplomacy. The itinerary of the mission was to take in not only the major Western powers with a significant naval presence in the Pacific and Asia, America, England, France and Holland, but also quite an extraordinary array of other major and minor powers including Germany, Belgium, Denmark, Sweden, Switzerland, Italy, and, of course, Russia. In terms of the proportion of time spent in these countries respectively, America and Britain received by far the greater portion with just over six months in America and four months in Britain; practically half of the entire time spent abroad. Next was France with just over three months, Germany and Switzerland with approximately four weeks each, Italy with three and the remaining states, including Russia, being given itineraries lasting approximately two weeks at most. A notable exception among the minor powers was, of course, Switzerland where the mission relaxed at leisure as it had earlier done in Scotland.[1]

The official objective of the mission was three-fold: primarily to present a credible face to the Western powers following the Restoration and thereby secure recognition; secondly, to investigate the social and economic conditions of the various powers and clarify the basis of their 'enlightened civilization'; and, finally, to investigate the possibility of renegotiating the unequal trade-treaty provisions existent at the time. The first of these objectives was obviously of such importance as to warrant the touring *en masse* of some of the most significant figures in the Restoration, men who arguably could ill afford to turn their attention away from the domestic front. The second objective signified an attempt to address a further practical issue which probably doubled the urgency in undertaking such a mission in the first place; namely, the clarification of how domestic policy should proceed in detail.

The Restoration leadership realized that further domestic reforms would be necessary but they were not agreed on the proper course and, moreover, they also realized that, if the wrong policies were enacted, the consequences would be disastrous. Consequently, using the concrete examples provided by the Western powers as a set of references was an indispensable means to clarifying the way ahead. The third objective, treaty revision, was recognized as being 'difficult' to carry out to say the least. Yet there was hope that, given favourable circumstances, things might transpire in such a way as to enable them to achieve such a favourable outcome. Nevertheless, it was always intended to be a relatively secondary priority, the speedy resolution of which would be a bonus rather than an absolute necessity.

This chapter deals with the progress of the mission with regard to the above objectives while sojourning in the United States from 15 January to 6 August 1872. As an overall theme, the motif of 'Enlightenment', particularly in the sense of what it came to mean for the Japanese in their own terms, will be focused on. While the mission was fundamentally a diplomatic initiative it was, most significantly, also an exercise in initiation and discovery as well.[2] In the process of discussing the American sojourn under the aforementioned theme it is hoped that some distinction between the mythology surrounding early 'Enlightenment' thought in Japan and the vision of enlightenment and civilization that actually crystalized in the minds of contemporary Japanese commentators can be brought into clearer relief.[3]

The standard record of the mission's activities is Kume Kunitake's *Beio Kairan Jikki* which details the events and outcomes of the encounters with various Western powers on an almost day-to-day basis. This work is naturally indispensable. But another record of the visit, including transcripts of various speeches in English, was compiled by

Charles Lanman and entitled *The Japanese in America*. A significant aspect of these speeches, both those made by the Japanese and the Americans, was the regularity with which they referred to 'enlightenment' and 'progress'. Iwakura Tomomi stated boldly in Washington: 'We came for enlightenment, and gladly find it here.' Ito Hirobumi proudly detailed the internal development that had been carried out since the Restoration and how rapidly the country was advancing in emulation of its model, the United States.[4]

As for how the Americans themselves perceived the presence of such an unusual company, we find that the reception was almost without exception warm and enthusiastic. Commerce was the keynote for scores of businessmen attending various public functions and this should not be surprising given that America was entering into that period of extraordinary technological and entrepreneurial vigour which came to be termed the 'Gilded Age'. As far as one can tell, the local media were eager to report on the mission's activities and it was not merely for the sake of novelty. Lanman implies that there were some colourful, if inaccurate, depictions of the mission in some newspaper reports, yet he is also careful to note the more serious commentaries as well. In particular, we may note the following (perhaps overdone comment) from the *Daily Evening Bulletin* in San Francisco.

> Japan is today, all the circumstances of her previous condition considered, the most progressive nation on the globe. . . . Unlike the Chinese, its people readily make changes in clothing, food, manufactures, and modes of living, when they see improvement therein. They are, as a race, impulsive, highly intelligent, brave to rashness, cleanly in their habits, have a high sense of personal honor, and are universally polite, from the highest dignitary to the lowest in the land, and withal are kindly disposed towards foreigners, especially Americans.[5]

Apart from the positive reception amongst businessmen and in certain media reports, one finds that the political reception was, if anything, even more cordial. It is certainly the case that the mission did not succeed in securing treaty revision as was at one point anticipated, yet the Japanese received quite extraordinary support from Congress itself when it voted that the money received for the Shimonoseki Indemnity be returned to the Japanese mission in total. It is also significant that the Japanese were accorded such favour given that the American government, on both the domestic and the international fronts, had plenty of other matters to hold their attention. President Grant's administration was becoming embroiled in increasingly embarrassing corruption and scandals. In diplomatic affairs, there were several weighty problems to be resolved between America and Britain which included the Alabama claims and the issue of the future alignment of Canada. Consequently, the Japanese might well interpret the degree of cordiality and cooperation encountered from President Grant's administration as being indicative of quite extraordinary goodwill indeed.[6]

As Iwakura's words regarding the search for enlightenment, and indeed the undertaking of the mission itself, suggest, there was a desire amongst the Meiji leadership to gain some kind of meaningful appreciation of what was meant by 'enlightenment', both in the sense of what it meant to their Western counterparts and what it should mean for them. To be sure, there was an element of window-dressing in the exercise but it would not be adequate to dismiss the mission or Iwakura's expressions regarding 'enlightenment' purely in those terms. Though more keenly felt by some than others, there was a broad realization that institutional reforms were inadequate by themselves and that some kind of *internal reform* was required as well. It can be said that the word 'enlightenment' was used by the members of Iwakura mission as a kind of catch-phrase for the particular mind-set or consciousness that would be required in the 'modern age'.

Perhaps indicative of Japan's preparedness for pursuing better relations with the outside world and attaining a deeper understanding of 'enlightenment' was the fact that Japan's first formal representative in the United States was Mori Arinori, a young member of the Satsuma oligarchy who had spent several years in England and the United States, including a year-long stint in a reclusive religious sect. Mori was distinguished by his immense courage (he was one of the earliest proponents of the abolition of swords), mixed with extraordinary impetuosity.[7] Nevertheless, Mori warrants special mention in relation to the Iwakura mission in that he was one of the leading authorities on American affairs at the time, was consulted on matters relating to the kind of image that ought to be projected to the foreign powers and, more importantly, was himself an extremely significant figure within the broader movement of '*bunmei kaika*' that was initiated from this time onward. For these reasons he is incorporated quite significantly in the ensuing discussion.

CONCEPTIONS OF 'ENLIGHTENMENT'

It should be acknowledged that conceptions of enlightenment are extremely broad-ranging and hard to pin down. Enlightenment is a word that has come down to us suffering from ravages of extraordinary over-use and acquiring some less than helpful nuances along the way. Much like the word 'modern', which merely denotes that something is contemporary or of the current mode, it came to function, for the most part, as a *de facto* synonym for 'good' or 'excellent'. Enlightenment has connotations of moral or intellectual excellence, it indicates a higher or better form of consciousness, however it has evolved with a decreasing sense of what is practically excellent or what makes one form of consciousness 'higher' than another. Such terms tend to become largely 'dead' through overuse as terms of approbation and, to be sure, this was increasingly the way that the word 'enlightenment' had come to be used in the nineteenth century (the irony of such usage was not lost on some of the more acute Japanese observers of Western society and morals).[8]

However, in order to establish some kind of useful delineation of the core substance of what for the Japanese Enlightenment might mean, I propose first to consider the possibility of a less culture-specific definition which springs from a socio-historical view of what 'enlightenment' signifies within the broader context of social development toward industrialization. The kind of 'industrial society' constituting this context is intended as simply a social configuration that exhibits the organizational traits requisite for the establishment of large-scale human cohabitations: an advanced governmental and bureaucratic structure along with a productive sector that is characterized by the forms of division of labour that enable mass-manufacture of goods and their efficient distribution. Enlightenment on a cultural level is profoundly related to the promotion of rational enquiry, both in the sense of scientific investigation in the physical realm or rational fathoming of less tangible entities such as society, the market, or the mind. It is also tied in, as Gellner rather deftly illustrates, with the universalization of intellectual discourses which are made accessible through generic educational and literary institutions. Enlightenment discourse, therefore, relates to the aforementioned mode of enquiry which occurs as part of an intellectual reorientation that is a *sine qua non* in the establishment of an industrial society.[9]

In the West, that which is referred to as 'the Enlightenment' was a very particular incarnation of rationality and it would pay to note some of the historical peculiarities that form the basis of Western conceptions of a proper mind-set for the modern world. Furthermore, we must make these peculiarities clear if we are to approach some more concrete and distinct notion of what came to be understood by Enlightenment by the Japanese during their stay in the United States.[10]

Perhaps the single most distinctive element in Enlightenment thinking in the West is Christianity. Not that there was one uniform conception thereof, nor even a uniform attitude in response to the demands that the various traditions made on their adherents. There were, of course, those who made opposition to the Church a point of priority outstripping other concerns. Certain ideologues of the French Revolution furnish us with several examples and one also finds examples of atheistic intellectualism among the English-speakers as well (Hume being perhaps the most obvious example). In contrast to these, however, there were also those who, far from seeing Christianity being inimical to Enlightenment, determined it was an integral part of it. We can trace this more conservative lineage from Locke through to Burke. Either way, the Christian doctrines conditioned the emergent conceptions of Enlightenment profoundly. In an ironic sense, the appeals for liberty (and sometimes equality as well) drew very directly on the history of religious enthusiasm from the preceding two-and-a-half centuries.[11] Moreover, it is tempting to draw parallels between state of nature theories and the biblical notions of the Garden of Eden and the Fall. It was precisely the presence of these Christian traditions which made the Pandora's box of rational enquiry so iconoclastic, often engendering bitter disputes in the West.

A second major distinguishing factor in Western Enlightenment is arguably the experience of relatively intense international contact, with concomitant intense interaction and competition. As the interconnections between the royal families of Europe amply indicate, the nations of Europe had been in each other's orbit over many successive generations. The intensity of interaction ensured that social developments, and indeed intellectual developments, would proceed with extraordinary rapidity. A military advantage gained today could well be lost tomorrow; the heresy of today could become the dogma of tomorrow. Under these conditions only the most hybrid and convincing forms of intellectual discourse would survive. Perhaps it is primarily to this factor that we can attribute the rise of universalized discourses that brook no plea based on particular interest or superstition, but rather demand an answer that holds water within a unitary cultural sphere. When we consider that this 'unitary' sphere was necessarily unitary only within the bounds of the known world and therefore somewhat relative, we may then perceive the peculiarities of rationalism and speculative philosophy in the Western context with greater clarity. Through rational measurement and speculation, universal measures and ideals were established. This is not to say, however, that all the results of this intellectual activity were necessarily universal in an absolute sense. The scientific and materially quantitative activities had a transparency that was perhaps more or less beyond dispute, yet there remained areas of speculative philosophy which, at least in some cases, won out not because they were necessarily verifiable or quantifiable, but simply because they made sense to European sentiment and experience.[12]

THE HISTORICAL CONTEXT OF JAPANESE ENLIGHTENMENT

The above peculiarities have particular significance as we consider the initiation towards Enlightenment that followed the Meiji Restoration. We must note that Christianity was for the new government, philosophically speaking at least, a non-issue. The revoking of the ban on Christianity in 1873 signified the pragmatic recognition of the necessity of not provoking the Western powers needlessly. Kume's record of the mission suggests that rather than being overawed by Christianity they were somewhat relieved. They did not underestimate its function in Western societies in general, but they were also aware of the potential incompatibilities between the Christian doctrines and the march of progress, and knew that it was by and large so alien in sentiment to the Japanese as to pose in all likelihood a minimal social threat.[13]

As for the language of internationalism and universalism, this was indeed to pose a greater difficulty. Japan's isolation and almost negligible experience of intercourse with any foreign country in recent times, let alone the extremely foreboding industrialized Western powers, was a great hurdle by any estimation. As a result, the Japanese found themselves having to dance to a new tune and it was one they were scarcely familiar with. For the mission, the language of Enlightenment and Progress was evidently a necessary part of the liturgy that they were required to follow in order to join the top rank of nations; but, as suggested earlier, the members themselves knew that it would not be enough simply to make the right noises but to actually establish an understanding of what these fetish-concepts really signified, and, more importantly, what they should mean for the Japanese people.

Apart from the aforementioned rather general observations, there are two more specific conventional associations with Japanese enlightenment that arguably require rejection if one is to have perhaps a more accurate appreciation of the intellectual direction such a discourse took in the Japanese context. The first is the tendency to make associations with the ideas and intellectual figures of the late eighteenth century. Certainly, the classical figures of the Enlightenment, regardless of whether we are speaking of France, Germany or Scotland, are of such significance that their ongoing influence into the nineteenth century cannot be ignored. Nevertheless, there are significantly new aspects to 'enlightenment thinking' in the nineteenth century which should give us reason to be cautious of treating it as essentially made of the same stuff.[14] To put it simply, 'enlightenment' in the mid-to-late-nineteenth century, especially with regard to the English-speaking world, is conditioned by quite profoundly different intellectual and social circumstances. Evolutionary conceptions of the human condition had an unprecedented influence on the nature and scope of philosophical investigation into human morality and human society. Whether fully justified or not, it gave fresh impetus to the drive to establish a scientific understanding of human affairs, even holding out the prospect of a scientific morality. As such it gave rise to a drier, less literate form of enlightenment thinking. Accordingly, the harbingers of this new movement were not great men of letters. On the contrary, they were practically minded technologists: men such as Samuel Smiles and Herbert Spencer, engineers by trade before they became household names as leading lights in the grand march of human progress. Enlightenment from the mid-nineteenth century onwards was tinged with almost unnerving optimism with regard to the human capacity for perfection through the advance of industrial technology. It was an enlightenment of steam locomotives and gas-lit streets. As should become fully apparent to anyone that reads the text of *Beio Kairan Jikki*, the enlightenment that the Japanese subscribed to was very much of this nature.

A second caveat should be issued with regard to drawing premature associations with the more radical or liberal branches of the eighteenth-century tradition and its successors. Perhaps one of the most unhelpful preconceptions regarding the Japanese Enlightenment has been generated by the tendency to see figures such as Mori, Fukuzawa Yukichi or Kato Hiroyuki as liberal '*Philosophes*' at the centre of the Meiroku Society. These images simply do not apply in the case of Mori, nor indeed arguably the majority of those involved in the Meiroku Society as 'charter' members. Almost all of them, with the notable exception of Fukuzawa, were in the government's employ in some form or another as *Goyo Gakusha*. Mori was no exception, indeed he was quite particular that the Meiroku Society place a distance between itself and the political activism of the Liberal Democratic Movement.[15]

If there is some legitimate association to be made between the eighteenth-century European Enlightenment and the Japanese incarnation, it is in the sense of what Pocock has most aptly termed the 'conservative enlightenment', in which we would include figures such as Burke and even Gibbon. This branch of the Enlightenment arose precisely as a reasoned response to the Utopian 'enthusiasm' of the more radical branch, and, on balance, the Meiroku Society more closely approximates the conservative incarnation of the Enlightenment than the Radical one. Certainly, when the respective writings of Mori and Kume are examined it is difficult not to arrive at such a conclusion.

It is important to recognize that a conservative enlightenment orientation was still compatible with a progressive outlook which countenanced radical social reforms. Indeed, this intellectual configuration was very reflective of the essence of the Restoration. Most of the members of the Meiroku Society, for example, accepted the retrospective premise of the Restoration while actively promoting radical intellectual and institutional reforms.

TREATY RENEGOTIATION: THE FIRST LESSON IN ENLIGHTENMENT

If the Japanese were initially awed by the achievements of contemporary Western societies and perhaps apt to take their rhetoric at face value, one series of events was to give them cause to reconsider radically the practicalities of emulating Western civilization. To see how the mission began to become practically initiated in the reality of nineteenth-century 'Enlightenment', we can consider the sojourn in the United States, in particular the three-month period spent in Washington lured on by the hopes of a swift resolution to the unequal treaties issue.

Mori's experiences as the new minister to the United States were indicative of the potential for misadventure in Japan's attempts to forge international ties. Fortunately for Mori, he was blessed with exceptional goodwill from the likes of Joseph Henry, an internationally famous physicist at the time and first curator of the Smithsonion Institution. He also received the aid of even the likes of Secretary of State Hamilton Fish who displayed remarkably good-natured prompting in the etiquette of diplomacy from time to time. To complicate the situation, however, there were thorny issues that would require more than a capacity to socialize within Washington's upper circles successfully. The issue of the unequal treaties which existed between Japan and her new diplomatic colleagues was a particular case in point and it was success in this field which was, in a sense, to provide the Litmus test for Japan's success in learning the new game and winning the acceptance from often rather patronizing international neighbours.[16]

The mission arrived in the United States in January 1872 but did not reach Washington until the end of February. The visitors were to spend over three months there in pursuit of a settlement of the treaties issue, an endeavour that ultimately proved to be futile. Such an extended length of stay for the enormous retinue of the mission was an obvious burden for the American government. Indicative of the very great degree of goodwill on the part of the Americans was the return of the indemnity exacted from the Japanese after the armed confrontation at Shimonoseki. This came about at the suggestion of Joseph Henry who, through his regular contact with Mori, was well aware of the Japanese government's straitened financial circumstances and much inclined due to his positive estimation of the same to intervene on the mission's behalf.[17]

Much has been written about the attempted renegotiation of the treaty between America and Japan, and in certain respects it has tended to be quite negative. Certainly, there was an almost farcical aspect to the proceedings as the first interview between Iwakura, his Vice-ambassadors and Secretary of State Hamilton Fish indicates. Fish more or less grilled his Japanese counterpart as he sought clarification of the mission's aims with regard to the renegotiation of the American treaty which was due to expire that year on 1 July.[18] The official line of thinking prior to departure was merely to seek an extension of the *status quo*, effectively in order to give the Japanese more time to undertake the kind of administrative and legal reforms that would strengthen the Japanese position when the time came to renegotiate issues of extraterritoriality and tariff controls. The letter from the Emperor Meiji to President Grant, which constituted the mission's credentials, was clear in charging Iwakura and his colleagues with the task of discussing substantive issues regarding renegotiation, but it was more ambiguous about the scope of authority of the mission if it had to sign documents that would form the basis of formalized treaties. Fish picked up on this vagueness immediately and tossed the mission into a panic of sorts when he pressed Iwakura for more precise definitions of the mission's aims and its authority to carry them out.[19]

It should be remembered that this event was in recent diplomatic history extremely novel. Here, for the first time, an Oriental power had of its own volition undertaken to enter the system of international bargaining that had up to that point largely been confined to interrelations between a people that shared a profound commonality of culture; linguistically speaking, the Americans, for example, could conduct diplomatic relations with almost any of the European powers with relative ease. French, literally the *lingua Franca*, was now well established as an international medium of diplomacy. And if not French, German, English and Italian or Spanish were languages which posed no great inconvenience in terms of linguistic difficulty and a clerisy of polyphones were readily available to facilitate communication. Culturally speaking, despite the mutual antagonisms that were legend amongst the European powers, the legacy of the Roman Empire and indeed the early Church bequeathed an intellectual *Lingua Franca* that constituted at least a set of commonly recognizable parameters, even if there were areas within those parameters that they did not perceive in quite the same light. Into this system of cultural interaction entered the Japanese with a patent lack of secretarial personnel to engage their new protagonists and no Latinate-cum-Christian cosmology or terminology to fall back on. We should not, therefore, be too harsh on the Japanese ambassadors if their first steps into the international diplomatic arena were shaky indeed.

Furthermore, Fish's role in adding perplexity to the situation ought also to be recognized.[20] The brief of the mission was clear enough: seek a postponement of full renegotiation, present a credible face to the Western powers in their own countries and, while pursuing those ends, 'sound out' the various powers on the degree of their willingness to accommodate the Japanese for Treaty revisions. Fish immediately sought clarification of what the mission intended to be the ultimate force of any documents they would sign. This in itself was, of course, a legitimate question and, to be fair, the Japanese were vague about what degree of significance ought to be accorded any such documents. But Fish's questioning was framed in such a way as to suggest that what the Japanese really wanted was a formal draft treaty, a protocol which would be tantamount to a treaty itself once formally ratified by the respective governments. If this were the case, Fish argued, then the mission would need a whole new set of credentials to authorize the signing of such a document.

While there was nothing necessarily sinister about Fish's approach to the Mission, it was less than helpful. The simple fact was that the Japanese did not know, and could not know, what kind of document they would care to assign themselves to without actually sitting down and thrashing out all the practical issues and then assessing whether the *status quo* or some new arrangement would be more salutary. What the Japanese really needed was a working document that would form the basis of later formal renegotiation and could also be taken with them to Europe and compared with the kind of similar documents that would emerge with the remaining treaty-powers there. Ideally, if discussions had gone well, the document produced in discussions with the Americans might well have been used as a *de facto* draft of a final agreement. This, however, was a degree of flexibility which the ageing Fish, with his perhaps slightly ponderous mind-set, had little predeliction to accept. In hindsight, the mission became flustered and was brought into a level of discussion that it originally had no intention of engaging in.[21]

The move of the mission to over-reach itself was aided by the enthusiasm of Ito and Mori seeking an avenue for maximizing the potential for a full renegotiation. Buoyed up by the exceptional goodwill displayed, first of all towards Mori and later towards the Japanese contingent as a whole since their arrival, Ito and Mori seized on the moment and urged the mission to call for new credentials and initiate a full renegotiation in earnest.

Traditionally, a large degree of blame has been attributed to Ito and Mori for diverting the original plans of the mission and ultimately sending the nation's top representatives on a wild goose-chase. Yet it is important to note in their defence that, first and foremost, there was already a deadline for renegotiation looming on 1 July, and that the Americans, so far as can be ascertained, fully expected (or at least fully desired) such a renegotiation to proceed as planned. Mori, in particular, would have been aware of this and also conscious of the fact that in March of the following year, a fresh set of gubernatorial elections would be held and that this might well void the possibility of making good the arrangements agreed upon prior to that event.[22] It was, under the circumstances, therefore, not unreasonable to pursue the talks to any extent if a significantly beneficial result could be attained. The actual problem was simply how to document and maintain officially such an accord in the interim while pursuing discussions with the other treaty powers in Europe. It was, in fact, this point that proved to be fatal to the mission's attempts at renegotiation rather than necessarily a misjudgement of the moment. Nevertheless, the most significant difficulty that arose was arguably with regard to the mission's attempt at a delayed concert of diplomacy at the end of its tour in Europe. The fact was that Fish vehemently opposed the possibility of the signing of a treaty by anyone other than himself or anywhere other than either the United States or Japan. The Japanese requested that an American envoy be sent to a conference in Europe to facilitate their concerted renegotiation. This was something the Secretary of State would under no circumstances countenance. What the mission needed to do was seek an accommodation from the Secretary of State for such a move, if necessary, by engaging in active lobbying of other politicians and even the President himself in order to obtain it. In the end, however, a combination of a lack of diplomacy and a lack of experience conspired to render the negotiations futile.[23]

The above circumstances were also compounded by internal strife within the mission itself. There were some, notably Kido, who had always been sceptical of the advisability of charging ahead with seeking an expanded brief from the Emperor and entering into full negotiations. In a sense, he was right in that, as I have already indicated, it was simply too early to know what kind of result would ensue from any such negotiations. Moreover, there was indeed a certain unseemliness about the way in which Ito was hastily despatched back to Japan to obtain fresh credentials. Add to this the distrust of Ito and Mori, Mori in particular, concerning the depth of their knowledge of Western diplomacy and even the degree of their patriotism.

An event that sparked open condemnation of Mori by Iwakura was, ironically enough, not related to foreign policy but to domestic policy. While the mission was in the United States, the interim government had hit upon the scheme of sending an envoy to join the mission with the express object of raising loans to facilitate the buying off of the samurai with an offer of a lump-sum payment in place of regular stipends. Yoshida Kiyonari had been despatched for that purpose. The move was greeted with disquiet by the senior members of the mission, as a strict agreement had been made that while the mission was overseas, no significant domestic policy initiatives were to be undertaken. Mori, not content to see things take their own course, apart from vehemently denouncing the plan in closed session, ultimately took to the American English-language press to prosecute his argument. This, by any standard, was highly inappropriate behaviour and entrenched in the minds of Mori's adversaries their suspicions of his unreliability and lack of patriotism.

Perhaps the event that proved to be the final undermining of the confidence of Iwakura and the senior members of the mission was a visit from Maximilian von Brandt, the German envoy to Japan, who was travelling back to Germany through the United States at the time. He pointed out to Iwakura that the most-favoured nation clauses contained in all the extant treaties meant that any advantageous provisions gained by the United States through a new treaty would automatically be open to claim from the remaining powers. Although this did not necessarily mean that substantial negotiations could no longer proceed nor be embodied in the form of a signed record of the negotiations, the decision was made soon after somehow to withdraw the intent of renegotiation tactfully, and proceed to Europe as originally planned.[24]

So ended the diplomatic aspect of the mission's activities in the United States. They were in one sense a failure; a failure in that a full renegotiation did not come off as hoped. Although we have seen that this aim itself was not so much misconceived as relatively incidental, the fact remains that it was an immeasurably valuable lesson in the new game of international diplomacy and one that, if recriminations could be laid aside, would prove to strengthen the capacity of the mission to fulfil its brief in the remainder of its tour. To be sure, if there were a nation that Japan could afford to irritate and yet remain friendly with at the end, it was certainly the United States. There was, after all, a significant gap between the diplomatic culture of the Americans and the more cloistered and mutually suspicious nature of European diplomacy. Better to stumble in America than to fail utterly in Europe. As subsequent events proved, good relations between the US and Japan were not significantly jeopardized by the events of 1872. Indeed, the foundations for the enormously successful visit of President Grant and his wife to Japan in 1879 were laid at this time.[25] At any rate, perhaps the most significant lesson with regard to Enlightenment in relation to the field of diplomacy was that a rational system of international law and diplomatic protocol did not guarantee successful resolutions to conflicts of interest, it merely made peaceful resolutions possible. The fundamental realities of relative military and economic strength were never mitigated by this process and a short sharp lesson in this regard was arguably to provide a stimulus toward a much more conservative and pragmatic view of international relations which would confirm the current of intellectual inquiry all the more towards an essentially 'conservative', almost reactive, conception of enlightenment.[26]

THE EMERGING CONSERVATIVE CONCEPTION OF ENLIGHTENMENT

The above lesson in the pitfalls of diplomacy was to sharpen the wits of those particularly concerned with clarifying the cultural aspect of the mission's search for Enlightenment. As mentioned earlier, the mission was feted and entertained from its arrival in San Francisco right through the journey to Washington where they remained for several months. As platitudes regarding 'enlightenment' and 'progress' were being exchanged in the public speeches, a more serious attempt at clarification of these terms was being undertaken. The records of both Lanman and Kume indicate that the mission, which included various specialists in all branches of government and the arts, spent considerable time visiting strategically important institutions within the United States, including telegraph installations, military bases and training camps, factories, offices of government and, of course, ultimately the Houses of Congress as well.

Although Kume's record of the mission's activities was published some time after the mission's return to Japan, and was therefore subject to a degree of re-editing with the benefit of hindsight, it is possible to get a sense of the gradual clarification within the minds of the Japanese of the overwhelming significance of the commercial and productive capacity of American society. The significance of the effective application of technological innovations, which enabled extraordinary quantities of high quality goods to be produced and sold, was strongly impressed upon their minds.[27] A further aspect that became clear to the Japanese (though it was perhaps not so consciously articulated by the Americans themselves) was the breadth of planning and strategy required in all levels of society to make such a phenomenon possible. They were aware that what had happened in the United States, although comparatively recent, was nonetheless the outcome of an extremely long period of gestation covering many centuries. Kume interestingly referred to museums as the record of the nation's course of Enlightenment and he was himself keenly aware of the interrelation between the material and intellectual elements of America's social development. It is in this sense that the mission developed a more holistic conception of Enlightenment, perhaps an almost sociological conception of it – as indeed a people possessing a radically different cultural and historical background would be apt to conceive. There were many elements in the Western experience of Enlightenment and Progress which Westerners themselves did not consciously acknowledge, precisely because these were elements that had developed without conscious engineering. This partially unconscious social devlopment was nonetheless a luxury the Japanese could not afford.[28]

The growing awareness of the interchange between the material and intellectual aspects of social progress was accompanied by a keen sense that it would be the latter that would prove to be most difficult to emulate. The Japanese could not and did not wish to take on board the spiritual edifice of Western Christianity and, at any rate, neither could they.[29] Thus, while answers were being found to immediate problems, somewhat more intractable difficulties with regard to the intellectual and spiritual background to 'Enlightenment' were also becoming apparent in the long term. This called for more concerted investigation.

A figure whose significance should not be underestimated in this regard was of course Mori Arinori, the young Chargé d'Affaires who later founded the Meiroku Society upon his return to Japan in 1874. Fortunately, unlike Mori's exploits in treaty negotiations, his endeavours in this realm were much happier.

CONSERVATIVE ENLIGHTENMENT AS SEEN IN MORI

Prior to the mission's arrival in the United States, Mori had already been working on compiling materials for both English and Japanese publications to promote mutual understanding. Mori recognized the cultural gulf and endeavoured to bridge it by all means. Indeed he became a kind of roving cultural ambassador in addition to his normal legation activities, making contacts in various culturally and politically important institutions and collating his observations for broader consumption. Mori's entree into the top flight of American society was smoother than perhaps might have been expected. He was recognized as an earnest and sincere person which endeared him to the Americans he met in spite of his tendency to speak with considerable bluntness. One of the happiest associations he formed early on was with Joseph Henry, the renowned physicist who had been exceptionally active in obtaining financial assistance for the mission. It was in relation to some marine surveys that were being undertaken by the Smithsonian Institution in the vicinity of Japan that contact was first made between the two but before long Henry came to be a close confidant of Mori, providing personal advice and even assistance with the recruitment of American staff for the Embassy.

Among those recruits was Charles Lanman who, apart from compiling a record of the mission's sojourn in the US, also played a pivotal role in aiding Mori in the compilation of works written in English regarding the social conditions of Japan and the United States. The titles of these works were *Life and Resources in America* (September, 1871), *Religious Freedom in Japan* (November, 1872), and *Education in Japan* (January, 1873). These English works are of great significance in terms of providing us with a view of Mori's thought in a relatively systematic form as it was applied to practical issues. They are also valuable in that they provide some of the first attempts at clarification of what enlightenment and progress might mean for the Japanese in the wake of the Restoration.

Mori's conception of Enlightenment was, nevertheless, problematic in some respects. It is customary to depict Mori as a Westernizer or liberal during this early phase while his later orientation is often characterized as being essentially statist. The real picture is somewhat more complex.

It was undoubtedly Mori's stand on the abolition of the carrying of samurai swords that contributed greatly to the image of Mori as a radical Westernizer or liberal reformer. However, an examination of the English works of his American period, as well as the works written during the existence of the Meirokusha, creates problems for such an interpretation. Throughout this period Mori does indeed reveal a position that endorses radical social reform and progress, yet there are elements within that position which cannot be comfortably placed within a conventional liberal viewpoint. Mori's thought contains a rather particularized notion of progress and it is this which lies at the heart of what is ultimately a very idiosyncratic conception of enlightenment.

As we saw in the case of the attempted treaty renegotiations, Mori had great confidence in the potential for the new government to promote Japanese foreign policy on the basis of rational principles and law. This was an orientation Mori had maintained since his first experience of the West prior to the Meiji Restoration and it became more firmly entrenched upon his second visit. In spite of the fact that the negotiations were not successful and Mori clashed with various members of the mission his faith in pursuing a rational and legal solution to Japan's social and political problems remained intact. Nevertheless, he was also capable of acts that seem to contradict the image of Westernizer and Enlightener quite profoundly. For example, in the case of the clash with Yoshida Kiyonari over the home government's attempts to raise loans to finance a 'one-off' settlement of the stipendiary claims of samurai, Mori, quite apart from the radical way in which he sought to promote his argument, actually maintained a position that was extremely conservative. To the surprise of many, he vehemently opposed the plan calling it 'an act of robbery'. Publicly, his opinions were disowned by the Japanese government yet we see what an extraordinarily conservative attitude to social restructuring he in fact had at the time. The stipend was, after all, at the heart of the feudal system and dismantling it was arguably an indispensable step towards the modernizing of Japan. To understand Mori's thinking on the matter we must consider his activities and thoughts more broadly.[30]

According to Mori's biographer, Kimura Kyo, Mori spent considerable time, in addition to that devoted to his ambassadorial duties, developing his knowledge of Western institutions and customs, as well as clarifying his opinions on what was required for the advancement of Japanese society. Mori greatly valued Japan's contact with the United States for the development of civilization in the sense of the establishment of educational and political reform. The following passage reveals a recognition of the significance that commerce between the two nations would have within the civilizing process:

> Ever since the Japanese began to throw aside the old restrictions, commerce has been steadily increasing, and the present disposition of the Government is to have the freest possible intercourse with all

> the world. It was the great ignorance which prevailed among the people of Japan, which prevented the development of commerce. The channel is now open, and all that is wanted is to have the people sail into it with great determination.
> *The aim is now to educate and elevate the people.* [my italics].[31]

Nevertheless, it can be said that the central focus of Mori's civilizing crusade lay with the issue of education.

> No civilization, or enlightened state of human society can be attained, so long as we remain beneath our proper degree of manhood. It has justly been illustrated by the renowned Horace Mann, one of the most distinguished American characters and a most eminent writer on education, in the following expression: 'As an apple is not in any proper sense an apple until it is ripe, so a human being is not in any proper sense a human being until he is educated.' Another sagacious and emphatic word by the same great personage may not less appropriately be quoted: 'Education,' says he, 'is our only political safety; outside of this ark is deluge.'[32]

Indeed, the success of the reforms, whether it be in commerce, politics or even in familial relations lay, at a pragmatic level, in the realm of education. This is most clearly stated in his comments regarding the republican political system.

> Another fact that should not be forgotten has reference to the educational qualifications necessary to secure success in a Republican form of government. . . . A prosperous, happy, and permanent Republican government can only be secured when the people who live under it are virtuous and well educated.[33]

There were elements in Mori's conception of how a society could progress towards higher levels of civilization and enlightenment that suggest a political philosophy quite extraordinarily liberal and radical even by the standards of the day in Western societies. Nevertheless, there is also a conservative undercurrent that informs almost all of Mori's statements and constitutes a gradualist perspective quite at variance with the radical reformist view of social advance at the time. In its ideal form, Western Enlightenment discourse on naturally and inviolably-held rights logically required immediate conformity to the dictates of this reasoning and brooked no discussion regarding the qualifications of the citizenry to take up these rights, beyond the fact that they belonged to the same society. The area where Mori's departure from this logic is most prominently displayed is in his comments on the American political system.

> The Japanese people have been much fascinated by what they have

> seen of the American government and institutions, and it is of the utmost importance that they should well consider the subject in all its bearings, before adopting any of its features into their own form of government. *The evils resulting from the misuse of freedom in America, are among the most difficult to correct or reform, and ought to be avoided* [my italics].[34]

For many liberal or radical proponents of democratic institutions, this reference to 'the evils that result from the misuse of freedom' would seem to be tantamount to reactionary conservativism. Moreover, this ambivalence with regard to the liberation of the citizenry would certainly seem to fly in the face of the sort of French Enlightenment thinking typified by, for example, Rousseau. Yet Mori is openly critical of the expansion of the vote in the American political system.

> It has been so profitable with designing and selfish men to increase the number of voters, that they have secured the passage of laws which allow all men to vote, in view of the single idea of personal freedom. This is undoubtedly all wrong, and the evil effects of this state of things are being manifested every day.[35]

He does not specify what these evil effects are but the assertion that the extension of the franchise has been the result of the machinations of 'designing and selfish men' is an important qualification of his radically progressive image.

The key to resolving the apparent contradiction above is to realize the fact that Mori was indeed a reformer with radical and, in most respects, liberal objectives; yet he is also an advocate of a carefully thought out gradualist programme of reform. This position is spelled out clearly in his essay, 'Religious Freedom in Japan'. In criticism of what we can assume was the Confucian school of political thought he states:

> To those who have been brought up in the strange school of that political economy which advocates the superior excellence of ignorance over knowledge for all the governed, . . . such doctrines as the rights of man or the liberty of conscience may appear as something strange and dreadful.

He follows with an extraordinary admission:

> *Even our government may not find itself in a position practically to adopt these views.* [The government] has wisely to overcome all the influences of prejudice and ignorance, which are still blindly hostile to the light of the new idea. [my italics][36]

Political reform, or any other reform for that matter, required the fulfilment of practical conditions so that any such move would be borne out by broad consent rather than by fiat. Mori's concern was for taking precautions against dangerous eventualities rather than assuming that, because it was in the power of the government to do something and seemed the most expedient policy, there was no need to worry further. This attitude of Mori's explains something of why he exhibited such surprisingly strong resistance in the Yoshida affair, although it is extraordinary how a person presenting such a conservative view could at the same time be so reckless.

Certainly, the above assertions regarding caution may seem strange for one as impetuous as Mori, yet he was adamant about the necessity for extreme caution when pursuing social and political reform. The theme of caution is indeed emphasized even more strongly later on in the same essay.

> In all matters we deal with, true precaution is important, nay, absolutely essential. The precaution that we exercise in accomplishing a difficult purpose is a part of the action, and is an assistance in reaching the result. The precaution that forbids any attempt to undertake the task is not precaution; it is rather neglect. . . .

Mori went on to spell out the practical requirements as follows:

> The best and most practical precautions for progress are as follows: The establishment of proper laws by which all the proper rights of man shall be recognized and protected from violence; and the organization of an educational system by which the whole condition of our people shall be so elevated that their moral strength will sufficiently protect their rights, even without the additional dry and unsatisfactory shield of the written law of the state.[37]

Here we see that he recognized the possibility of achieving long- term political changes only by cultivating an underlying cultural and social transformation. Moreover, we can detect an extraordinarily pragmatic perception of the limits of law (and by extension other rational systems) in a society not yet developed sufficiently to enable them to function. 'Enlightenment' came to be recognized for what it truly was: a form of discourse appropriate to a particular stage of human social development and not a disembodied set of fetish concepts and institutional totems.

CONSERVATIVE ENLIGHTENMENT AS SEEN IN KUME

When considering the significance of Mori's writing in relation to the record compiled by Kume Kunitake two aspects ought to be noted: the first is that Mori's observations were recorded more or less around the same time as the Mission was in the United States whereas Kume's were compiled quite some time after the events. The second is that Kume's work is the official perspective on what happened during those eventful months whereas Mori tended, perhaps more than was advisable, to pursue purely his own concerns independently. What makes these records interesting despite this political and chronological 'distance' is the extraordinary degree of similarity in outlook that emerges in both cases. Indeed, it suggests the possibility that a consistent view of an Enlightenment of a particularly Japanese conception was being established independently in quite separate quarters.

There are several key areas that display obvious similarity. Not all of them are necessarily purely Japanese in origin (indeed that would be a rather unexpected outcome). Nevertheless, they signify the clarification of what enlightenment ought to mean for the Japanese quite apart from the standard Western interpretation by placing more emphasis on key aspects of the orthodoxy and venturing into areas that indicated a significant departure from their 'mentors' only occasionally.

As with Mori it is commerce that emerges as an extraordinarily impressive aspect of American society in *Beio Kairan Jikki*. For a ruling class accustomed to regarding commercial activities as decadent, industrial institutions were certainly novel and in the passages in the *Jikki* which enthuse about the broad social significance of commerce, there is an element of genuine wonderment combined with an atmosphere of religious conversion expressed.

> The commodities which together make up the nation's wealth are scattered throughout the world; they have value when they have been collected. By then thoroughly distributing what others have gathered, middlemen further increase the value of these commodities.[38]

Their Western hosts, to be sure, never left their Japanese guests in any doubt as to how significant they themselves regarded commercial enterprises.

> Even when we had audiences with emperors, kings, and queens, when we were entertained by foreign ministers, these two words [commerce and industry] always appeared in their speeches. As we travelled, commercial and industrial companies in every city vied with each other to welcome us. . . .Each time a speech was made to the crowds, when there was talk of friendly relations with our country and flourishing trade, all threw up their hats and stamped their feet.[39]

Nevertheless, Kume, possibly given the benefit of hindsight once he had returned to Japan, was able to perceive the significance of the organizational implications of commercial activity in a way that was perhaps less typical of Western participants themselves. The following quote suggests an idealized view of entrepreneurial activity which nonetheless reveals an appreciation of what ultimately mattered in commercial success; constant planning and review:

> When the Westerner engages in a business venture, as he constructs his plans he concentrates intensely on his aims. His detailed consideration of every matter is the complete opposite of the Japanese tendency. . . . Based on strict accounting of profit and business volume, factory buildings and machinery are steadily increased, improved, and perfected.[40]

As a further point of intersection with Mori's writings the *Jikki* stresses the significance of character and education as having a primacy ahead of the material and institutional trappings of civilization:

> If the will of the people is not strong, they cannot extend their power over great distances. The waxing and waning of nations is related to the will of their people. *Skill and wealth are secondary considerations.* [my italics][41]

Furthermore, in a vein extremely reminiscent of Mori's later educational concerns Kume notes the significance of technical and commercial education as being an important adjunct to successful industrialization. The existence of commercial schools and other specialist educational institutions were aspects of the American educational system that greatly impressed.[42]

However, beyond the material that dealt with the institutional and educational background to 'enlightenment', there was also an extremely cautious political outlook that revealed itself when it came to the issue of how social progress is generated.

> When one goes through a museum, the order of a country's enlightenment reveals itself spontaneously to the eye. If one studies the basic reasons when a country flourishes, one learns that it is not a sudden thing. There is always an order. Those who learn first transmit their knowledge to those who learn later. Those who open their eyes first awaken those who awaken later. By degrees there are advances. We give this phenomenon a name and call it progress. By progress we do not mean merely throwing away the old and planning the new. . . . As one sees the order of progress, one feels obliged to work hard thereafter. Ideas for learning spring up, and one cannot control them. Thus books are collected and schools built for the purpose of acquainting people with the practical arts.[43]

In the above we see a brief but fairly comprehensive outline of what the experience of Western enlightenment had taught the Japanese. In the following we see that it was to have very conservative implications with regard to the matter of settling domestic social policy:

> Since the Western theory of progress is being transmitted and planted in Japan, things are being carried out carelessly and without forethought. The old is abandoned and there is competition for what is new. These 'new things' cannot always be obtained. What should be preserved of the old is destroyed, and in the end there is no trace of it. Ah! how indeed can this be spoken of as daily advancement? How can it be called progress?[44]

Indeed, according to this perception a thorough-going conception of political gradualism was to become established which would cause the Meiji leadership to rethink the necessity of wholesale 'Westernization'.[45] This reticence was most pronounced with regard to the applicability of Western political models. The reason for departing from the Western model in political matters was based on cultural, if not racial, differences.[46] Yet there were also specifically practical reservations regarding Western political institutions which the Japanese came to be increasingly aware of. The American republican model in fact came under quite barbed criticism. Kume notes in his discussion of the American Congress that there was indeed already a body of critical opinion emanating from the other side of the Atlantic which viewed American political arrangements in less than flattering terms.

> The people of the constitutional monarchies of Europe have viewed the American people's recent war while they themselves are at peace with some derision and regard themselves as fortunate not to be the citizens of a republic. They regard that nothing perfect can be created through man-made laws. If power is extended to the people, proper government decreases. If too great a degree of freedom is apportioned, the rule of law becomes lax. To them, these positive and negative outcomes are perfectly natural.[47]

Nevertheless, Kume does not conceal his criticism behind European opinion. He goes on to discuss in detail the specific vices that the contemporary American system displayed. These criticisms revolve around the institutional antagonisms that exist between the various branches of government, particularly the executive and legislative branches.

> When President Johnson took over from President Lincoln after his assassination, he vetoed Bills of Congress repeatedly. Since Congress was the only organ of state whereby laws could be promulgated, legislation could only be passed after numerous amendments had been made. . . . The power of Congress in relation to such problems requires further consideration. In America entering the upper House

> as a Senator is a great honour and entails responsibilities regarding the election of public officials and giving final assent to legislation. On the surface this arrangement seems perfectly open and just. However, there is no guarantee that the elected representatives to the upper and lower Houses are the most gifted or intelligent. Perceptive and far- sighted opinions are not always recognized by ordinary people and when a matter comes up for serious and protracted debate the result is determined simply according to the agreement of the majority. As a consequence, there is the constant situation of having good policies rejected and bad policies adopted.[48]

The objection raised here is that the American constitutional arrangements seemed to interfere with the requirements of efficient government and, when the above is considered in relation to the direction taken in Japanese constitutional developments towards the end of the eighteen-eighties, there is something almost prophetic in its nature. Perhaps the most concise criticism of the American system was summed up in the statement that the '. . . political merit of a particular policy is not determined according to good argument but simply on the basis of considerations of how to get the right political document [that no-one in the House would oppose]'.[49]

CONCLUSION.

The events of the period covered by the Iwakura Mission's stay in the United States indicates an initially unclarified and sometimes contradictory perception of enlightenment and progress amongst the Japanese. Nevertheless, with remarkable speed the rules of the new game of international diplomacy along with some of the fundamental elements of Western economic and military supremacy were recognized and assimilated. Yet, as mentioned earlier, there were new, more subtle problems that emerged in the wake of finding answers to some of the initial questions about Western society; in particular, problems that related to how the Japanese, enjoying a fundamentally different intellectual tradition, could emulate the successes of their new international partners. In Mori Arinori we have an example of how this sort of problem was being tackled such that a more purely Japanese conception of enlightenment and progress was being articulated and applied to practical issues. What is more intriguing, however, is the degree to which the conception of enlightenment as expressed by Mori was very much in tune with the thinking expressed in Kume Kunitake's record of the mission's activities and summation of the mission's findings. I propose that in both of these cases, we see the emergence of a form of enlightenment much closer in type to the English experience as proposed by Pocock; a conception of enlightenment more eager to hedge in 'enthusiasms' of all kinds and pursue a pragmatic, gradualistic middle path. We have seen how this shift emerged in the American milieu during the early 1870s, and we can also see how it set arguably a precedent for later conservative developments in the 1880s and beyond.

SELECT BIBLIOGRAPHY

Kume Kunitake (Ed), *Tokumei Zenken Taishi Bei O Kairan Jikki*, Tokyo, 1878. Reproduced with a commentary by Tanaka Akira through Iwanami Shoten, 1996.

Lanman, Charles, *The Japanese in America*, in *Mori Arinori Zenshuu*, Vol. II, Okubo Toshiaki et al (Eds), Senbunshoten, 1972.

Mayo, Marlene, 'A Catechism of Diplomacy: The Japanese and Hamilton Fish, 1872', in *The Journal of Asian Studies*, Vol. XXVI, No. 3, Association for Asian Studies, 1967.

Mayo, Marlene, 'Rationality in the Meiji Restoration: The Iwakura Mission' in *Modern Japanese Leadership: Tradition and Change*, B.S. Silberman & H.D. Harootunian (Eds), University of Arizona Press, 1966.

Mori Arinori, *Life and Resources in America* (September, 1871), in *Mori Arinori Zenshuu*, Okubo Toshiaki et al (Eds), Senbunshoten, 1972, Vol. III.

Mori Arinori, *Religious Freedom in Japan* (November, 1872), in *Mori Arinori Zenshuu*, Okubo Toshiaki et al (Eds), Senbunshoten, 1972, Vol. I.

Mori Arinori, *Education in Japan* (January, 1873), in *Mori Arinori Zenshuu*, Okubo Toshiaki et al (Eds), Senbunshoten, 1972, Vol. III.

Nish, Ian, *Japanese Foreign Policy 1869-1942: Kasumigaseki to Miyakezaka*, Routledge & Kegan Paul, 1977.

Nishikawa Nagao & Matsumiya Hideharu, *Beio Kairan Jikki wo Yomu*, Horitsu Bunka Sha, 1995.

Oka Yoshitake, *Meiji Seiji Shiso Shi*, Iwanami, Shoten, 1992.

Pocock, J. G. A., 'Conservative Enlightenment and Democratic Revolutions: The American and French Cases in British Perspective', the text of the Government and Opposition/Leonard Schapiro Lecture delivered at the London School of Economics, 19 October 1988. Published in *Government and Opposition*, Weidenfeld and Nicolson, 1989, Vol. 24, No. 1.

Soviak, Eugene, 'On the Nature of Western Progress: The Journal of the Iwakura Embassy' in *Tradition and Modernization in Japanese Culture*, D.H. Shively (Ed.), Princeton, 1971.

Tanaka Akira, 'Iwakura Shisetsudan no Obei Ninshiki to Kindai Tennosei' in *Meiji Kokka no Kenryoku to Shiso*, Konishi Shiro & Toyama Shigeki (Eds), Yoshikawa Kobunkan, 1979.

2

BRITAIN

[1]

17 AUGUST-16 DECEMBER 1872

Early Meiji Travel Encounters

Andrew Cobbing

DURING the four months that the Iwakura mission spent in Britain towards the end of 1872, the ambassador and his entourage were engaged in a busy programme of official engagements. There were factories and museums to visit, banquets to attend and speeches to be made, culminating in an audience with Queen Victoria herself on 5 December. It was on such occasions that Iwakura and his retinue encountered their official hosts in the public eye, and where their visits were most often recorded by the Victorian press. As a result, it was the images that the 'distinguished guests' conveyed on these occasions that underpinned British impressions of the Iwakura mission.

The party reached Britain after spending more than six months travelling in the United States, and Victorian journalists were keen to recapture any lost initiative by stressing the potential their visit might have in promoting Anglo-Japanese relations. *The Times* announced that 'an Embassy from such a people at such a time would always demand the highest consideration; but the character of the personages who have been selected as Ambassadors greatly enhances their claim'. In the eyes of the press, it was difficult to underestimate the importance of their stay. 'Upon the relations we cultivate with men of this spirit, intelligence and power must depend, to an incalculable degree, the prospects of English enterprise in Japan, and even of Japanese civilization.'[1]

The experience of the Iwakura mission, however, extended beyond the exchanges recorded during these official engagements. There were other events and dialogues with people living there, both Victorians and Japanese, which did much to shape their impressions of Britain in 1872. The records left by travellers in the party reveal some of the concerns and distractions that characterized their stay, and which combined to influence their perceptions of Victorian society. Of the vice ambassadors alone, for example, Kido Takayoshi kept a diary, while the letters of Itō Hirobumi and Ōkubo Toshimichi have also been preserved. By far the greatest wealth of information, however, was recorded by Kume Kunitake, Iwakura's personal secretary, who travelled with the ambassador throughout his tour of Britain, for in addition to writing up the official account of the mission following his return to Japan, he also dictated his memoirs some sixty years later.

Between them, such records convey a sense of the struggles which these early Meiji officials experienced in their efforts to understand the changing world around them. On the one hand, they faced the responsibility of government at a time of far-reaching domestic reforms. At the same time, they were keenly aware that, in order to plan for the future of Meiji Japan, they needed some explanation for what they saw in Britain, a country itself in the midst of rapid social change.

THE IWAKURA MISSION ARRIVES IN LONDON

In August 1872, the Japanese ambassadors travelled across the Atlantic Ocean bound for Liverpool and the first leg of their European tour. During the voyage, they were able to take stock of their observations so far as they looked forward to their stay in London. Their objectives had already shifted in emphasis, now that a decision had been taken during their recent stay in Washington not to rush into any hasty revisions of the unequal treaties. Richard Brunton, the Scottish engineer who sometimes accompanied Itō Hirobumi during his travels in Britain later observed: 'Absolutely nothing was made public of their intercourse with the officers of the British Government, which under any circumstances could not have been of much importance; but their desires seemed to be wholly pointed to an examination and study of the industries of the country.'[2]

Although this was not the first stage in the Iwakura mission's tour of the West, the prosperity of Victorian Britain in the early 1870s still proved to be a revelation. During the voyage across the Atlantic, for example, Kido and Ōkubo had warned Kume Kunitake in jest not to express amazement at anything he saw in London or Paris, as he had already exhausted his supply of superlatives in New York, Philadelphia and Boston. To the despair of the vice ambassadors, Kume's resolve cracked on the day their ship arrived in Liverpool, for the grandeur of the North Western Hotel and the sheer volume of traffic at Lime Street Station seemed quite unlike anything they had yet seen on their travels.[3]

The Iwakura mission was visiting Britain in circumstances very different from those of the first *bakufu* missions to Europe in the early 1860s. These had been singularly insular in outlook, and official interest in the conditions they saw there had been largely confined to matters of military security and the management of the treaty ports. Western studies, however, were no longer a minority interest more often pursued by younger samurai of low rank. The vogue for Western ideas had rapidly become accepted among many levels of Japanese society, and even the sons of aristocrats and prominent statesmen were now making their way to study in Europe. Both Sanjō Kimiyasu, the son of Sanjō Sanetomi, and Kido's adopted son, Kido Shōjirō, were already in Britain, while members of the Hachisuka, Nabeshima and Iwakura families were also on their way to pursue studies at Oxford.

This sea change in attitudes had been clearly spelt out in the Charter Oath in 1868, at the onset of the Meiji period, which declared that 'knowledge shall be sought throughout the world'.[4] The theme had been further developed in the letter of credence which the Iwakura mission had recently presented to President Grant in Washington: 'It is our purpose to select from the various institutions prevailing among enlightened nations as are best suited to our present conditions, and adopt them, in gradual reforms and amendments of our customs.'[5] The shift in popular attitudes in favour of Western customs and fashions had been so precipitous, however, that opinion in Japanese government circles was sharply divided in the early 1870s. As a result, there were distinct radical and traditionalist factions to be found within the Iwakura mission itself.

The mission was travelling around America and Europe at a time when enthusiasm for the West was reaching unparalleled heights. Statesmen like Mori Arinori and Itō Hirobumi were seriously considering replacing Japanese with English or trying to persuade the Emperor to convert to Christianity. This was an understandable trait to be found among younger politicians, particularly among those who had studied abroad and partly owed their rise in public life to their specialist knowledge in Western affairs. At the same time, there were other members of the Iwakura mission who found it more difficult to contemplate surrendering traditional customs in Japan.

Kido Takayoshi, for example, was scathing in his criticism of overseas students such as Mori, whose infatuation with Western customs he thought reflected their ignorance of Japanese tradition. During the mission's stay in Washington, he was appalled to hear that 'there are some like Mori, now a minister of our country no less, who openly scorn the customs of their own land indiscriminately in the presence of foreigners'.[6] Although he was just thirty-three years old at the time, Kume Kunitake's Confucian education had also instilled a tendency to be relatively sceptical of Western fashion. In addition, Ōkubo Toshimichi, himself only in his early forties, told Iwakura, Kido and Kume during their stay in Britain that 'those with older learning like ourselves' had a duty to educate the radical s, and stressed: 'It is up to those with older heads to provide stability, by striving to accomplish what must be done without chasing after novelties.'[7]

Debate among these factions within the Iwakura mission evolved during their travels, shaped not only by their observations but also by chance encounters and news of developments in Japan. The correspondence of Ōkubo and Itō shows that, throughout their travels, the vice ambassadors' thoughts were constantly bound up with affairs at home. The mission's arrival in Britain, for example, coincided with important events in Japan such as the proclamation of the Education Ordinance, and the Yokohama-Tokyo railway, the country's first regular railway service, was opened during their tour of the industrial north.

Against this background of ongoing changes, arguments for and against future reforms constantly framed the ambassadors' enquiries during their observations in the West. Even the most trivial incident could provoke serious debate between radical and traditionalist factions within the party. On their arrival in London, for example, it was discovered that the mirror in Kido's room at the Buckingham Palace Hotel was broken. For want of any evidence, however, the porter suspected of causing the damage escaped any bills for compensation, and Kume recalled how 'the devotees of Western ideas among us extolled this as evidence of British justice, but we thought it hardly worth such glowing admiration'.[8]

Their task was further complicated by the distractions and contributions of the Japanese student community in London. These were a feature of overseas travel which the first *bakufu* missions had never encountered because, until the mid-1860s, there were hardly any Japanese people to be found at all in Europe or America. During the mission's first weeks in London, however, Iwakura and the vice ambassadors were often besieged by a continuous stream of Japanese students calling to pay their respects at the Buckingham Palace Hotel.

In fact, the question of what to do with these students in Britain was a matter of some concern for the Iwakura mission. Most of them had been sent abroad by their respective domains which had since been abolished in 1871, leaving the Meiji government responsible for funding their research. In a report prepared in December 1871, one member of Iwakura's party, Hatakeyama Yoshinari, had pointed out that there were already over 80 Japanese students in London, but that many of them appeared to be wasting their energies on fruitless research.[9] This theme was taken up by Itō Hirobumi during the mission's stay in Britain when he sent his own recommendations to Tokyo, and these formed the basis of a new set of regulations for overseas students in 1873.[10]

To some extent, communications between members of the Iwakura mission and the Japanese students in London reflected regional *han* loyalties. Kume Kunitake, for example, was in contact with Nabeshima Nabehiro, the former daimyō of his native Hizen who had just arrived and settled into a house in Bayswater.[11] Later in the Iwakura mission's travels the following year, there was to be quite a sizeable reunion of men from Satsuma in Paris, and also a gathering of men from Hizen in Vienna.

One student from Hizen whom Kume came across in London was Tanba Yūkurō. At the time, there were growing calls among some overseas students to reform the Japanese language and replace Chinese characters with Roman letters, but Tanba had acquired a reputation for his outspoken campaign to replace them with indigenous *kana* characters instead. His principal critic was Mori Arinori, the most prominent advocate of Westernising the Japanese language, and the two later met in Washington to debate the strength of their cases. Mori even went as far as arguing that English should replace Japanese altogether, inspiring Baba Tatsui, another student in London, to defend his native language by writing the first systematic Japanese grammar book, which was published in 1873.[12]

Perhaps the one student in London who was to have a significant impact on the Iwakura mission's travels was Minami Teisuke from Chōshū, a nephew of the late Takasugi Shinsaku. He had made the journey across the Atlantic to join the party in the United States, and travelled with them on the voyage to Britain. There he was often seen in the company of his Chōshū compatriot Kido Takayoshi; he was with the vice ambassador when he toured the streets of London by carriage, and he acted as a guide on his visit to London Zoo.[13]

During the voyage from America, Minami had also been seen locked in talks with two American entrepreneurs, the Bowles brothers. All became clear after the mission arrived in London when the brothers opened a branch of the American Joint National Bank at an imposing office in Charing Cross. Minami was employed as a director, taking home a monthly salary of £200 for his efforts in quickly persuading many of the Japanese in London to deposit their money there. He apparently cut an impressive figure when he invited potential customers to his large house, served them wine and held forth on the future of Japanese business overseas.[14]

Minami once entertained Kido to lunch at his office, and the vice ambassador noted that 'many of the Japanese students and members of the mission have deposited their money in this bank. I am one of them'. Minami even tried to persuade Tanaka Mitsuaki, Fourth Secretary of the Treasury Department, to deposit government funds with his bank. Tanaka daily handled much of the mission's funds, but rejected the idea after consulting with his superior officer, Fukuchi Gen'ichirō.[14]

Not only were Minami's business activities a conspicuous feature of the Iwakura mission's stay in London, but his private life was also the subject of some debate. Partly through the influence of one Liza Pitman from Surrey, he had become convinced that the infusion of some Anglo-Saxon blood would help the development of Japan. International marriages, however, had not yet been legalized by the Meiji authorities. 'When I made my case to the ambassadors', Minami later recalled, 'Itō told me that the time had not yet come for such a plan. Ōkubo said it would be permissible as long as I spent several more years in Britain.' He advised, however that 'it might be dangerous for the two of us to proceed directly to Japan together'.[16]

Minami went ahead with his marriage on 20 September 1872, a week before Iwakura and his party embarked on their tour of the north. He was the first to register his match with the Ministry of Foreign Affairs when international marriages became legal in 1873, and later took Liza with him to Japan. Ten years later, their liaison ended in divorce because, according to Minami, 'she made no attempt to adapt to Japanese culture'.[17]

During their one-month stay in London in the summer of 1872, Iwakura and the vice ambassadors spent much of their time meeting Japanese students. While they were able to gather a wealth of information in conversation with them, their days at the Buckingham Palace Hotel gave them only limited scope to observe life in Britain for themselves. It was not until they embarked on a tour of the north that they were to have any extensive opportunities to establish direct contact with their Victorian hosts.

THE IWAKURA MISSION'S INLAND TOUR OF BRITAIN

Queen Victoria was at Balmoral when Iwakura and the vice ambassadors arrived in London, and they had to wait until her return south before they could receive a royal audience at Windsor Castle. This enforced delay allowed them to embark on an extensive tour of England and Scotland. There were nine in the party that left Euston Station for Liverpool on 27 August, including Iwakura, Kido, Ōkubo and Itō. The other vice ambassador, Yamaguchi Masuka, was unwell and travelled up the next day to join them together with Kume, his fellow countryman from Hizen.[18]

The party was accompanied by three British officials. Major-General George Alexander was there in his role as the mission's official host, together with W. G. Aston from the British legation in Tokyo who travelled with them as their interpreter. In addition, Sir Harry Parkes, the British minister in Japan, was also on home leave at the time and joined Iwakura's party for the tour. In effect, it was he who took control of arrangements for their journey through Lancashire, Scotland, the North East, Yorkshire and the West Midlands.

Now that the ambassadors had left the relative seclusion of their London hotel and packed their cases for the journey north, the influence of Parkes was to become a constant feature of their travels in Britain. One member of the retinue who remembered him well was Hayashi Tadasu, who was later to become the Japanese Ambassador to Britain. Hayashi thought of Parkes as a fair but impatient man, who constantly endeavoured to promote the development of Japanese trade and industry to Britain's advantage, so much so in fact that, 'in his dealings with the Japanese, he was often like a woman tormenting her son's new bride'. His sincerity was beyond question, however, and he never used his rank for personal advantage. 'He was thus maligned while in Japan', Hayashi recalled, 'but sorely missed following his subsequent transfer to Beijing'.[19]

In 1872, Hayashi was a promising young diplomat attached to the Iwakura mission, and he was surprised to find that Parkes cut an apparently insignificant figure during their stay in London, in spite of the considerable power he exercised in Japan. Throughout the ambassadors' negotiations with Lord Granville, the Foreign Secretary, Parkes had simply sat mute at one end of the table, speaking only when spoken to. According to Hayashi, Granville did not even seem fully aware of who Parkes actually was.[20]

Once out of London, however, the British minister had more opportunities to show his mettle as a man of action. Although he remained guarded in Iwakura's presence, Parkes assumed an air of authority whenever the ambassador was out of sight. During the long train journeys across the English countryside, he would lecture his Japanese guests on the significance of the institutions they were en route to inspect. On one occasion when they were travelling by road, he even took the reins of one carriage himself, and after they missed their train connection to Beeston Castle in Cheshire, he drove for two hours at headlong speed, reaching the village in time to find the station there decked out in flags with the entire population still on the platform. They were all in a state of shock following the Japanese ambassadors' failure to appear on their scheduled train only minutes before.[21]

During the course of their travels, the party formed a favourable impression of transport in Britain. In a letter home to Japan, Ōkubo wrote: 'What is particularly impressive is the emphasis on convenience achieved by endeavouring to build roads and bridges to even the remotest places, so that there is nowhere out of reach by road or rail.' He was also struck by the fact that, before the invention of steam power, a network of canals had been constructed to enable boats to travel inland.[22]

At the onset of their tour, Iwakura and his retinue spent ten days in Liverpool and Manchester, where they were kept busy with a gruelling schedule of observation tours and official receptions. Within a week, the relentless pace of their itinerary was already beginning to take its toll. As soon as they arrived in Manchester, for example, they were treated to a performance of Sheridan Knowles's *The Love Chase* at the Theatre Royal. 'I am sure it was with the best intentions that we were invited', Kume recalled, 'but after being dragged around a factory all day, and as we had only just arrived, washed and begun to relax at last, it was more than I could bear to be strapped up again in these tight-fitting Western clothes, and have to watch a performance that I could not understand at all.'[23]

Clearly, their suits looked as uncomfortable as they felt, as a British journalist noted how the ambassadors wore 'plain European clothes, which did not sit gracefully on them'.[24] Rather than endure the theatre, most members of the party finally admitted defeat and opted for a quiet evening at the Queens Hotel. 'Just two or three of those who could understand English decided to go', Kume confessed, 'and I stayed behind to write up my observations for the day'.[25]

An intensive schedule of factory visits was to be the dominant feature of the Iwakura mission's tour of urban Lancashire. On the train bound for Manchester, Parkes announced to Iwakura and the vice ambassadors that 'Lancashire is said to have more factories than anywhere else in the world'. He confidently told them that, 'as far as Japan's future traffic with the world and the promotion of new enterprise is concerned, this is the single most significant tour of inspection you are likely to have'.[26]

In the event, however, the ambassadors' experience of industry in the United States in previous months somewhat reduced the impact of the Lancashire factories. The mills they visited were apparently not so dissimilar to those they had seen in Philadelphia and Boston where there was also a vigorous new textiles industry. While the sense of novelty had begun to wear off, even a Confucian scholar like Kume was at last beginning to understand some of what he saw. A few weeks later, they were once again shown the Bessemer process in Sheffield, and he remembered: 'I had seen a similar process in Crewe the month before, but perhaps as I was gradually becoming accustomed to these factory tours, I was now able to understand the explanation quite clearly.'[27]

As the ambassadors continued their round of factory visits, they realized that much of Britain's industrial power seemed to be the result of quite recent developments. In a letter home to Japan, Ōkubo pointed out that the prodigious wealth of trade and industry he had seen in these cities had only come about within the last fifty years since the invention of steam power.[28] In the official chronicle of Iwakura's travels, Kume declared that 'the remarkable wealth and prosperity to be seen in Europe today dates to a large extent from 1800, and took a mere forty years to create'. He justified this observation by pointing out that 'this is evident from travelling to factories around the country (Britain) and seeing the records of their foundations. The expansion of one part of Glasgow in Scotland from a settlement of less than 8,000 to a large metropolis of 50,000 has occurred over the last 45 years alone. Talking to the old people who have seen this happen, it seems the people of the city were driven almost out of their senses during the first years of this development'.[29]

If this was the case, it was possible for the ambassadors to envisage rapid industrialization in Japan, a conclusion not lost on Ōkubo who campaigned vigorously to develop the infrastructure of the Meiji state. In this light, it is worth pointing out Kume's thoughts some sixty years later in the 1920s when he remembered the Iwakura mission's visit to Gray's spinning mill in Manchester. 'During World War One', he observed, 'Japan began producing fine-quality textiles to the astonishment of the British, and recently Japanese cloth has penetrated the

British market to angry protests of unfair competition. When our party toured around Britain, however, Victorian confidence was so high that they believed Oriental people could not hope to compete with them, and they never dreamed that Japanese textiles could ever pose them any problems.'[30]

After visiting Liverpool and Manchester, Iwakura's party then travelled north to Glasgow. Their tour of industrial centres exposed them in quick succession to some of the most polluted areas in Britain, and Kume's chronicle vividly records the smog that the party encountered in these Victorian cities. Of Liverpool, he wrote that, 'seen from afar on the south banks of the Mersey, the sky is always darkened by a cloud of coal smoke rising two or three hundred *shaku* into the air. Our guides pointed out that the people live their lives breathing this blackened air, and there is so much smoke that life expectancy here is 35 years for the upper classes, 25 years for the middle classes, and just fifteen years for the working classes'. In Manchester too, he noted: 'Throughout the city, coal smoke fills the heavens, darkening the sky.' In Glasgow, the party was surprised not to encounter any rain, but there was barely any sunshine to be seen, and they were mystified when people in the city complimented the Japanese ambassadors for bringing such good weather with them.[31]

It soon became apparent that their tour of Britain's industrial heartland was beginning to take its toll on Iwakura's health. As a result, Parkes recommended a change of air following their stay in Edinburgh to tour the renowned scenery of the Scottish Highlands. Leaving the vice ambassadors behind, Iwakura set out in a small party on 17 October for four quiet days in the country. Apart from the three British guides, he was accompanied only by Kume, Hatakeyama and Fukui Junzō, their physician.

On their first night in the village of Birnam, all the guests at their hotel sat at the same table for dinner, and after all the formality of their official engagements, they were delighted not only by the warm welcome they received, but also by the locals' simple and unaffected ways. As they travelled by train through the hills, even Parkes, Alexander and Aston had to admit that they could not understand the dialect of the railway staff, but the language barrier did not prevent the Japanese visitors from discerning the sincerity of the Highlanders. On one occasion in the village of Killin, an old man who had just shown them around the local castle revealed that his son was a merchant in Yokohama, and invited the party back to his house where his wife and daughter held out their hands in welcome. 'It was a remote village in the mountains', Kume recalled, 'so chairs were placed in front of the hearth, wood was added to the fire, drinks were served, and we just talked together in a simple expression of mutual goodwill.'[32]

On the first night of their mountain excursion, Iwakura himself said how relieved he was to forget his official duties for a while, and become just another traveller in the Highlands. By the following day, it seems he had managed to cast off his worldly cares, for he was heard whistling happily to himself in a little clearing by a waterfall near Birnam. Another indelible memory of their tour was contrived by the owners of the Trossachs Hotel, who not only provided the party with transport for a day and accompanied them throughout, but also arranged for a piper to lead the way in the front carriage. Kume remembered that 'it was a fine day with brilliant colours and not the slightest wind, so that we could even hear the rustling sound of falling leaves'. Describing their journey through the Trossachs, he wrote: 'We entered a wood of golden leaves, and it was as if we had passed in a trance into some other world, as we drove through the glimmering light and shade with the sound of the bagpipes leading us on our way. The trees were not thickly clustered together or at all oppressive, and looking to our left from the carriage, we saw a rocky peak covered in mist.'[33]

After the tour of the Highlands, Iwakura and his party resumed their observations of Victorian industry with more factory visits in the North East, Yorkshire and the West Midlands. At the same time, they also received invitations to stay at some country houses. They had already stayed at Erskine House near Glasgow at the invitation of Lord Blantyre, and later spent a night at Peckforton Castle in Cheshire, the home of the local member of Parliament, John Tollemache.

Although their tour had been planned with industry foremost in mind, these visits to country houses allowed Iwakura and his party to form some impression of the state of agriculture in Victorian Britain. Just as they had found many of the factories they had seen to be a relatively new addition to the urban environment, rural land management also appeared to have undergone rapid changes in recent years. Their observations suggested that the efforts of the landed aristocracy had promoted this development. 'Traditionally this has been the preserve of poor folk', Kume reported, 'and it is less than a hundred years since the gentry first began to give it their attention.' He noted that 'France and Germany are renowned for their agricultural prosperity, but the British too have made great strides over the last ten years'.[34]

During the party's visit to Chatsworth House in Derbyshire, Kume was also impressed by the care he saw being taken to preserve and restore examples of old Imari ware. He pointed out that the great houses of Europe had been keeping such collections for centuries, and suggested that Imari ware of such high quality might even be harder to find in Japan. Of all the customs in the West, it was perhaps this trait that aroused Kume's most unreserved admiration. On one occasion after dinner with the Mayor of Warwick, for example, the children of the house took their Japanese guests by the hand and led them away to show them their collection of personal treasures. These turned out to be no more than worthless curiosities, but Kume was struck by their presence of mind, an attitude he thought was fostered by the great variety of museums and exhibitions he had seen during his stay in Britain.[35]

In Kume's view, it was only through their recent exhibitions that the British themselves had finally realized the need to abandon their debilitating habit of imitating French fashion. He employed this theme in the official chronicle to attack the sometimes undiscriminating enthusiasm for Western fashions in Japan. 'My readers should consider what lessons can be learned for Japan', he declared. 'The present day is for us very much like that earlier time in European history when everyone was fascinated by the brilliance of Louis XIV and France. If we ignore our traditions and rush to model ourselves on Europe, is it not conceivable that we shall fall into the same delusion as European countries before the Great Exhibition?'[36]

During their inland tour, Iwakura and his party encountered many people and observed their customs, whether among crowds on the way, at official receptions or in the quieter surroundings of country homes. They were surprised to find that, contrary to their assumption that the British travelled far and wide and were used to foreign travel, many of the people in the countryside were visibly astonished at the sight of Japanese visitors. When they reached Bolton Abbey in Yorkshire for example, 'the villagers crowded around to look at us just as in every other place we had been. The fact is', explained Kume, 'that only a small minority of British people are used to seeing foreigners, and many people in regional districts look upon them with curiosity, just as in any other country'. This point was brought home sharply one day near the lighthouse at Tynemouth. The party was watching the launching of rockets used for life-saving when a crowd gathered round them and Kume was suddenly struck on the back of the neck by an unseen hand. That evening, Parkes announced that he had identified and questioned the culprit, a woman who explained her action by declaring: 'He was warm-blooded after all'.[37]

Kume generally found British women somewhat reserved and more respectful than those he had seen in the United States. In his view, they were less stridently individualistic in outlook, and showed a reassuring attachment to family values. Aristocratic ladies, in particular, were, he thought, most refined. His assailant in Tynemouth may have been something of an exception, but her actions nevertheless exemplified the enquiring mind he identified as a characteristic feature of Victorian women. Some ladies they met at a reception in Manchester, for example, appeared to know little about Japan, but were delighted to learn that silk was produced there, and promptly asked them: 'Why then are you wearing this dull cloth and not your own beautiful silk?'[38]

Iwakura's most formidable inquisitor during the inland tour, however, may have been the wife of John Tollemache, who Kume thought epitomized the Western obsession with clarity. When beef and mutton were served at dinner, she asked him which of the two he preferred, and was not satisfied by his polite insistence that he liked them both. 'Were you not repelled', she asked, 'by the characteristic smell of mutton when you tried it for the first time?' At this point, Ōkubo turned to Kume and whispered: 'Prince Iwakura has been driven into a corner now.' Quite unruffled, however, Iwakura replied: 'Yes, you are right. I did notice the smell at first, but I am used to it now', and she inferred that he was a confirmed convert to mutton after all. Kume thought this exchange was a good example of the way in which Iwakura employed his Oriental sense of diplomacy to deflect the abrasive enquiries he often faced. As he explained: 'Western people do not like leaving matters unclarified, and will never be satisfied until the relative merits of one thing and another are weighed together.'[39]

THE IWAKURA MISSION'S LAST WEEKS IN LONDON

After leaving the Tollemache estate on Saturday 9 November, Iwakura and his party visited Chester and travelled back to London later the same day. Forty-two days had passed since they had set out on their inland tour. If they had intended to spend the next day recovering after their long journey, however, their plans were soon disrupted, for they arrived back to find the Japanese community in London in a state of near shock over the collapse of Minami Teisuke's bank. During their absence, the American Joint National Bank had collapsed without warning, and when Japanese customers had gone to the office in Charing Cross to rescue their deposits, they found a notice in the window announcing that business had been suspended, with Minami inside trying in vain to placate his clients. The Bowles brothers, meanwhile, had made good their escape.[40]

On Sunday 10 November, the day after their return, Itō came to report to Kido on the matter, and when Kido then met Minami, his worst fears were confirmed.'Everybody is dismayed over the trouble at the bank', he declared.'The confusion is too great to be described with the writing brush.' A number of officials in Iwakura's party, and more than fifty Japanese students in Britain had lost substantial amounts of money, having deposited more than £20,000 between them. The victims included aristocrats like Nabeshima Naohiro, and also senior members of the mission such as Kido and Ōkubo.[41]

Among Iwakura's retinue, there were some particularly heavy casualties of the Minami affair, and their misfortune became a talking point among the Japanese in London. Shioda Saburō, the First Secretary in the Foreign Department, for example, lost as much as £600, and he was so notoriously mean with money that some students rejoiced at his demise. Kume Kunitake, a man renowned for his frugality. also lost £150.[42] Perhaps the greatest victim, however, was Minami himself. One student, Ozaki Saburō, thought he was to be pitied, for 'he had no inkling of the swindle he was caught up in, and believed throughout that he was engaged in a sound business, but was simply used as a machine by the Americans'. As a result, he added, Minami's standing in Japanese circles 'crashed to the ground'.[43]

The Iwakura mission and the Japanese students in London never recovered their money from Minami's bank. With the help of Yoshida Kiyonari of the Treasury Department, however, Ōkubo managed to use his status as Minister of Finance to secure a loan of £15,000 from the Oriental Bank in the name of the Japanese government, so that the threat of immediate hardship was largely averted.[44] Nevertheless, the travel plans of some members of the mission were severely disrupted. Sasaki Takayuki and his party, for example, found themselves unable to leave Vienna when, after packing their luggage, they tried to pay their hotel bill with a cheque from the Joint American National Bank. They had to stay there until one of them had been to London and back to collect the money they needed from Iwakura.[45]

At the end of their stay in Britain, Iwakura and his party spent a month in London before embarking on their tour of continental Europe in mid-December. They used this time to inspect a number of institutions from hospitals and law courts to gas works and biscuit factories. By this time the schedule of official visits had become less frantic, and in the weeks before the ambassadors finally received their audience with Queen Victoria at Windsor Castle on 5 December, they had some time to pursue their own interests. Kido, for example, followed up his ongoing investigations into the constitutions of the West by visiting Yasukawa Shigenari, a member of the party who had stayed in London to visit the Houses of Parliament no less than 39 times and prepare a detailed report on British politics. Kume later described Parliament in his official chronicle, stressing the power of the landed gentry in the House of Lords, and emphasising the balance struck by the two-party system between conservatism and reform.[46]

After dark on 12 December, Kido, Ōkubo and Hatakeyama experienced one of their most startling adventures, when Alexander took them on a tour of some of the poorer back streets in the East End. This was not their first encounter with poverty in Britain. They had already seen a surprising number of poor people during their tour of the northern cities, many of whom walked around barefoot, destroying their impression that everyone in Britain wore shoes. They had also been disturbed by the death of Alice Blanche Oswald, a destitute twenty-year-old woman from America, who caused a sensation in London when she committed suicide by throwing herself off Waterloo Bridge on 5 September.[47]

Nevertheless, their tour of the East End made a lasting impression on the vice ambassadors. After returning to their hotel, Kido reported: 'It is not so much a den of poverty as a nest of vice. What we saw there was indescribable.' Ōkubo was so depressed that he declared: 'After seeing that, the whole world appears despicable.'[48] The intensity of these impressions was later reflected in Kume's official chronicle of the Iwakura mission: 'I heard that in London', he wrote, 'there is a never-ending stream of destitute men and women throwing themselves into the river, and there are halls of ill-repute, where every shade of villainous character can be found congregating in pernicious gatherings, and pursuing all manner of vices from devising fraudulent schemes to the smoking of opium'.[49]

On 16 December 1872, four days after the vice ambassadors' sobering visit to the East End, the Iwakura mission travelled to Dover and crossed the English Channel to embark on their continental tour. The memories of Britain they took with them were a bewildering mixture of images, ranging from exchanges with Japanese students in London to their encounters with Victorian people in smoky cities, quiet villages and country houses. After the Minami affair, few of them left the country with their trust in Western banking entirely intact. Following their inland tour, however, they had developed an overall awareness that Britain's industrial power and agricultural wealth were all the result of comparatively recent developments. While radical members of the party continued to marshall their evidence in support of Western progress, self-confessed sceptics like Kido, Ōkubo and Kume also drew some comfort from their discovery that tradition and innovation did not necessarily appear to be mutually exclusive in the Victorian world. While the ambassadors were certainly impressed by the new technology paraded before them by ranks of proud factory owners, it was with a renewed sense of faith in the value of continuity that they left Britain at the end of 1872.

LONDON *TIMES* 1872

THE JAPANESE EMBASSY

The members of the Embassy are not only great officials and great nobles in a kingdom more ancient than our own, they are also statesmen who, with their lives in their hands, have worked out an immense and most beneficent revolution in their own country. The power they wield is more potent for good or evil than we can easily realise. The announcement, which sounded so strange to us the other day, of the intended proclamation of a new religion by the Japanese Government, is a conspicuous illustration of the extent of their influence. Upon the relations we cultivate with men of this spirit, intelligence, and power must depend, to an incalculable degree, the prospects of English enterprise in Japan, and even of Japanese civilisation. The occasion, in short, demands the best attention from all who are responsible for the reception of the Embassy. While the Ambassadors deserve at least as much respect as the representatives of most European kingdoms, it should be remembered that their habits induce them to expect even more. The highest attention was paid to the Duke of Edinburgh during his recent visit to Japan, and it is now our opportunity to make a becoming return. It is most unfortunate the Embassy should have reached our shores at a time when the unbending habits of English life compel the absence of the greater part of our Court and of our Government, and it is an additional misfortune that London should be unusually empty even for the present season. It will be the duty of those who wait on the Ambassadors to make this circumstance perfectly clear to them, and to prevent their entertaining the least idea that the dullness of the Court or the capital indicates any disrespect to them. The feeling of the English people is one of profound interest in one of the most remarkable races of the Old World, and we trust our Government will not fail to give due expression to this sentiment.

OCT. 12, 1872 *THE JAPAN WEEKLY MAIL*

THE JAPANESE EMBASSY

The members of the Japanese Embassy, headed by Sionii Tomomi Iwakura, arrived at Liverpool on the 17th inst. by the Cunard steamer *Olympus*, and were received by General Alexander, representing the Government, the Mayor of Liverpool, and the Secretary to the Chamber of Commerce, who presented the address, which appeared in our last issue, to Iwakura. The Ambassadors proceeded direct to London, and were entertained to dinner by Lord and Lady Granville on the 19th inst., and afterwards visited the International Exhibition, which was brilliantly lighted up for the occasion. On the following day they proceeded to Brighton, were present at the reading of a paper before the Geographical Section of the British Association by Mr. Mossman and were subsequently entertained at luncheon by Mr. Burrows the Mayor of Brighton. There were no speeches, but the Mayor, in a few sentences, assured Iwakura of the welcome Brighton gave him as chief Ambassador from Japan. Iwakura replied in his own language, with thanks to his host and hostess, and expressed on behalf of himself and colleagues their deep feeling at the warm reception they had received. The Ambassadors returned to London in the evening, and attended a concert held in the Albert Hall.

On the 21st the Embassy paid a second visit to Brighton, and in company with Sir Harry Parkes they inspected the aquarium which was opened last week. Their next provincial visit will be to Liverpool, where, as we have already stated, a banquet is to be given in their honour by the Chamber of Commerce of that town. We understand that Mr. Robert Sloan, surgeon to the Embassy, is engaged in writing a work descriptive of its establishment and objects, which is shortly to be published.

2

BRITAIN

[2]

17 AUGUST-16 DECEMBER 1872

The Mission's Aims, Objectives and Results

Ian Ruxton

THE IWAKURA MISSION arrived in Liverpool on board the Cunard steamer *Olympus* on 17 August 1872. It stayed in Britain for a total of 122 days, leaving London for Paris on 16 December. This mission was the most important and largest of all the Japanese missions sent to Western countries between the end of the Edo period and the beginning of the Meiji era, that is, between 1860 and 1873. It was the first official diplomatic mission abroad since the Meiji Restoration, the first Japanese mission designed according to Western diplomatic principles, and perhaps the first overseas mission in world history to include such a large proportion of a country's leadership.[1]

In the official record *A true account of the tour in America and Europe of the Special Embassy* (*Tokumei Zenken Taishi Bei-O Kairan Jikki*) compiled by the Confucian scholar Kume Kunitake (1839-1931) and published in 1878 under the auspices of the Grand Council of State (*Dajokan*), the total number of pages devoted to the tour of Britain was 443. This was 46 pages more than the total for the United States of America which was only 397, despite the fact that 205 days (i.e. 83 days more than in Britain) were spent in the USA. The reasons for this are probably twofold: first, there was simply less of interest to report on in the United States, still recovering from the devastation of the American Civil War which had ended only seven years earlier; second, the Mission had failed to bring appropriate credentials to present to the American government, as Secretary of State Hamilton Fish pointed out to them. Other countries in Europe received less than half the number of pages devoted to Britain (Germany, France) and in some cases less than one quarter (Italy, Russia). The total number of days spent in each of these countries was also less than that spent in Britain.[2]

The aims of the Mission's members were: (i) to achieve recognition for the new imperial regime; (ii) to initiate a renegotiation of the treaties which had been signed with foreign powers (or at least to find out the reforms necessary as preconditions for renegotiation); and (iii) to judge for themselves the achievements of Western societies with a view to adopting those parts of value to Japan.[3] This study will concentrate mainly on the third objective, as this was the most important one in the visit to Britain; a satisfactory renegotiation of the unequal treaties (including the abolition of extraterritoriality) was not achieved until 1894.

The ambassadors and their assistants were responsible for three different sets of enquiries. One was to study the law and government, and to examine British political institutions including both Houses of Parliament. This task was undertaken mainly by Kume Kunitake himself.[4] The second was to study the economic structure including industry, transport and communications, banking, currency and taxation and how these all affected trade. The third was to examine education in all its aspects, together with the equipment and training of military and naval personnel. These lines of enquiry had all been suggested by Guido Verbeck, who had gone to Japan as a Christian missionary in 1859, in his *Brief Sketch* first presented to Okuma Shigenobu in June 1869.[5]

The principal British cities and areas visited were: London, Liverpool, Manchester, Glasgow, Edinburgh, The Scottish Highlands, Newcastle, Bradford, Halifax, Sheffield, Burton-upon-Trent, Birmingham, Coventry, Warwick, Worcester and Chester. However the Mission did not travel everywhere *en masse*. Occasionally, splinter groups formed, and Kido Takayoshi (1833-77) briefly visited Dublin with three other members of the Mission, while three experts in mining and mineralogy (including Oshima Takato who had studied the reverbatory furnace before the Restoration and later worked on the problems of iron-smelting at Kamaishi) visited the Cornish tin-mines, and even went as far as the Welsh coal mines near Cardiff.

RED CARPET TREATMENT

Each country visited by the Mission, including the USA, Britain, France, Germany, Holland and Russia mounted a comprehensive programme designed to impress the Japanese with its enterprise and achievements. Every host country was eager to entertain such a distinguished delegation and show off its modern industry and infrastructure. Swift steamships and steam trains running at up to 100 km/h, comprehensive rail networks, efficient post office and telegraph systems were all on display to impress the visitors who constantly discussed among themselves what they had seen. In Britain the main railway lines which exist today were already in place.

The kinds of questions which were uppermost in the minds of the visitors were: did industrialization depend on an educated population for its success? Who was responsible for the financing and development of trade and industry? Was the educated élite responsible for Western industrial supremacy?

Although Britain had many visitors from abroad at this time who were greatly impressed by what they saw, few can have received such careful attention as the Iwakura Mission, with comprehensive and well-ordered tours undertaken on a daily basis. The *Bradford Observer* of 3 August 1872 reprinted an article from *The Times* which drew a comparison between the reception of the ambassadors in the United States and Britain: 'It is not necessary, or even advisable, that we should emulate the bombastic reception which has been given to the Japanese in America. But it is most important that due value should be attached to the significance of the Mission, and that the Japanese Government should be met in the same spirit with which it has come forward to assert itself in the world.' The writer regretted however that the members had been so charmed by the 'fascinations of Washington' that they were arriving when Parliament was in recess, and the Queen and most government ministers were not in London.

As the visit drew to a close *The Times* noted with typical understatement on 7 December: '. . .as they came to learn, and found no obstacles in the way of acquiring information, we may hope that their satisfaction is substantially complete'.

It was the 'industrial grand tour' of the north of England and Scotland, inspecting key factories and being entertained frequently by eminent local industrialists, which brought home the strength of the manufacturing base on which British imperial power rested. Throughout the visitors were accompanied by the British Minister in Japan Sir Harry Parkes (who was on leave) and one of his consular officials, W. G. Aston who acted as interpreter. Major-General Alexander was seconded by the British government to supervise arrangements.

Sir Harry Parkes, who stayed with Iwakura throughout the Mission's tour of Britain and was responsible for the overall supervision of arrangements, was well-known to the Japanese. Born in 1828, he had arrived in Japan in June 1865 to take up his appointment as minister. He returned to England on 9 August 1871 via the United States for home leave, departing once more for Japan on 16 January 1873, after the embassy had left. Before the mission arrived in England, Parkes and his family were installed at 1 Lancaster Street, Lancaster Gate, so that he could be near the Foreign Office where he worked during his leave. He received instructions from his superiors that he was to act in such a way as to give a favourable impression to the high-ranking visitors which would assist future Anglo-Japanese relations.[6]

Before the mission arrived, Parkes was called on to defend his policies with regard to the lack of protection of Christians in Japan by a deputation from the Evangelical Alliance on 9 February 1972. This he managed successfully, balancing sympathy with the aims of the Evangelicals with a strong defence of the Japanese government from foreign pressure. In April Parkes was called as a special witness on diplomacy in East Asia before a special Committee of the House of Commons.

Despite Parkes's well-known irascibility and roughness of manner, the Japanese envoys were apparently grateful for his help during their investigative tour of Britain. A long note of thanks was sent to him from Paris. *The Times* of 17 January 1873 praised his courtesy, which drew this comment from Gordon Daniels, his recent biographer: 'No valedictory statement could have better highlighted the great divide between Parkes' behaviour and reputation in Britain, and among the Japanese.'[7] In other words, Parkes was apparently on his best behaviour when close to his bosses, but less so when he was only accessible by irregular despatches at his far-away posting!

William George Aston, an Ulsterman and graduate of the Queen's University Belfast, was serving as a consular official at the Tokyo legation, and he was provided as interpreter. Born in 1841, he had arrived in Japan in 1864. He was probably the most proficient in the Japanese language of the new breed of consular interpreters after Ernest Satow who had arrived in Japan two years before him. Later, Aston was to become well-known for his pioneering work in Japanology.

Major General G. G. Alexander of the Royal Marines was a Chinese linguist who had published a book on Confucius. He was suggested by Parkes, and assigned to escort the mission through an arrangement made by the Foreign Office. In Brunton's words he 'had been specially appointed as the representative of the Queen to see to their comfort and well-being'. He accompanied the embassy on its visit to Parliament, and assisted with occasional running commentaries. Although one supposes that Alexander was at his most useful in his explanation of military facilities and demonstrations, he was also present at visits to non-military factories and institutions. It would be quite incorrect to infer from his presence that the mission was only interested in military matters. Indeed, Professor Beasley has observed that 'the attention paid to non-military matters remains the most striking feature of the embassy's investigations in Britain'.[8]

Another person who was close to the ambassadors was Richard Henry Brunton, a forthright but capable Scottish engineer born in the Kincardine district of Aberdeenshire on 26 December 1841. He was employed as an *o-yatoi gaikokujin* (foreign employee) in Japan from 1868 to 1876, after Parkes had insisted that Japan fulfil its treaty obligations by making its ports and waters safe for navigation. His main work was to build 34 lighthouses, but he also charted the Inland Sea and the approaches to the major ports, as well as acting as a consultant on various other engineering projects.

Brunton, having obtained leave of absence, had arrived in London on 18 June 1872, and called on the embassy at the Buckingham Palace Hotel as soon as they arrived. He wrote in his memoirs: 'While Iwakura, Kido and Okubo were escorted by General Alexander and Sir Harry Parkes, to the great Government establishments at Woolwich, Chatham, Portsmouth etc., Ito, as [Vice] Minister of Public Works, together with a number of intelligent young attachés, put himself under my wing, and by me was introduced to a large number of manufacturers.' During September they visited no fewer than twenty-eight factories in London involved in such diverse activities as making candles, glue, cement, clocks, gunpowder, and meat-preserving. Brunton added that he accompanied Ito and his group via Birmingham, Manchester and Liverpool (where they visited the most important factories) up to Edinburgh where they rejoined Iwakura and Parkes early in October.

THE ITINERARY

Kume Kunitake in his official account assumed that the mission was where Iwakura himself was at any one time. The same convention is followed here. The itinerary was largely decided as the group travelled around the country, not in advance.

London and the South of England (17 August-29 September)

During the early weeks in the South of England the Japanese delegation made it a priority to see army manoeuvres and equipment, and naval installations. The British had begun to train the Japanese navy in 1867, so there was a particular interest in naval matters.[9]

On 26 August Parkes, Alexander and Aston escorted the visitors to Blandford Forum in Dorset. The next day they observed troops drilling, a sight which Kido found spectacular. Field camp equipment, provisions storehouses, bridges, the telegraphy system, a printing press and a courier office were all on display. The next day the mission was in Portsmouth as guests of the Royal Navy. They boarded a midshipmen's training vessel, and observed the manufacture of bricks, a dock under construction, and a steel warship, *HMS Monarch*, being made. (At that time steel ships were newly invented. Steel was lighter and stronger than iron, but corroded more easily. On the deck of the *Monarch* there were four 700-pound guns housed in steel shields.)

On 29 August the mission witnessed a demonstration of the firepower of big guns on a warship, and the court martial of two naval officers. The captain of *HMS Hercules* ordered a nineteen-gun salute to be fired, and the party went inside one of three forts placed in the sea. They were structures surrounded by three-foot iron walls on top of stone bases. The next day six battalions of troops drilled in front of the mission's hotel, a fort equipped with forty guns was visited, and a soldiers' camp. The party returned to London by train the same day.

Back in London there was a great variety of things to see and places to visit. On 31 August Kido went to a photography studio and Madame Tussaud's waxwork museum which had been established in Baker Street in 1835. He boarded the carriage of Napoleon I and found it equipped with numerous interesting devices. On 3 September Iwakura led the party to see Buckingham Palace, and the next day they looked in on every single room of the Houses of Parliament.

On 7 September the mission was taken to Windsor Castle. They were astonished by the splendour of the state rooms and their contents, and took a carriage ride through the grounds. Someone told Kido that the road through the grounds was over 200 miles in length, an obvious exaggeration which he recorded in his diary.

Three days later there was an important visit to the Woolwich cannon factory. Kido was impressed and wrote as follows:

> We took a steamship from Westminster Bridge down the Thames to the factory; the huge size of the bridges over the river is astonishing. . . We looked over the Woolwich cannon foundry. There are about 700 workers. We did not see any such factory with so much

> activity in America . . . we went to various departments to see the manufacture of cannon, gun carriages, shells, and rifle bullets. Altogether some 8,000 workers are employed in this factory daily. Wages are £4 weekly for craftsmen of the first class; £2 per week for those of the middle class; and £1 per week for those of the bottom class. Several cannon captured from the Chinese and from the Russians at Sebastopol were displayed.

The next day the mission saw St Paul's Cathedral and the Bank of England where they watched gold and silver being weighed. Weights were used instead of counting the coins. They also looked over the Queen's carriages, and found the Lord Mayor's residence (Mansion House) much finer than the White House in America. They dined with the Lord Mayor and Mayoress in the splendour of the Egyptian Hall.

On 12 September the ambassadors travelled 80 miles by train to Beaconhill near Southampton to observe the army parade at the end of autumn manoeuvres. It was a grand display including 35,000 cavalry and 10,000 artillerymen, observed by the Prince of Wales and senior officers from several European countries. The following day, back in London, Kido recorded that they had dinner in the Mercer's Hall with one of the city livery companies. During the dinner everyone drank out of a large bowl which was passed around, and perfumed face towels not unlike *oshibori* were used.

On 18 September the delegates went to the Tower of London where they saw the crown jewels and an armoury which included a set of Japanese armour and weapons. In a separate building they saw 60,000 Snider rifles. They also visited the telegraph office which contained state-of-the-art equipment they had not previously seen.

Crystal Palace, the giant glass-and-iron exhibition hall in Hyde Park (later moved to Sydenham in South London) that had housed the Great Exhibition of 1851, was visited on 19 September in the company of Alexander and Aston. It was a remarkable construction of prefabricated parts; its dimensions were 1,851 feet long, 456 feet wide, 66 feet high, with a floor area of more than 800,000 square feet. Kido noted that 'the architectural style of the building, and the design of its garden are among the best to be found in this country'. He was especially taken with models of a Grecian building erected in 1717 BC and the Coliseum.

Two days later Kido travelled in an underground train. The first underground railway line in the world was the Metropolitan Railway. Construction had begun in 1860 by cut-and-cover methods, and the line had been opened on 10 January 1863. It used steam locomotives that burned coke and so gave off sulfurous fumes, but it was popular from the beginning. In the first year of its existence it had carried almost ten million passengers. In 1890 the first electric underground railway began to operate in London. In Budapest an electric subway was opened in 1896. It was the first subway on the European continent.

On 27 September the mission visited the British Museum, established by act of parliament in 1759. The library was a revelation. Kido wrote that he had never seen so many books. He must have seen the circular reading room which was completed in 1857, and he also noted the collections of Japanese and Chinese books. Yet it was the museum's holdings which impressed him the most, especially the Egyptian antiquities and Greek stone sculptures of people and animals. This reflection of the wealth of upper-class British collectors, and the power of the British Empire was surely not lost on the Japanese visitors. But the mere fact of the existence of such a collection was compelling testimony of the need to learn from, and embrace, the past.

The North West: Liverpool and Manchester (29 September-9 October)

Kido's first impression on arriving at Liverpool had not been a favourable one. He wrote in his diary (17 August) that it had the largest shipyards in England, and it looked prosperous, but had a dreary appearance compared with America. The mission did not officially visit Liverpool until 30 September. At that time they saw the floating dockyard, a five-storeyed grain elevator, countless tobacco warehouses with tobacco from all over the world including Japan, and the yards of Cammell Laird at Birkenhead.

From Liverpool they travelled to Manchester via Crewe and St Helens. At Crewe they saw the train and rail factory where thousands of miles of rail had already been made. Kido noted that 90,000 people were connected with the North-Western railway, and that the total factory wage bill (always carefully recorded at each factory along with hourly rates) was a colossal £250,000. At the latter they saw Pilkington's glass factory (established in 1869, though glass-making had started in 1773). Kido made a brief note of the manufacturing process using quartz and sodium carbonate which he apparently did not understand in any detail.

In Manchester, from 5 October, they concentrated on the cotton textile industry, but also saw a steel mill with an 8,000-ton press used to manufacture large guns. They found time to see the rubber factory owned by waterproof fabric manufacturer C. Macintosh & Co. and were visited by members of the Temperance Society. Child labour was common in the spinning and weaving factories, but the most impressive thing for Kido was 'the rule that those under fourteen or fifteen should work only five hours per day, and go to school for three hours'. The importance of attempting to maintain education in these trying circumstances clearly moved him.

In the afternoon of 7 October a full meeting of the City Council was held at Manchester Town Hall in which the Mayor William Booth welcomed the mission. He showed himself quite well informed about recent changes in Japan, remarking:

> We have witnessed with the deepest interest the numerous and important changes which have lately taken place in Japan. . . Especially we would allude to the patriotic self-sacrifice of the Daimios in the surrender of their property to State purposes, – to the abolition of the feudal system, firmly established many centuries ago, – to the greater liberty granted to the humbler classes, – to the extension of higher education to women, – to the abolition of the office of the Shiogun, – and to the labours of the Great Council [Dajokan] in favour of representative government.

With due humility and perspicacity he concluded:

> We cannot pretend to equal your people in the matchless finish and subtle delicacy of their work, as shown in the polished lacquer ware, in the richness and beauty of their silks, or the fineness of their porcelain; but we can offer you our manufactures, machinery, books, scientific apparatus, and works of art, and we hope that your sojourn will lead to a larger exchange of these commodities.

Replying through an interpreter, Iwakura responded by expressing his thanks on behalf of the Emperor and the people of Japan. He said he would have been glad, if time had permitted, to discuss in detail the 'revolution which brought us into new relations with other nations of the world', but the purpose of the visit was to learn rather than teach. He continued:

> It is our intention to treasure up the knowledge we shall gain, so that we may follow the example of your energy and industry, which have made you so prominent among the nations of the world. The result of your many centuries' experience will be of great value to us. We desire to introduce every facility for improving the condition of our people. We shall send young men to your shores to be educated, as we have already done. We shall ask for your machinery, your engines, and such modern appliances as will help us to begin properly in this new stage of our national development. . . We have investigated with great interest your factories with their wonderful machinery, and have thus seen for ourselves that your nation's greatness is largely centred in her manufacturing and commercial interests.[10]

On 9 October the party left Manchester with a salute fired from a gun activated by the steam locomotive as it passed over rails wired with electricity.

Scotland: Glasgow, Edinburgh and The Highlands (9-21 October)

In the west of Scotland the mission were the guests of Lord Blantyre from 9 October for three days at Erskine House, which commanded a fine view of the River Clyde. Visits were made to Glasgow where the Lord Provost welcomed them. The itinerary included a cotton mill producing 130,000 handkerchiefs per day; a steel mill, the stock market, Corporation Galleries and the Chamber of Commerce. Kume Kunitake was impressed by the Glasgow waterworks.[11] A visit to Caird's shipyard in Greenock and Walker's sugar refinery which converted South American brown sugar into white were also included. On 12 October Kido was astonished by the efficiency of steam-powered machinery used on Lord Blantyre's home farm to thresh wheat.

Edinburgh provided a chance for sightseeing at the Castle, the Palace of Holyroodhouse and the Museum of Science and Art before continuing the industrial tour. The party also saw a traction-engine works, the North British Rubber Company's factory, and a paper mill. On 16 October, as guests of the Commissioners for Northern Lights, they steamed 40 miles on the ship *Pharos* to the Bell Rock Lighthouse designed by the firm of the Stevenson brothers, David and Thomas. For this visit they were accompanied by R. H. Brunton, the 'Father of the Japan Lights' who had trained at Stevenson's.[12] Brunton had written a letter to *The Times* published on 29 June 1872 in which he had described Japan's lighthouse building programme which he supervised from 1868 to 1876: 'About 20 lighthouses of the best description, fitted with the newest and most expensive optical apparatus have been erected, and are in excellent working order.' The next day a coal oil refinery was visited, and the mission divided into three groups. Iwakura and Kume headed for Blair Atholl in the Highlands, Ito went to Glasgow, and Kido stayed in Edinburgh.

While Kido visited one of the Merchant Company's Schools with Professor Archer of Edinburgh University, and the presses of *The Scotsman* newspaper, Iwakura's party were surprised to discover that neither Parkes nor Aston could understand Scottish Gaelic. On 21 October the reunited groups left Edinburgh, with Kido expressing profound regret at leaving such a quiet and cordial place.

Newcastle and Yorkshire (21-31 October)

The mission arrived the same day in Newcastle-upon-Tyne. The next morning they were met by Sir William Armstrong, whose guns had played a vital part in the bombardments of Kagoshima (1863) and Shimonoseki (1864). Armstrong escorted them around the Elswick Engine and Ordnance Works and Gosforth Colliery. Kume made detailed notes of the various stages of manufacture of Armstrong and Gatling guns. From this time a personal contact with Armstrong (who himself never went to Japan) was established, and this led to significant orders for guns and cruisers from the Japanese government.

On 24 October the Japanese were welcomed to Bradford by the Mayor, M.W. Thompson. He addressed them as follows:

> May it please your Excellences, we, the Mayor, Aldermen and Borough of Bradford. . . receive the honour of your visit with sentiments of profound esteem. We tender you a hearty welcome, and trust that this interview may be the commencement of an intimate and abiding friendship between the Japanese nation and the people of this district, the seat of the worsted trade of England.

He went on to praise the 'enlightened blessings of commerce' and to recognize the Emperor's wisdom in sending an embassy 'to gather information from younger communities of the West with reference to such of their arts, manufactures and social regulations as may be rendered conducive to the welfare of His Majesty's subjects'.

The Mayor had in fact received a Burmese embassy and their suite (23 persons in all) on 2 September, so by this time he was no doubt well rehearsed.

On 25 October the mission travelled to the woollen manufacturing area of Yorkshire, and like the Burmese who preceded them visited Saltaire, a model village three miles from Bradford built near the Manningham woollen mills in 1853 by Sir Titus Salt (1803-76). It was named after Salt himself and the river Aire that runs through the town. He had developed a method for weaving the fur of the *alpaca* (a South American animal similar to a llama). Kido noted approvingly the generosity of Sir Titus who had built houses, schools, hospitals and homes for the aged. It was 'a vivid demonstration of Victorian paternalism'[13] with facilities for 4,000 employees provided at a cost in excess of one million pounds. The next day the mission was in Halifax to see the Crossley carpet factory, a wool-carding factory and an orphanage.

On their way down south on 30 October the ambassadors visited Chatsworth House, the magnificent estate near Sheffield of Richard Cavendish, Duke of Devonshire, which literally overwhelmed Kume. The duke personally welcomed the Japanese to the stately home, with its well-stocked libraries, wine cellars and spectacular interiors. Kume tried hard to appreciate the famous works of art (Titian, Tintoretto,

Rembrandt and Van Dyke), though he was more pleased by the extensive landscaped gardens. Chatsworth in Derbyshire was the only country house visited by the mission.

Birmingham and the Midlands (1-9 November)

Arriving in Birmingham on 1 November by way of the breweries of Burton-upon-Trent, the delegation first met and exchanged speeches with the Chamber of Commerce and then went on to Chance's Glass Factory where the glass for the Stevenson-built lighthouses in Japan was made. The rest of the day included visits to a needle factory, Walls steel pen factory (output 5 million pens per week!) and the Aston button factory.

The next day included visits to Cornworth wire factory, Osler's glass craft factory and Elkington's factory which made nickel, silver and gold-plated tableware. Kido noted that Japanese copperware was praised and that 'they wanted to hire some craftsmen from Japan'. In the afternoon they saw the privately-owned Mint and the Small Arms factory which was in the process of making 30,000 Belden rifles ordered by Russia. A newly-invented weapon called the 'machine gun' was also on view.

On 6 November the mission attended an unsuccessful fox hunt in Worcester before observing the manufacture of porcelain at the Royal Porcelain Works. The following day they saw Minton's factory in Stoke-on-Trent. In both places their hosts expressed regret that modern Japanese porcelain had changed from the traditional style, tending to imitate Western mass-produced goods of inferior quality. The 8 November found the mission in Cheshire visiting a salt mine which Kido found a spectacular sight, with several thousand candles blazing underground. After a brief visit to Chester to admire the old-fashioned city streets, the delegation members returned to London on an express train on 9 November.

Return to London (9 November-16 December)

On 13 November the Meiji Emperor's birthday was celebrated at a dinner for 40 persons, including the ambassadors, commissioners, attendants, Japanese nobles living in England, Alexander, Aston, Brunton and the president of the Oriental Bank. It was the Oriental Bank which had been appointed by the Japanese government to manage the loan for the first railway between Edo and Hyogo, in the wake of some double dealing by Horatio Nelson Lay C.B., a former British government employee in China. Lay had attempted to skim 3% profit for himself off loans raised in London at 9% interest by charging the Japanese government 12%, even though he was acting as agent for them.

On 20 November Okubo, Sugiura (a Satsuma samurai) and Kido went to the Customs House. They looked over various departments, and found two separate departments for analyzing liquors and sugar. In the evening there was yet another banquet, this time with the goldsmith's guild which had been in existence for more than 200 years. A toast to the Queen was followed by some patriotic songs. On the next day, after a trip to a Turkish bath, Kido was escorted to the India Museum by a Professor Beer. There he saw Indian-made craft goods of astonishingly exquisite quality, and countless books. On the way home Alexander took Kido to his London club where large-framed paintings of kings, generals and famous battles caught Kido's attention.

One week later the mission visited a hospital, described by Kido as 'the best hospital in England'. Built at a cost of £600,000, it included a chapel, a medical school, a pharmacy and an autopsy room. It was worthy of note that the nurses were women. On 1 December Kido was again in Brighton where he requested the help of a Dr Gill in caring for his adopted son Shojiro who was a student there, and he pointed out an aquarium to the party which he had first seen in August.

On 3 December Kido was in Dublin for the briefest of tours: the Bank of Ireland, St Patrick's Cathedral, the Guinness brewery and Phoenix Park were all visited by carriage in one day. The speed of the visit compares favourably with modern tourism as the four travellers were back at Euston the next morning! The following day all the envoys put on full formal dress for the presentation of credentials to Queen Victoria at Windsor Castle. Another audience with the Prince of Wales took place at Sandringham on 9 December.

An agricultural show was visited on 11 December, with prizes for the best livestock. Kido approved the prize-giving as a way of ensuring that the quality of cattle, sheep and farm implements improved year after year. The next day Okubo, Sugiura and Kido visited a police station, low-class music-halls, and destitute opium addicts living in an alley. It was exactly one year since the mission had left Japan. On the morning of 16 December the mission went by train from Victoria to Dover, arriving by steamship at Calais at 11.30 am.

A SUCCESSFUL MISSION?

Was the mission successful? Were the objectives of the British and Japanese achieved? Olive Checkland (1989) has suggested that the outcome was satisfactory for the British, who were pleased to entertain potential customers and encourage a relationship based on trade. It was an opportunity also to express disapproval about the repression of Christianity in Japan. *The Times* reported that a deputation from the Council of the Evangelical Alliance was received by the Mission on 10 December. A note from Iwakura was presented to Lord Ebury assuring him that imperial laws against Christianity had not been repromulgated. After hearing similar opinions in other Western countries, the restrictions on those Japanese professing to be Christians were removed on 24 February 1873.[14] Yet *The Times* noted in an editorial assessment: 'It is probable that the Japanese Ambassadors know more about us at this moment than we know about them.' (7 December 1872).

For the Japanese, matters were not so clear-cut. It is true that the Iwakura Mission successfully reasserted the status and authority of the Emperor with the Western powers, which had been one of Iwakura's main concerns. The treaty-making powers which the Shogun had wrongfully appropriated were thus restored to the Emperor. Yet the Mission was unable to begin treaty renegotiation, although the senior delegates understood more clearly the constitutional and legislative reforms needed in Japan before the West would renegotiate the 'unequal' treaties. Finally, a great boost was given to the industrialization of Japan as a result of the many factory visits, some of which have been detailed above.

In conclusion, it is worth noting that Ambassador Fujii gave a lecture to the Japan Society of London on 9 June 1997 in which he repeatedly raised the significance of the Iwakura Mission. He quoted from *The Times* editorial of 20 August 1872 which referred to Japan as 'this Eastern Great Britain', and emphasized the shared capacity for change – without compromising the essence of their traditions – which characterizes the two ancient island kingdoms. Fujii pointed out that Japan was completely alone in the Meiji era as it sought to modernise itself through trial and error. 'The energy and perseverance with which Japan tackled the challenges posed by the need for modernization in the mid-nineteenth century must surely have some lessons for us today.' The mission's unrelenting schedule is fitting testimony to that energy and perseverance.[15]

BIBLIOGRAPHY

Books

D.W. Anthony and G.H. Healey, *Itinerary of the Iwakura Mission in Britain*, Occasional Papers No. 1, Centre for Japanese Studies, University of Sheffield, 1987 (revised and updated October 1997, published by the Cardiff Japanese Studies Centre, University of Wales)

W.G. Beasley, *Japan Encounters the Barbarian: Japanese Travellers in America and Europe*, Yale University Press, 1995

S.D. Brown and A. Hirota (eds), *The Diary of Kido Takayoshi*, Vol. II, 1871-1874 . University of Tokyo Press, 1985

R. H. Brunton, *Building Japan 1868-1876*. With an introduction and notes by Sir Hugh Cortazzi, GCMG. Japan Library, 1991.

O. Checkland, Chapter 7, *Britain's Encounter with Meiji Japan, 1868-1912*, London: Macmillan, 1989

G. Daniels, *Sir Harry Parkes: British Representative in Japan 1865-83*, Japan Library, 1996

G. Fox, *Britain and Japan, 1858-1883*, Oxford University Press, 1969

H. Imai, *Nihonjin to Igirisu*, Tokyo: Chikuma Shinsho, 1994

Kume Kunitake, *Tokumei Zenken Taishi Bei-O Kairan Jikki*, 5 vols. Tokyo: Iwanami Bunko (12th edition, 1996) with notes by Tanaka Akira

Kume Museum of Art, *Rekishika Kume Kunitake*, Tokyo: Kume Bijutsukan, 1997 (Museum pamplet)

T. Miyanaga, *Shiroi Gake no Kuni wo Tazunete – Iwakura Shisetsudan no tabi; Kido Takayoshi no mita Igirisu*, Tokyo: Shueisha 1997

A. Tanaka and S. Takata (eds), Interdisciplinary Studies on *Bei-O Kairan Jikki*, [Bei-O Kairan Jikki no Gakusaiteki Kenkyuu] Hokkaido University Press, 1993

Articles

A. Altman, 'Guido Verbeck and the Iwakura Embassy', *Japan Quarterly*, XIII (1966), 54-62

Marlene Mayo, 'The Western Education of Kume Kunitake, 1871-6', *Monumenta Nipponica*, XXVIII (1973), 3-67

Marlene Mayo, 'Rationality in the Meiji Restoration: the Iwakura embassy', in B.S. Silberman and H.D. Harootunian, eds, *Modern Japanese Leadership* (Tucson, 1966) pp. 323-69

Eugene Soviak, 'On the nature of Western progress: the journal of the Iwakura embassy', in Donald Shively, ed., *Tradition and Modernization in Japanese Culture* (Princeton, 1971), 7-34

3

FRANCE

16 DECEMBER 1872-17 FEBRUARY 1873

Richard Sims

THE VISIT of the Iwakura mission to France has not generally been regarded as of great significance, and it has certainly attracted much less attention from historians than the immediately preceding stays in America and Britain. This neglect is understandable. The mission spent only two months – from 16 December 1872 to 17 February 1873 – in France, and apart from its journeys from Calais and to Marseille (via Lyon) and a brief excursion by one of the four vice-ambassadors, Ito Hirobumi, to the textile centre of Elbeuf, its activities were confined to Paris or to the environs of the French capital. By the time the embassy reached Europe, its members had already spent a year abroad and were less likely to be impressed by what they saw and heard. The fact that some of the ambassadors opted out of a number of trips to places of interest in France suggests that they did not always make the fullest possible use of their time there.[1]

It is not only historians who have paid little attention to the Iwakura mission's visit to France: the same was true of the contemporary French press. An examination of the pages of *Le Temps* and *Le Figaro* shows that, after reporting the fact of the mission's arrival on 16 December, these mainstream newspapers contented themselves with brief notices of the official reception of the ambassadors by French President Thiers on Boxing Day and with even more cursory mentions of their attendance at diplomatic receptions on 29 and 30 December and their visit to Versailles on 15 January 1873. The radical *Le Siècle*, which had earlier reported that the foreign minister, the Comte de Rémusat, entertained them on 23 December, provided a few different details about the initial presidential audience, including a description of what the Japanese envoys wore, and also noting that a large crowd assembled an hour in advance to see their arrival.[2] More unusually, it further recorded their lengthy visit to the Bibliothèque Nationale on 6 January. The Japanese mission was also featured in *Le Monde Illustré*, which printed a large, half-page, artist's impression of its ceremonial reception by Thiers, together with several ministers and aides, on 26 December, as well as publishing a fairly detailed description of Iwakura's 3-hour tour of a perfume factory in February. Neither *Le Siècle* nor *Le Monde Illustré* so much as mentioned any of the mission's other inspections and investigations, however, and neither of them informed their readers of its departure. Still more surprisingly, the *Journal Officiel de la République Française*, despite the fact that it regularly included news from Japan, made even less attempt to chart the embassy's activities. Notwithstanding its official character, it restricted its account of the initial presidential reception to a mere three sentences and ignored all the other activities of the Japanese ambassadors, including their New Year's Day courtesy call on the President and their attendance at an official dinner hosted by him on the day before their departure. Nor was it only the press which paid little heed to Iwakura and his associates. Even Edmond de Goncourt, a Japanophile of over ten years' standing, failed to note the mission's presence in Paris in his journal.[3]

The low level of French interest in Iwakura's visit is surprising in the light of the impression Japanese art had already begun to make not only on opinion-formers and innovative artists but also on French taste at a broader level. If the Japanese triumph at the 1878 Paris Exposition was still to come, the first revelation of Japanese artistic skill to a wide audience had already taken place at the preceding exposition of 1867.[4] Part of the explanation of why the mission attracted so little attention may lie in the fact that it was not seeking any controversial diplomatic concessions. It is also possible, though, that by 1872-3 Japanese visitors had lost something of their novelty. There had been official Bakufu missions in 1862, 1864, 1865, and 1867, as well as visits by groups from Satsuma and Saga and, more recently, officials and private individuals. Japanese students had also been arriving in some numbers, and since 1870 the Meiji government had been represented in Paris by a Japanese diplomat, Samejima (or Sameshima) Hisanobu.[5]

Although the Iwakura mission may not have created a stir in France, it should not be concluded that it met with any lack of official courtesy. Apart from the three presidential receptions, the ambassadors were invited to the Quai d'Orsay to meet the Comte de Rémusat on no fewer than three occasions, and the French foreign minister also visited the mission on 26 December. Admittedly the Japanese visitors found that most of the eight ministers on whom they paid calls on 27 December were absent from their ministries, but either six of them (according to Kido) or five (in Ito's version) attended a formal dinner with the mission on 31 January. The French government took the trouble to send General Appert and Commandant Chanoine (the head of the short-lived military mission which had been sent – too late – to help the Tokugawa Bakufu) to meet the mission at Calais where the garrison received it with military honours; and in Paris it provided the Japanese visitors with accommodation (though not food or other everyday requirements) in the conveniently situated previous Turkish embassy at 10 Rue de Presbourg, a favour which the ambassadors appreciated, according to *Le Siècle*.[6]

When they went to the Élysée Palace to be presented to the President, the envoys were escorted by two troops of cavalry, and when they arrived, they were met by a guard of honour, supported by a band. The reception, during which Iwakura handed over the mission's credentials, lasted no more than twenty minutes, but was apparently friendly, and the Japanese were presented also to the President's wife. According to *Le Temps*, the visiting dignitaries made a favourable impression. 'Throughout the interview', it reported, 'the ambassadors did not appear to be at a loss in the very slightest; they wore their dress with the greatest assurance'.[7] President Thiers himself was encouraging rather than patronizing when, in response to Iwakura's declaration that the mission's intention was 'to visit all the nations of Europe in order to know them, study them, and open relations between them and [Japan]', he expressed his desire for as complete and friendly relations as possible and stated that he 'would make it his duty to take all measures which may facilitate the ambassadors' mission in France'.[8] His promise seems to have been a genuine one. There is no indication that the Japanese visitors were unable to go anywhere or see anything they wished, and in some cases they were conducted by representatives of the French government – either Chanoine or the diplomat who had returned from Japan in 1871 after three years' service there, Ange-Maxime Outrey. More frequently, a French escort was unnecessary, and they were either guided by chargé d'affaires Samejima, or by his assistant, Frederick Marshall, or ventured out in small groups unaccompanied.

ITINERARY

An often very detailed picture of what the mission saw in France is provided by its official chronicler, Kume Kunitake, in the third of the five volumes which was published in Tokyo in 1878 under the title *Tokumei Zenken Taishi Bei-O Kairan Jikki*. From Kume's account it is clear that whatever the geographical limitations of the embassy's visits, its investigation of French civilization, and especially French institutions, was commendably wide-ranging. It is true that in their visits to Napoleon's tomb, to the palaces at Versailles, Fontainebleau, St Germain and Saint-Cloud, to Notre Dame cathedral, to the parks of the Bois de Boulogne and Buttes-Chaumont, to the Luxembourg Museum, to the Academy of Fine Arts and to the Arc de Triomphe, the ambassadors resembled tourists.[9] Such sight-seeing, however, was not entirely without an educational side, for – if Kume's account is any guide – it encouraged reflection on the history and nature of political, military and technological change. The excursion to the Paris Observatory, for instance, prompted Kume to write about the historical development of astronomy.[10] At a different level, the discovery that the park of Buttes-Chaumont in eastern Paris had been constructed by Napoleon III for the benefit of the workers in the neighbouring tenements led Kume to praise the ex-emperor and no doubt drew not just his attention, but also that of other members of the mission, to the question of how to deal with the problems presented by the growth of an urban proletariat.[11]

A number of other excursions more obviously linked investigation with sight-seeing. A visit on 15 January to the military academy at St Cyr, for example, was combined with one on the same day to Versailles, which the ambassadors had not had time to explore on 26 December.[12] But the majority of excursions were mainly or wholly serious in intent. On 3 January, for instance, Marshall conducted mission members to a foundling hospital; and on 6 January some of them toured not only the Bibliothèque Nationale but also the Conservatoire des Arts et Sciences, which displayed agricultural and industrial machinery. The next day a visit to the Mint was followed by one to a pawnshop, an institution which Kume regarded as socially important and described in great detail. On 10 January, after viewing the Père Lachaise cemetery, where Kume was struck by the difference in quality between the tombstones of the rich and those of the poor, the mission was taken to an ironworks. The week was rounded off on 11 January, a Saturday, with a trip to Sèvres to see the government-owned porcelain factory.[13]

During the following week the Japanese interest in military affairs came to the fore. After their visit to St Cyr on 15 January, the ambassadors again went westward on 17 January to the gun emplacement at Mont Valérien where the evidence of the German attack in the recent war remained clearly visible. Next day they went in the opposite direction to the artillery school and barracks at Vincennes. In between, on 16 January, they fitted in a visit to the impressive new Paris waterworks.[14]

The itinerary during the rest of January was more varied. On the 20th the embassy visited not only the École de Ponts et Chaussées, the leading institution for teaching construction and engineering, but also the École des Mines, while on the following day no less than three establishments were toured: the Bank of France, the Gobelins weaving factory, and a chocolate (or, according to Kido's diary, a coffee cake) factory. This hectic pace was maintained on the 22nd, when visits were paid to the Paris Observatory, a law court, and a major prison. On 23 January industrial art received attention when the mission members were guests of a leading metalwork company, Christofle. On the same day, a school for deaf and dumb children was inspected, and this was complemented by a visit to a school for blind children two days later.[15] Not until 27 January, surprisingly, when Kido again travelled to Versailles, did any of the Japanese leaders attend a session of the Assemblée Nationale.

Kido also pursued his constitutional and political interests in a series of meetings with Professor Maurice Block, a naturalised ex-German who had become known to the vice-ambassador through his position as a teacher of a Japanese student, Nishioka Yumei. Block is said to have been the only academic visited by mission members, not only in France but also in America and Britain,[16] and as well as meeting with Kido on at least four occasions, he also gave him a book and a map as farewell presents. For the most part, however, the mission was much less active in February than it had been in January, making only two further inspections, both of factories.

IMPRESSIONS OF FRANCE

What sort of impression did France make on the Iwakura mission? The short answer, if one judges from Kume's *Kairan Jikki*, is that it was still seen as a leading state and that its reputation had not suffered in Japanese eyes from its recent defeat at the hands of Germany. Its reverses in 1870-1 were attributed by Kume not to any basic deficiency, and certainly not to any lack of fighting spirit among its rank-and-file soldiers, but rather to its relative weakness in numbers compared with Germany and to the inferiority of its officer corps. Neither of these deficiencies was irreparable, and French willingness to learn from

Germany was indicated when, on their visit to Vincennes, the Japanese were given to understand that 'formerly the French had never imagined copying, but very regrettably, if they did not do this, France might not be able to remain France. . .'[17] Such a sentiment would no doubt have struck a chord with the ambassadors, who were all too conscious of the need to maintain Japan's distinctive character while borrowing from the West.

It was not only expectations of French adaptation that made France still appear worthy of respect, but also its economic standing. According to Kume, Britain had been surprised and Germany dismayed by the speed and ease with which the war indemnity imposed by Germany had been paid off, and this fact was adduced to confirm not only that France's financial and commercial position was healthy but that it had a rich reservoir of talented men, especially in the fields of economics and commercial law.[18] Elsewhere Kume described Paris as ranking with London and New York as one of the three great trading capitals of the world, and it was largely because he saw Paris as the fashion and industrial arts centre of Europe that he maintained that France was not inferior to Britain. While acknowledging that Britain led the way in mass production, he stressed that it could not match French elegance and delicacy.[19] His admiration for France was also evident when he wrote in the introduction to his account of the mission's visit to France that 'British industry depends on machines; in France there is a balance between human skills and machines'.[20]

France was rated highly by Kume on other grounds too. It was, he asserted, superior to Britain in refinement despite the latter's economic wealth; and although he reported the view that Germany had attained a higher level in some respects, he still held France to be the most enlightened country.[21] Not only was France seen as the pinnacle of elegance and civilization because of the reputation of French painting, sculpture, jewellery, clocks, buttons and dress styles, but its language was the medium of the European aristocracy. Moreover, it had held this preeminent position for over two centuries.[22] Admittedly, it was also a Catholic country with a financially burdensome priesthood, but Kume found that in France Christianity seemed to intrude less into everyday life than in the Anglo-Saxon countries. He remarked on the holiday-like feeling of Parisian Sundays, adding that 'when one goes from America to Britain the atmosphere of religion diminishes, and when one goes from Britain to France it is halved'.[23] Kume's lack of enthusiasm for Western religion did not, however, prevent him from admiring Notre Dame, and it was his visit there which prompted the comment that in comparison with the great Western cathedrals the Honganji in Kyoto seemed hut-like.[24]

It is doubtful whether many of the mission's other members were as enthusiastic about France as Kume,[25] but at least some of his sentiments do seem to have been shared. Okubo Toshimichi and Kido Takayoshi both found the often bright weather and clear air of Paris a welcome change after London, and Okubo was sufficiently impressed by this and by the architecture of the French capital to accept that it might well be the world's number one city.[26] He was particularly struck by the Bois de Boulogne and, in a letter to Oyama Iwao, he waxed lyrical about the spectacular waterfall there and the fragrant flowers that bloomed out of season and which created the impression of entering a pure land away from the real world. [27] Okubo also seems to have shared with Kume an admiration for the French President, whose rise to national prominence from a relatively poor background would have been appreciated by those among the ambassadors who had similarly achieved power by their own endeavours. It should be noted, however, that Okubo regarded France, like Britain and America, as too advanced for Japan to emulate. Instead, he suggested in a letter from Paris to Nishi Tokujiro, Germany and Russia would be more appropriate models for Japan.[28]

Okubo's comment raises the question of whether what the Iwakura mission learned in France was of any real value. The answer may well be that although their stay in France undoubtedly gave the Japanese leaders a fuller understanding of Western civilization, it ultimately did little more than reinforce a number of established convictions. The chief of these, arguably, was that although change, based on new knowledge, was essential, it was important to recognize and build on the achievements of the past. With its museums and libraries Paris was one of the best places to remind the Japanese of the legacy of the past and the way in which it helped to shape the national identity. At the same time, however, the extensive new building carried out under the Second Empire and the various developments in social policy noted by Kume (such as the creation of housing, parks, and agencies of social and economic assistance for workers and the disadvantaged) would also have shown that reform and innovation could work. Apart from these two contrasting lessons, the embassy certainly encountered evidence of how France had suffered from the Franco-Prussian War and the Paris Commune, but whether Japanese leaders who had lived through the turbulent 1860s needed to be alerted to the dangers of military defeat and civil war is highly questionable. Nor did they need to visit France and be told about the frequent changes of regime in that country in the previous eighty-four years to be aware that newly-established political systems might easily be overthrown. One other possible lesson which the mission might have learned was the desirability of acquiring a colonial empire. Kume noted that colonies provided France with profitable access to raw materials, and he suggested that Algeria's geographical position vis-à-vis France resembled that of Korea towards Japan.[29] In the light of Iwakura and Okubo's defeat of the expansionists in Japan in the dispute over Korea later in 1873, however, it would seem that this lesson was premature.

The remaining question for consideration is whether the Iwakura mission had any impact on diplomacy. One reason for suspecting that it did not is that diplomatic issues were discussed on only one occasion – when Iwakura (aided by Samejima) met foreign minister Rémusat (supported by Outrey) on 24 January 1873. The fact that this encounter was not recorded by Kume, and also not mentioned in Kido's diary, Okubo's letters or Ito's biography, would suggest that it was not regarded as significant, at any rate by the Japanese.

TROOPS AND TREATIES

It would, in fact, have been surprising if serious negotiations had taken place in Paris, for the current issues in Franco-Japanese relations were ones which could not be decided by bilateral talks. The Japanese wish for the withdrawal of foreign troops from Yokohama, for instance, involved Britain as well as France, since both countries had maintained forces to protect their nationals in that port for nearly ten years. After 1868 the Meiji government had objected to the foreign military presence, but no progress had been made towards securing their removal. What made the issue difficult was that whenever either Britain or France showed an inclination to accept withdrawal, the other country always discovered some pretext for maintaining the status quo. Behind such obstructionism there sometimes existed an ulterior motive. In 1869, for instance, when the then French minister in Japan, Outrey, rejected a British suggestion that troops might be withdrawn, he did so nominally on the grounds that they were still needed to provide security but really because he considered that the existing situation put France on a level of equality with Britain and in a position of superiority to other Powers.[30] Subsequently the prospects of withdrawal had improved when the French Navy Ministry came to advocate withdrawal, but this counted for little because Britain generally opposed any change and because in September 1871 Rémusat adopted the dubious position that the presence of the French troops might be a useful 'means of action' if the Meiji government pursued its recently declared intention of revising its treaties with foreign countries.[31]

This insistence on maintaining the status quo was still the official French policy when Iwakura arrived in Paris, despite a recommendation from the Comte de Turenne, the chargé d'affaires in Tokyo, that it was safe to withdraw the forces and that it would improve France's standing in Japan if the French government took the initiative in doing so.[32] The fact that the British foreign secretary, Lord Granville, had recently informed Iwakura that troops were still needed for security purposes confirmed the French foreign minister in his judgement and deprived the Japanese ambassador of any expectation of success in Paris. Iwakura did present a new request for withdrawal, but that he was only going through the motions was shown by the fact that he made no attempt to press the point when Rémusat observed that it was important not to act precipitately and offered the less than precise assurance that withdrawal would take place 'dans un avenir plus ou moins rapproché'.[33] As it happened, it took another year before any French troops were withdrawn; and the Meiji government had to wait for a complete withdrawal until March 1875.

If the Iwakura mission had little reason to hope for success in this relatively simple matter, it had even less cause for optimism with regard to the much more difficult task of securing revision of the 'unequal treaties' which the Meiji government had inherited from the Tokugawa Bakufu. The likelihood that the Western powers would damage the interests of their own merchants by allowing Japan tariff autonomy was extremely remote, while the chances of ending the provision for foreigners to be tried, when they were defendants, in their own country's consular court were scarcely less slim. The fact that Japan had no realistic expectation of achieving concessions at this stage meant that the ambassadors had brought no concrete proposals with them when they left Japan in December 1871; and although their hopes were briefly raised in Washington, they had quickly learned that to try to embark upon treaty revision would be premature. As a result Iwakura was reluctant to negotiate with the British government; and in Paris it was the French foreign minister who broached the matter at their 24 January meeting.

Rémusat began by stating that France was satisfied with the treaties but that he had no objection to examining any Japanese proposals and that he believed that 'an exchange of ideas, by facilitating relations between the two countries, can only contribute to tightening the bonds which unite them'. In response Iwakura was evasive. He informed Rémusat that the mission's purpose was to express the sentiments which Japan felt towards the Powers and that, although it wished to discover the various governments' opinions, it was 'only on the embassy's return to Japan that they would proceed to revision'. Iwakura's evident desire to put off serious negotiation did not deter Rémusat from indicating French wishes. While praising Japan's progress so far, he also emphasised the desirability of the eradication of all anti-foreign prejudice, and to that end he urged that it was 'essential for relations between the indigenous population and foreigners to be more frequent'. He recognized that the Japanese government had reservations about the complete opening of Japan, and he conceded that so radical a measure might be premature; but he offered the opinion that 'the moment is come when there would be advantage for everybody in the granting of new facilities to foreigners'. That, he suggested, could take the form of the 'opening of the country subject to certain restrictions and on special conditions which would be regulated by a joint agreement'.[34]

Rémusat was by no means overbearing, but what he said could hardly be welcome to the ambassador, for it revealed that France had its own treaty revision agenda and that this ran counter to Japan's. Until the meeting of 24 January this fact had not been evident. In Tokyo the Comte de Turenne had evinced some (albeit limited) sympathy for the Meiji government's grievances about consular jurisdiction and, because he regarded the system of extraterritoriality as unsatisfactory in practice, he was even prepared to give mixed tribunals a trial.[35] In this he may have been influenced by Albert Dubousquet, an ex-member of the French military mission who had been recruited to the service of the Meiji government. In July 1872 Turenne sent to Paris a memorandum in which Dubousquet proposed a transitional system whereby consular courts would continue to take decisions in reality but in formal terms would only make recommendations which newly established Japanese courts of justice would confirm.[36] Clearly, these suggestions offered some hope of future concessions .

In France itself thoughts of revision had proceeded in a different direction. On 17 December 1872 a memorandum by Outrey suggested (highly implausibly) that in order to be relieved of payment of the remainder of the indemnity imposed after the allied expedition against Shimonoseki in 1864 Japan might offer the opening of new ports or even of the whole country. Although the French diplomat considered the latter possibility to be premature, he felt that merchants bearing passports should be allowed access to other commercial centres and that foreign ships should be permitted to trade at ports which had not been opened.[37] Such a proposal may appear to have been an obvious one, but it actually represented a departure from previous French acceptance of the view that it was better to limit Western access to the interior of Japan because recent experience seemed to show that increased exports would lead to a drop in the quality of Japanese silkworms, on which the French silk industry had come to rely. Although there is no direct evidence that the change of policy was prompted by the Iwakura visit, the date of the memorandum and the fact that no other explanation immediately suggests itself makes that a distinct possibility.

Whether or not the Iwakura mission unintentionally stimulated such a change in French policy, the situation soon became even more unsatisfactory from the Meiji government's standpoint. The French minister in Washington, Jules Berthemy, was appointed to Tokyo with the express task of negotiating treaty revision, and, in conjunction with the British and German ministers, he went significantly further than Rémusat by pressing for the unrestricted opening of the whole of Japan. It is noteworthy that in justifying to his own government the position he had adopted he made what appears to have been an indirect allusion to the Iwakura mission: 'It is when the Japanese government claims to have seriously embarked on the way of progress, when it boasts of a truly liberal policy and sends its officials and its students around America and Europe to find an often too eager welcome, that at that moment one sees it without any avowable reason deny to businessmen, to traders, to foreign travellers permission to go more than six leagues into the interior of the country'.[38] As it turned out, Berthemy's diplomatic colleagues were less single-minded; and when the Meiji government conceded the right of travel in the interior for most non-commercial purposes, they were willing to accept what was offered, leaving Berthemy to make empty threats to the Meiji government about the consequences of what he chose to regard as its unreasonable attitude. Nevertheless, his attempt to make the treaties even more unequal than they already were had placed the Meiji government in a difficult position and may have been one of the least desired consequences of the Iwakura mission.

IN DEFENCE OF CHRISTIANS

Ironically, the Japanese ambassadors had had much more reason to be apprehensive about a quite different issue. The treatment of Japanese Christians had been a cause for complaint against the Meiji government from its inception, because it had inherited from the Bakufu the problem of what to do with the hidden believers whose existence had come to light when French Catholic priests built a cathedral in

Nagasaki in 1865. The new leaders of Japan were by no means disposed to abandon the two-and-a-half-centuries-old proscription of Christianity. Indeed, they sought to force the newly discovered Christians, most of whom came from the Urakami valley, to apostasize, eventually going so far as to split up their families, exile their members to different provinces, and set them to forced labour. Because France claimed the right to protect Catholics in the East, it was natural that French diplomacy should be particularly concerned with the Urakami question. Its capacity for action was limited, however, by several factors, beginning with the special position of Outrey's predecessor, Léon Roches. His close relationship with the Bakufu inhibited him from protesting at the initial arrests as strongly as the French missionaries who were encouraging the native Christians wished. Indeed, when the Catholic periodical, *Les Missions Catholiques*, published a series of articles about the Urakami question at the time of the Iwakura mission's visit to France, the allegation was made that the French diplomat had converted to Islam during his earlier service in North Africa.[39] More important than Roches' own attitude, however, was the fact that after his departure in June 1868 it became one of his successor's main priorities to dispel any suspicion on the part of the Meiji government that France might seek to undermine the new regime. In consequence, Outrey played down France's special religious role and protested against Japanese religious intolerance only verbally or when the other treaty powers did so.

There was a brief moment in 1870 when persecution intensified and the French minister contemplated recommending the use of threats backed by an 'imposing demonstration'.[40] This quickly passed, however, and even though missionaries continued to complain of harsh treatment of Japanese Christians, in 1872 the Comte de Turenne sent a series of reports which indicated that the situation was improving.[41] Not only did he inform the Quai d'Orsay that some arrested Christians had been released and that the edict imposing severe penalties had been revoked, he also stated that Japanese would now be permitted to practise Christianity provided they did not attempt to convert others.

Turenne's acceptance of the Meiji government's protestations that it was moving as fast as was practicable towards toleration was significant, for it counteracted pressure from missionaries and their supporters for the government to adopt a critical tone towards the Iwakura mission in Paris. This was publicly evident when, on 7 December, just before the embassy's arrival, an emotional attack was made on Japanese religious intolerance by a deputy in the French National Assembly. The deputy, the Comte de Richemont, began by noting Japan's recent progress: 'Shaking off its age-old lethargy, emerging from the absolute seclusion which specially characterized its policy, this empire has been seized with a taste, I will almost say passion, for occidental civilization'. But this, he continued, made the recent news that a third of the 3,000 exiled Christians had died all the more shocking. He then proceeded to point out that Japan was 'at this very moment sending a solemn embassy to visit the different European powers', and to the acclaim of other deputies he suggested that this was 'an opportune circumstance for making the voice of France heard on this subject, so profoundly serious and so profoundly grievous'. He concluded by appealing to France's tradition: 'France has remained ahead of the world and, despite its misfortunes, the first of the Christian nations. . . . France will never cease to provide a protection which is perhaps the greatest honour of its history'.[42]

So clamorous was the support for Richemont that Rémusat, even though he ventured to suggest that the persecution might be less than had been alleged, was obliged to promise that he would use French influence to secure 'behaviour more befitting a nation which wished to have itself counted among the civilized nations'. Referring specifically to the mission's impending arrival, he observed that its purpose was 'to study the arts of Europe, the railways, the electric telegraphs, all the curiosities, all the novelties which have made our country illustrious', and he assured the Assembly that 'not only will we be eager to make known to it all these precious things, to initiate it into the material benefits of modern civilization, but we will neglect no opportunity to ensure that when it returns to Asia it teaches the Japanese something more precious: humanity and tolerance'.[43]

Rémusat kept his promises, but in a way which Richemont would undoubtedly have considered half-hearted and unsatisfactory. Turenne was instructed to remind the Japanese government of 'the duties imposed on it by its generous ambition of securing for Japan a rank among the truly civilized Powers', but not for nearly two weeks.[44] The chargé d'affaires was not told to hint at any threat of retaliation, and Rémusat himself abstained from any suggestion of pressure in his own conversation with Iwakura on 24 January. Rather than stressing French displeasure, he emphasized that a change in Japan's religious policy would serve its best interests: 'The most appropriate means of attracting to Japan the sympathies of Europe and America would be for the Japanese government to abandon the errors followed by it until today and to show itself benevolent towards the Christians. The political situation of the country may be an obstacle to the proclamation of full freedom of worship; but nothing seems to block an entry into the way of religious toleration.' He further implied that such a move 'would predispose the French government to enter on its side into the way of concessions'. In his response Iwakura, while avoiding any definite commitment, indicated that the Japanese government was aiming at religious toleration and would achieve it at an opportune moment. Had he chosen, the French foreign minister might have pressed him on his reasons for delay, but instead, the Quai d'Orsay procès-verbal recorded, he took note 'with satisfaction of the declarations which the Ambassador has just made'.[45]

The fact that Rémusat had taken a conciliatory line towards Iwakura may not have escaped the attention of the missionaries and their supporters. Five weeks after the mission's departure from France, six members of the National Assembly renewed the call for the French government to take advantage of the current opportunity 'to resume, within the limits imposed by circumstances but with the firmness which its honour and its interests enjoin, its traditional policy in the Far East'. They demanded the 'active intervention of French agents' in support of religious liberty and asserted that France had the right to require from Japan 'guarantees analogous to those given to us by the Chinese government in the treaty of Tientsin'.[46] Their appeal, however, had already been rendered irrelevant by a telegram from Turenne announcing that 'the Japanese government has just abrogated the edicts against Christianity and it is going to proceed to free the Christians exiled in 1870'.[47] This evidently satisfied Rémusat, although his successor, the arch-conservative Duc de Broglie, tried to reopen the issue in August, when he instructed Berthemy to insist that missionaries be allowed to preach throughout Japan, not just in the open ports.[48] The minister in Tokyo, however, poured cold water on the idea and it was very quickly dropped by a new foreign minister, the Duc de Decazes, in December 1873.[49]

The action which had prompted Turenne's telegram in February was the removal of the notice-boards prohibiting Christianity in Japan, and in view of their proximity in time it might be tempting to assume that this measure and the Iwakura mission's stay in France were connected. The evidence for this supposition, however, is at best circumstantial and runs counter to the recent argument that even if Ito Hirobumi became convinced – at a rather earlier stage – of the desirability of religious freedom, the senior ambassadors remained unpersuaded, however much Iwakura sought to give a different impression in his diplomatic encounters.[50] Furthermore, as Berthemy pointed out at the time, the removal of the anti-Christian notice-boards did not necessarily mean that the prohibition of Christianity had been formally ended.[51] From a rather different angle, it also needs to be noted that the caretaker government in Japan sometimes acted without consulting the Iwakura mission. It should not be assumed, therefore, that the changes in the treatment of Christians reported by Turenne necessarily have to be explained in terms of a change of attitude or understanding on the part of the ambassadors.[52]

Nevertheless, before the significance of the Iwakura mission's visit to France is dismissed, a further factor needs to be taken into account. One of the original reasons for the proscription of Christianity was that Japanese leaders feared that it would enable Western countries to encroach upon Japan on the pretext of protecting co-believers in their own religion. The fact that the Iwakura mission emerged unscathed from its venture into (in religious terms) hostile country may have given the Japanese leaders some reassurance that Christianity was not quite the insidious vanguard of Western power that they had suspected. Since it was French missionaries who had the keenest interest in the Urakami Christians, and since France prided itself on protecting Catholics in the East, the French foreign minister's abstention from any attempt to intimidate the embassy over the religious issue may have been particularly important in reducing Japanese apprehensions. If so, the fact that in practice the ban on Christianity became a dead letter from 1873 onwards may have owed something to Iwakura's reception in Paris.

RESULTS OF THE VISIT

In conclusion, it seems possible that the Iwakura mission's visit to France had some impact, albeit probably a limited one, on both the treaty revision question and the Christian problem. The main significance of the mission, however, has generally been felt to have lain in the general impression of the new Japan which it created, and, above all, in what the ambassadors learned about Western civilization and its applicability to Japan. It seems reasonable to suppose that if the overall experience of the Iwakura mission was indeed of great value, then its time in France cannot have been unimportant. Nevertheless, to measure that impact seems impossible. If one considers the impression that the mission made on the French government, for instance, one might well accept that Rémusat's congratulations to Iwakura on Japan's civilizing efforts constitute evidence that a favourable image had been established. Such an image, however, was arguably created less by the Japanese mission itself than by the favourable reports on Japanese progress from Turenne in Tokyo and by gratification that Frenchmen were playing key roles in Japan's transformation.[53]

The French public image would similarly have been shaped by the mission itself only to a very limited extent, for although the ambassadors' seriousness and intelligence were favourably commented on, less attention was paid to their activities in Paris than to news of events and developments in Japan itself. The reception of the new French military mission by the Meiji emperor in October 1872, for instance, was given substantially more space in *Le Siècle* on 28 December than the paper had allotted the day before to the audience given by President Thiers to Iwakura; and the reports on the embassy in the *Journal Officiel de la République Française* were outnumbered by items on such varied topics as Japanese foreign trade, the extension to Tokyo of the submarine cable, Japanese students of industry abroad, the original opening of Japan, Japanese silkworms, reforms in Japan, and the contributions of various Frenchmen to Japan's progress. *Le Monde Illustré*, though less broad in its coverage, accompanied its (1 February 1873) account of the Emperor's reception of the French officers with a half-page artist's impression and two weeks later also had a whole page of eye-catching pictures illustrating the opening of Japan's first railway. In any case, even if the French image of a progressive new Japan was confirmed or enhanced by the visit of the Iwakura mission, the diplomatic effect was largely counteracted by the highly negative attitude of the new French minister in Tokyo, who believed that Iwakura had been received too favourably and that as a consequence the Japanese government was behaving like a spoilt child.[54]

When one turns to the even more fundamental question of what impact the Iwakura mission had on Japanese understanding of, and attitudes towards, the West, precise measurement is no easier. There are, of course, indications that the ambassadors were impressed by many of the things they saw. After his visit to the maison Violet, the largest and most up-to-date perfume manufacturer in France, for instance, Iwakura is reported to have said that 'he would never have thought that the perfume industry could possess such notable and perfectly maintained establishments'.[55] Moreover, it cannot be ignored that the mission's extraordinary journey brought Western statesmen (who, at least in France's case, rarely seem to have given Japan much thought) into direct contact with the top Meiji leaders in an unprecedented way and made it almost incumbent on them to offer their visitors advice. Rémusat certainly made an attempt to encourage Iwakura to accept Western liberal values, for as well as urging religious toleration he also went out of his way to advocate a change in attitude towards the merchant class. He understood, he informed the ambassador, 'that in Japan this very important part of society is not treated with all the respect and consideration with which it is surrounded in Europe. France', he went on, 'attaches importance to everything which has a bearing on industry and commerce, and it is desirable, in Japan's own interest, that the government takes upon itself to remove class distinctions which among us are completely unknown'.[56] Iwakura's response was vaguely favourable but it was far from the first time that such ideas had been suggested to Japanese leaders. Did it make a difference that on this occasion they were recommended by a Western statesman rather than an ordinary diplomat? That this, like other similar questions about the Iwakura mission, cannot be answered with any certainty makes it difficult to avoid the conclusion that to describe the mission's activities is easier than to assess its significance precisely.

4

BELGIUM

17-24 FEBRUARY 1873

Willy Vande Walle

THE IWAKURA MISSION had several objectives but, in view of the fact that its official aim was to enter into preliminary talks about revision of the unequal treaties, it was obvious that Belgium should be included in the itinerary. It had been the ninth Western country to conclude a Friendship and Commerce Treaty with the Bakufu, which had been signed on 1 August 1866. Putting aside the diplomatic rationale, we have to ask ourselves whether there might have been any other particular, and more specific, reason why Belgium was worth visiting.

For one thing, this was not the first Japanese mission to visit Belgium. A few years earlier, in 1865, part of a Satsuma mission to Great Britain had visited Belgium extensively, held talks with government representatives, and even signed a contract for the establishment of a Satsuma-Belgian joint venture company.[1] In 1867 the high-profile Bakufu mission to the Paris Exposition led by Tokugawa Akitake had also paid a goodwill visit to Belgium on its tour of the treaty powers.

Leaving aside the Satsuma mission which did not have an official character,[2] the purpose of both the Bakufu and the Iwakura missions was to promote goodwill and international recognition, to study the material and spiritual civilization of the West as well as its military aspects, with an eye to furthering the modernization of Japan.[3] A subsidiary objective appears to have been the control of the Japanese students studying abroad.[4]

When we compare the itineraries and the programmes of both the Bakufu and the Iwakura missions in Belgium, they show a striking resemblance: the hosts were largely the same or at least had the same perception of the relative importance and position of Japan in the world. Moreover many secretaries of the Iwakura mission were former Bakufu officials, selected precisely for their experience of travelling abroad.[5] This and other elements bear testimony to the continuity that spanned the overall aims governing both missions, whether in the format of the missions themselves or in their respective programmes. The programmes, incidentally, are not very different from present-day missions. They share similar obligatory official functions (e.g. official audience by King Leopold II) and courtesy calls, the cultural and society evening events (the Iwakura mission went to the Brussels première of Wagner's *Tannhäuser*, and attended a sumptuous soirée at the Royal Palace), the sightseeing excursions on Sunday (they visited the battlefield of Waterloo and the memorial hill there, and an Art Museum in Antwerp on Monday), as well as a tight schedule of company visits.

If we are to discern a difference between the Akitake and the Iwakura missions, it is in their emphasis on either military establishments and institutions or industrial facilities. Most of the industrial facilities the Bakufu mission visited had to do with the construction of military equipment, whereas the Iwakura mission squarely put its emphasis on coal mines, iron foundries, glassworks and textile factories. No visit to a canon foundry was included. That armament figured so prominently on the agenda of the Bakufu mission (as it did on that of the mission from Satsuma) had much more to do with internal problems than with any foreign threat: the growing antagonism between the Bakufu and the insurgent domains.

The Bakufu urgently needed to strengthen its army, but could not appeal to Great Britain, which showed itself less than committed to the Bakufu. Initially the Bakufu emissaries had intended to visit France, Britain, the Netherlands and Belgium, in that order. However, eventually they began to have doubts as to the kind of reception they would receive in Britain and therefore decided to change the order of the countries visited. They would first visit Holland, with whom Japan had a long-standing relationship of friendship, and then Belgium, with whom Japan had concluded a treaty just one year before, and only then Britain. They calculated that after the warm welcome Holland and Belgium had extended to the embassy, Britain could do no less.

BELGIUM'S INDUSTRIAL POWER

Why then was it important for the Iwakura mission to visit Belgium apart from the diplomatic niceties? In terms of armaments Belgium certainly had a lot to offer, but had it in terms of industry? The answer is yes. Belgium had actually been the second industrialized nation in

Europe, following Great Britain, and the first on the continent. Its coal mines, furnaces, glassworks, wool, cotton and linen mills ranked among the most modern and competitive on the continent. By 1850 Belgium had even grown into a considerable competitor for some of Great Britain's industry.[6] The major technological innovations had been implemented in the first quarter of the nineteenth century. Between 1800 and 1810, under French rule (1798-1815), cotton spinning (Ghent) and wool spinning (Verviers) had been mechanized. Between 1820 and 1830, during the period of the United Kingdom of the Netherlands (1815-30), metallurgical industry had gone through a series of innovations, highlighted by the introduction of the coke furnace (1821) and the puddling process (1822), a more efficient method of transforming cast-iron into iron.[7]

Kume Kunitake, the chronicler of the mission, quotes a Belgian spokesman as saying that until 1825 Belgium did not have any industry of note except for ceramics.[8] Ishizaka Akio contests this, claiming that, after a long period of stagnation, Belgium had entered the phase of industrial revolution under the rule of Napoleon and that it ranked among the vanguard of industrializing countries on the continent.[9] While it is true that the period of Napoleonic rule did away with most vestiges of the *ancien régime*, and firmly established bourgeois society, it took another decade before industrialization really took off. The Napoleonic period did create the necessary conditions however. The *Code de Commerce*, promulgated in 1807, established the *société anonyme* in Belgium.[10] Therefore Kume's spokesman is correct in his chronology, because it took some time to translate the new legislation into an institutional framework and the latter into a new type of economy. These were developments witnessed during the period of the United Kingdom of the Netherlands. The first joint stock company was established in 1819. In 1822 King Willem I of the Netherlands founded the *Algemeene Nederlandsche Maatschappij ter Begunstiging van de Volksvlijt*. In 1830, when Belgium became independent, its official name was changed to *Société générale pour favoriser l'industrie nationale* commonly referred to as the Société Générale. This powerful company would determine to a considerable extent the industrial development of Belgium.[11] Willem I pursued a vigorous policy of industrialization of the newly-acquired southern half of his kingdom in an attempt to bridge the many gaps that existed between the Dutch and the Belgian parts of the realm. He took a personal interest in many of the companies that were established during his reign. His policy soon began to bear fruit. For instance, *John Cockerill & Cie*, later to become one of Belgium's major steel mills, was established in 1825.[12]

Just how high Belgium ranked on the scale of the Japanese is hard to tell. That it was the fourth country visited was no doubt due more to its geographical position than to its rank on the scale of importance the Japanese had in their minds. If anything, it figured more prominently on the ranking scale of the Bakufu mission than on that of the Iwakura mission. With Britain keeping aloof and France the only major power dedicated to the Bakufu, Belgium was in the eyes of the Bakufu potentially a welcome supportive state. By 1873 the political landscape of Europe had changed dramatically. Napoleon III had been toppled, France was smarting from its defeat in the Franco-Prussian War and Germany had just become a unified empire. What I would like to call the *Eidokufutsu* mindset would soon dominate Japan's approach to Europe, but it had not yet at the time of the Iwakura mission.

Although they visited Belgium for a mere eight days, i.e. from 17-24 February 1873, whereas they stayed 12 days in Holland and 27 in Switzerland, Kume devoted three chapters each to these smaller countries. The first of the three chapters on Belgium is entitled *Berugī sōsetsu* (a general description of Belgium), and is a general treatise on the country, its history, topography, industry, agriculture and way of life, political institutions, morality and religion. The other two chapters are written in diary format, relating the visits to the industrial plants, fortifications and other noteworthy sights. The flow of diary notes is regularly interrupted with an essay-like digression on the processes and principles of the industrial activity they are visiting, in a format that is found throughout the *Bei-Ō kairan jikki*.[13] He inserts an outline of the industrial process of spinning and weaving cotton, when relating the visit to the *Filature et Tissage de Coton* of M.F. Lousbergs at Ghent, and of the process of treating flax and weaving linen, when describing their visit to La Lys in the same city. The visit to the famous glassworks at Val-Saint Lambert is an opportunity to give a description of the process of glass-blowing and decorating the finished products. When describing the visit to the *Société Anonyme Cockerill*, he gives a short description of the Bessemer process of iron-making (in Kume's transcription *Beshima no hō*), further referring to chapters 27 and 36, where he deals with the same process in Britain.

He makes a digression about mechanics: the lever, the slope and the pulley.[14] Often, when explaining a principle of physics or technology, a typically Western institution, or a technical device, he adds that because Japan or Asia does not have it, they are lagging far behind. For instance, after having described the manufacturing process of linen, he goes on to say that the flax is much coarser than the ramie found in

Japan. The ramie (*karamushi*) of Echigo e.g. has a lustre that is equal to that of silk. Yet, because Japan lacks the technology, the finished product (*nuno*) is far less refined than European linen cloth.[15]

Why was Belgium interested in receiving this mission? One reason is of course emulation. In internal correspondence of the Ministry of Foreign Affairs, one comes across arguments to the effect that, since other European countries have received the Japanese with pomp and circumstance, Belgium could do no less. Apart from that, the motive was first and foremost economic, arguably more so than for the other countries, for whom matters of hegemony, international prestige and influence or historical ties played a stronger role than they did for Belgium.

From 1834 onwards the fledgling Belgian state embarked upon a state-sponsored programme of railway construction. This was quite unique. No other country except for Britain had done so. In most other countries railway-building was entrusted to private companies. For the Belgian government railway-building was enough of a priority to sponsor the enterprise with state money. Now that Belgium had been deprived of the Rhine, and the Dutch colonies, it had to look for other markets, and these it found close by, in Germany and France, which could be reached by railway links. In 1844 the country counted 560 km of trunk lines. Adding the private branch lines that were subsequently built, the country could boast a total length of 3027 km in 1871.[16] The Belgian railways were important enough for Kume to devote a short essay to a comparison of the relative merits of the different types of railway company.[17]

With the proliferating railway system as a lever, the Belgian economy expanded dramatically. Two major banks, the *Société Générale* and the *Banque de Belgique* invested in iron-manufacturing, coal-mining and machinery. They imported the latest techniques and production methods from Great Britain, thus realizing the first industrial revolution on the continent. Belgium exported pig iron and railway equipment to Germany and France. When the world went through a railway construction boom during the sixties, Belgian industry found itself in an advantageous position to make the best of the opportunities offered and expanded its exports to other European countries as well, even financing the construction in those countries.[18]

In the wake of the crisis of 1867, however, the railway boom abated, while France and Germany had successfully completed their own industrial revolution and had less need for Belgian products. The country saw itself forced to look for new markets overseas, and this explains the great interest Belgium had for China and, to a lesser extent, for

Japan. Admittedly, interest in colonies dated from an earlier date. Even during the 1840s unsuccessful attempts had been made to acquire colonial possessions in Guatemala and Guinea[19] but during the sixties the need became more urgent. There were proposals to buy the Philippines from Spain, or to set up a venture in Taiwan. From 1868 on, missions put together by the *Société Générale* and the *Société Anonyme Cockerill* were dispatched to China to explore new possibilities, although the efforts to sponsor development projects in China would only bear fruit in the 1890s, when Belgium secured the concession to build the Beijing-Hankou railway.[20]

Belgium was indeed seeking new markets overseas for its capital exports and heavy industries, in an attempt at cushioning the effects of the economic crisis of 1867, which had put a temporary end to the railway-boom. This was the perspective from which the Belgians welcomed their Japanese guests. That explains, too, why the programme that the emissaries were presented with was heavily tilted to heavy industry, even leaving out a visit to the arms factory in Liège. Belgium was clearly eager to sell its industrial products to Japan, more than its weapons.[21]

TALKS WITH THE BELGIAN GOVERNMENT

On 23 February Iwakura had an interview with representatives of the Belgian government. Because the then minister of foreign affairs, Baron d'Aspremont-Lynden, was ill, he was replaced by Auguste Baron de Lambermont, who was secretary-general of the Ministry of Foreign Affairs, with the function of Envoy extraordinary and Minister plenipotentiary.[22] In the interview Iwakura had with Baron de Lambermont, the latter did most of the talking. He dealt at length with the possibilities of bilateral trade with Japan, including the export of weapons, technical assistance to the construction of artillery arsenals, Belgian participation in plans to build railways in Japan, accommodation of funds and sales of equipment.[23]

Although a Francophile elite had won Belgium's independence, the major threat to its independence was France. Therefore, Belgium had espoused perpetual neutrality, a status that was cemented in international treaties and guaranteed by Great Britain. As a result, Belgian diplomacy was largely predicated on British foreign policy. This was true in particular with regard to Japan, since Great Britain's representative to Japan, Sir Rutherford Alcock, had given substantial support to the Belgian envoy 't Kindt de Roodebeeke, in the process of negotiating a treaty with the Bakufu. On both these counts, it was evident that Belgium would align itself with the stance taken by Great Britain with regard to the Japanese insistence on treaty revision.

It comes as no surprise, therefore, to find in the file that contains all documents relating to the visit of the Iwakura embassy to Belgium in the Archives of the Ministry of Foreign Affairs, a number of documents and letters that originated in the British Foreign Office. Especially noteworthy are three memoranda, summaries of the three interviews Foreign Secretary Lord Granville had had with Iwakura. Equally interesting is the copy of the instructions Lord Granville had addressed afterwards to Sir Harry Parkes as to what course to follow in the negotiations for treaty revision that were to come. Sir Henry Barron had sent them to Lambermont.[24] The three memoranda recording the interviews between Granville and Iwakura are signed by W.G. Aston, interpreter.[25] All four documents were printed officially for wider distribution among British diplomats overseas.

In the margins of the memoranda in the archives at Brussels, someone has added in a careful hand, a few French words epitomizing the gist of the argument in the text, such as *tolerance, circulation libre de personnes*, etc. . . All the items appear in the memorandum of the meeting between Lambermont and Iwakura. On comparison Lambermont appears to reiterate many of the viewpoints already voiced by Granville. Lambermont had probably studied the British position very carefully in anticipation of his interview with Iwakura. From the British memoranda we learn that Iwakura had told Lord Granville that he was not charged with expressing the views of the Japanese government on the subject of treaty revision but only with ascertaining the views held on it by the British government. The British minister could scarcely conceal his exasperation at the noncommittal stance of his Japanese guest. At the second meeting of 27 November, the moot question of extraterritoriality and consular courts was broached. Lord Granville insisted on the necessity to ensure that British citizens got a fair trial. He adumbrated the possibility of following the experiment the British had set up in Egypt. There they had allowed Egyptian tribunals to administer the law in civil cases. If the experiment were to succeed, it would be tried in criminal cases also. If the mood that transpires from these records is anywhere near a faithful reflection of what was actually being said, then we cannot but conclude that the official contacts between the Japanese envoys and the representatives of the British government were rather unpleasant.

The meeting with Lambermont was on the surface less strained, although he struck a similarly condescending tone vis-à-vis Iwakura. The Belgian representative launched into a harangue about the strong points of Belgium's institutions, the merits of the free movement of goods and persons and the minimal import barriers as well as the need for religious tolerance. The question of extraterritoriality was not touched upon, whereas the exchange focused much more on industrial and commercial issues. Interestingly, all Iwakura's interventions boiled down to complimentary phrases except for one topic: several times during the meeting he reiterated his government's intention of revising the treaties, a topic that Lambermont kept steering clear of until the end.

Since this memorandum is the single most important documentary source about the contacts on an official level the mission had in Belgium, I will give a fairly extensive paraphrase of its contents.

The meeting begins with Lambermont reading a passage from the credentials of the Japanese mission. Thereupon he asks the envoy to give a brief overview of the prevailing situation in Japan and the existing relationship between the two countries. Iwakura says that this is the first mission sent abroad since a change of regime has occurred in Japan. Strangely enough, he seems to think that the treaty between Belgium and Japan had been concluded twelve years earlier. It is unclear whether this mistake is due to the secretary who took the minutes or to the envoy himself. He has been charged, Iwakura says, with studying the modifications that could be made to the treaties between the two countries. In an effort to justify this desire for treaty revision, he explains:

> For the last five years the feudal system has been abolished in our country; authority has been restored to the sovereign whose power has existed for centuries: our Emperor. We are assured that tranquility is completely guaranteed in the Empire. In order to consolidate this order of things, we are working hard to assimilate ourselves to the other civilized nations, in the field of politics, industry and the arts.

Next, Lambermont deems it useful to inform his guest about Belgium. He points out that Belgium is neutral, and does not take part in wars between other nations. It has no warships, but has an army of a hundred thousand men and fortresses to defend it. He assures the envoy of Belgium's willingness to help Japan, and implies that assistance from Belgium could not pose any threat to Japan's sovereignty. To this offer Iwakura replies that he would be most happy to hear any suggestion that might be of help in renewing Japan's treaties with the foreign powers.

Before talking about the treaty, Lambermont says he wants to give an outline of Belgium's administration, finances and public works, 'from the viewpoint of the relationship that has to be established between the two countries'. What follows is basically an overview of all the products and the expertise Belgium is willing to sell to Japan. He goes on to say that Belgium is a kingdom, has a bicameral assembly, and a provincial and a communal administration. With some pride he states that 'the general character of all our institutions is that they involve at the same time much freedom and much order'. He also enumerates the great variety of educational institutions and invites the Japanese to come and study in Belgium.

Belgium may be small in size, he says, but it is one of the richest countries in the world. The greatest care has been taken in the organization of its finances. The levy of taxes and the public expenditures are governed by extremely well conceived rules. Not only is there a special Ministry for Finance, but there is also a Board of Audit that oversees and controls all revenues and expenditures of the State. He carries on saying that he has read reports about the financial situation in Japan:

> I have noticed that the latest events have caused great expenditure, that some of the revenues have not been forthcoming and that the authorities have been forced to issue paper money. We know, he continues, that your government has commissioned research with a view to establishing a sound financial system. In that respect, Belgium can supply you with most useful information. We would even like to contribute to the creation in Japan of a financial system, which would have the double advantage of assisting your government and creating between the two countries banking relations of such a kind that neither side would any longer be obliged to rely on foreign intermediaries.

Next, Lambermont deals with the high-quality arms Belgium is producing and selling throughout the world. He expresses Belgium's eagerness to sell guns to Japan, canons and even warships. 'Belgian industry produces guns according to the most advanced system and canons after the Prussian system. Moreover, there are military schools and workshops of high renown, where Japanese officers and foremen sent by the Japanese government would be most welcome.'

The shipyards of Antwerp build large size vessels and boats of several types, even for Russia, especially designed for navigation on rivers and canals. He goes on to say that since Japan has an infinity of navigable waterways, Japan could purchase Belgium nautical equipment that is as advanced as that of any other country, yet available at a lower price.

Next, he vaunts, with some justification, the railroad network of Belgium. He points out that almost all railroads are government-owned. Belgium was indeed the first European country to implement a national programme of railway construction. In Seraing and Charleroi there are factories that produce rails, carriages, locomotives and all kinds of transport equipment. He says that he knows about the railroad between Edo and Osaka, the telegraph, the arms factories and the mint. He adds that he even had some personal connection with the company that built the first railroad in Japan. Belgium was on the point of being involved, but eventually, he says, the Americans have taken everything.

He expresses the hope that the embassy, after what it has seen in Belgium, will convince its government of the truth that for a country to prosper it needs an extensive railroad network. He hopes that the Japanese authorities will take note of the wide range of experts Belgium can offer in the field of railway construction: engineers, operators, accountants and all kinds of specialists for the preliminary research, the construction, administration and management of the railways. For the whole range of equipment no country could offer better conditions.

Moreover, the huge capital that lies accumulated in Belgium could be put to good use in Japan. For more than thirty years Belgium has been building railways, so that in terms of expertise no country can equal it. Lambermont deplores that so far commercial relations between the two countries have been limited. Belgium has been exporting window glass, nails, textiles, candles, paper and other articles. Apart from the glass, these products hardly represented innovative technologies. Then Lambermont hastens to say that he does not only want to sell, but is also interested in buying. He says that in Belgium there are great lovers of fine porcelains and lacquer objects. Japan could export cotton and silk to Belgium. It could also sell considerable amounts of rice and in the future probably also of sugar.

But before long, he returns to what he considers to be essential. He says:

> You will have noticed during your trip through America and Europe, especially through Belgium, that coal and iron are the essential elements of the industrial prosperity of nations. In Japan you have coal, iron, copper, gold and silver. These resources still lie buried in the ground, the laws of your country prohibiting their exploitation. They have to be unlocked. Your government and assembly will understand that the future of your country hinges on the use of these resources.

In the fields of coal-mining and metallurgy, too, Belgium is prepared to set up a company for the opening up of mines and the building of metallurgical works.

Iwakura replies that this is very interesting but, without further ado, takes up the issue of exchanging consuls. He says that he had intended to ask that Belgium appoint a new minister plenipotentiary in Tokyo, since the former representative had left Japan quite a while ago. He is glad to find out, upon arrival, that Belgium had just done so, for at the meeting, the new appointee, De Groote, was present. Lambermont intimates that Belgium intends to accredit a permanent representative in Japan, who will be assisted by a secretary and an engineer, whose job it will be to do market research and to follow industrial developments closely. Lambermont asks that the Japanese emperor equally accredit a diplomatic agent in Brussels. As a next step, he suggests that the Japanese appoint honorary consuls in Liège, Charleroi, Verviers and other industrial and commercial centres.

It is interesting to see how the two parties were talking on basically different wavelengths. Lambermont focuses on industrial development and commerce, Iwakura on purely diplomatic issues. Even the suggestion of appointing honorary consuls in the major centres bespeaks the mercantilist motivation of Lambermont. This spirit was omnipresent in all echelons of the Belgian administration and it even inspired the king himself.

Indicative of this difference in attitude is the following anecdote. When in 1867 King Leopold II received Tokugawa Akitake, the Belgian sovereign talked to the fourteen-year-old lad about trade. He told him that he should visit the foundries, that the use of iron is a sure measure of the wealth of a country and that Japan ought to buy lots of iron. The samurai in attendance on the young Tokugawa prince had been appalled by this blunt talk about business.[26] In the traditional Confucian scheme of things, those in government had to keep aloof from the pursuit of gain through commerce. Five years into the Meiji period, the same vision still largely prevailed among the erstwhile nobles and higher samurai, who were now in positions of power. This probably explains why Iwakura does not touch much upon the issues of commerce.

Then at last Lambermont touches upon the subject of the treaty. He says:

> When touring America, Great Britain and Belgium the ambassadors will have recognized that, in order to create a major industrial and commercial movement, one needs numerous means of communication and as few restrictions as possible. Just as industry needs coal and iron, trade requires economic and speedy means of transportation and much freedom as well. All formalities, all useless taxes have to be done away with. (. . .).

He refers to the ports that Japan has opened so far. Especially the port of Yokohama has been thriving. If Japan proceeds with the further opening of new ports, importing products into its interior and shipping its internal produce abroad through these ports, then Japan is sure, in his words, 'to become what it has to be, i.e. the Great Britain of the East'. He concludes this point stating:

> While admittedly import duties have to be maintained, it is vital that there are neither excessive taxes nor useless restrictions. It is in this spirit that in my opinion, we have to engage in revising the treaty.

Next he makes an appeal for allowing free movement of foreigners in the interior. He refers to the fact that Iwakura had promised to Linden, a Ghent horticulturist, whom the envoy had visited, that his agents would be allowed freely in the Japanese interior. He expresses the hope that this treatment may be extended to all Belgians wishing to travel in Japan.

Lambermont naturally also appeals for religious tolerance. As we shall see later, a considerable portion of public opinion was indignant at the news that had reached Europe about the inhumane treatment and persecution of the Christians. He lectures Iwakura about the freedom of religion that is guaranteed in Belgium and the system whereby priests of recognized faiths are even being paid a salary by the government. He admits that the prevailing treaty recognizes freedom of religion to Belgian citizens, but that it does not allow foreigners to interfere in the relationship between the Japanese authorities and their subjects. Yet, he insists, prosecution is contrary to the very progress the country is so eagerly pursuing. He refrains from protesting, but assumes a tone of friendly advice and is satisfied with the assurance by Iwakura that the Japanese government intends to allow religious freedom as the other nations do. Lambermont's soft approach was in line with the policy the other powers were pursuing with regard to the Urakami question and which might be characterized as positive engagement. Yet, it certainly would have displeased a large section of Belgian public opinion, had the contents of the meeting been made public.

KUME KUNITAKE'S VIEW OF BELGIUM

While Iwakura was concentrating on the diplomatic issues, Kume involved himself in as broad a study of the country as time would allow him. He has some interesting observations to make, which, needless to say, tell as much about him and the Japanese perception as they do about Belgium.

He begins his general description, the *Berugī sōsetsu*, as follows:

> In the previous volumes I have described America as an area of set-

> tlement for Europe, England as the world's market-place, France as the biggest market in Europe. These three big countries have a vast territory, and numerous population, they are mighty countries whose economic power (*eigyō no chikara*) reaches out over the entire globe (. . .) Our country Japan, when compared to these big countries in terms of territory, population or produce, does not necessarily fall that far behind. In my opinion, it is because the people are short-sighted and lacking in (the spirit of) community and perseverance that the economic power (of Japan) is weak and manifestly is not on a par with the power (of these states). Now that we have completed the tour of these three countries, I would like to take a look at one or two small countries (*shōkuku*), namely Belgium and Holland. In terms of territory or population these two countries may be compared with the island of Kyūshū. The land is unproductive and wet, yet they manage to survive among the big states, and maintain their sovereignty. Their economic power even surpasses that of the big states. They do not only maintain (commercial) ties with Europe, but influence world trade. This is due to nothing else but the diligence and concord of their populations. They have impressed me more deeply than the three big countries.[27]

It is evident that Kume believed that Japan had the inherent capacity of becoming a major country (*taikoku*), and therefore Belgium and Holland could not be models to emulate, yet they had a few lessons to teach that could be helpful to Japan.

Kume was struck by the fact that Belgium could survive in the midst of a hostile environment, surrounded as it was by the major powers of the world. That it could maintain its independence, he attributed in the first place to a strong army. He characterizes Belgians as valiant and hard working and obliquely refers to Caesar's statement in *De Bello Gallico* about the Belgians being the most valiant of all the peoples of Gaul, an idea that he directly or indirectly derived from a Belgian school textbook. Kume explains at some length why Belgium could so easily become the battlefield of Europe and why the country made such great outlays for the defence of its neutrality.

Leaving all rhetoric aside, it was true that Belgium put great stock by its defence. During the 1860s the politics of Napoleon III were growing into a major threat for Belgium. He attempted to purchase the Grand Duchy of Luxembourg in 1867, and tried to acquire the control over Belgian railway companies in 1869, so that in case of war there was a danger that warring parties would invade Belgium and violate its neutrality, which was guaranteed by international treaties. Therefore, between 1859 and 1868, Belgium embarked on a programme of fortifying Antwerp. It built a semi-circular wall around the city, supplemented by eight fortresses. This system of fortification was designed by H.A. Brialmont and constituted the newest in defence works.

The fortifications of Antwerp elicited keen interest among the Japanese. The Iwakura mission was preceded by the Tokugawa mission led by Akitake and an artillery officer named Harada Kazumichi had visited the place shortly before Iwakura.[28] The Satsuma mission, too, had gone to see it. At that time the works had not even been completed. Nevertheless, Godai writes about them with great interest. He comments that their size is not in proportion to the country and that they are the biggest of the recent fortifications anywhere in Europe.[29]

In Antwerp the Iwakura mission made a tour of the fortresses and batteries that protected the city. At the battery of Boechout they witnessed a demonstration by the artillery with ammunition. Kume concludes that the whole party was deeply impressed by the secure fortifications. He comments:

> Belgians all claim the following: When in a country there are few independent people, then the power of the state wanes, and the country cannot be preserved. The polity and legal system are all set up with an eye to fostering the capacity for independence. All strata of society are united in fostering a spirit of enterprise and setting up independent businesses. Up to 1825 there was not much in the way of industry, people worked the land and grew crops. The only industry was that of ceramics. Nowadays, although the population of the country is numerous, almost half of it are independent.[30]

In describing the political institutions of Belgium, Kume stresses their democratic character. He states that 'with regard to the sovereignty of the people, (it) even surpasses the republic'.[31] He is overstating the fact, however. For, while it may have been true that at the time of the foundation of the state in 1830, the new state adopted a very progressive and democratic constitution, which was hailed as such throughout Europe, by the time Iwakura arrived, it had not changed much, while the surrounding countries had witnessed seminal developments. In Belgium elective franchise was still limited to a small number of taxpayers. In this respect it was less democratic than the United States, Great Britain, the Third French Republic and the German Empire.[32]

THE ISSUE OF RELIGIOUS TOLERANCE

Although the Belgian press showed its interest in the visit of this exceptionally high-profile embassy, the happening did not figure as headline news. Most articles or notices about the embassy are subsumed under headings such as local news, referring to a visit to a city in the province, or as society news under the heading *Faits divers*. Belgian politics coloured off on the reporting of the visit. A sharp dividing line ran through Belgian society, pitting the Catholics against the free-thinkers. The acrimonious debate was not limited to Belgium alone, but it went on in most of the Catholic countries of Europe. The Pope had only recently been stripped of the Papal States, and the exile of Bishop Mermillod in Switzerland was causing a great uproar.

While the free-thinking press by and large gave a matter-of-fact report of the whereabouts of the embassy, what places they visited and what particularly impressed them, the Catholic press paid almost no attention to the socialite or economic and commercial aspects of the visit, but did not miss the occasion to criticize the Japanese government fiercely for its persecution of Christians. Notably the head of the embassy, Iwakura Tomomi, came under fire for having been an accessory to these abominable actions. The Catholic press urged the Belgian government and officials who had direct contact with the leaders of the embassy to press this point home with their guests. It will be recalled that persecution of Christians had been revived in 1867 under the Bakufu. When the new regime took over the reins of power, the missionaries had anticipated a more liberal attitude, but their hopes had been dashed, when the persecutions were resumed with a vengeance. The actions were inspired by a newly formulated nationalist ideology. All citizens of the new nation-state had to adhere to the native religion, since religion and state were supposedly one and the same thing (*saisei itchi*).[34]

In the spring of 1868 the government stepped up its efforts to clamp down on any show of adherence to the foreign religion. In April an imperial notification confirmed that Christianity remained prohibited as before, and anti-Christian notice-boards were put up again all over the country.[34] From the middle of the year the deportation of Christians began in earnest, a course of action that did not fail to elicit representations of protest from the consuls of the treaty powers. The foreign protests did bring temporary relief, but in the end imprisonment and deportation of Christians resumed on a massive scale.[35]

On 19 January 1870, at the request of the ministers of a few Western powers, a conference on religious matters was convened in Tokyo. Prime Minister Sanjō, the former Prime Minister Iwakura and the Minister of Foreign Affairs Terashima represented the Japanese government. The Western ministers were Harry Parkes of Great Britain,

Ange-Maxime Outrey of France, De Long of the United States and Max von Brandt of Prussia. While the foreign diplomats appealed to the Japanese to halt the persecution in the name of humanity and freedom of worship, the Japanese kept hammering away at the principle of the unity of religion and polity, invoking the right of the state to impose the native religion on all citizens. As a result further deportations were halted but the Catholic exiles, far from being immediately released, were kept for three more years in confinement.[36] To cap it all, four days before the Iwakura mission sailed for the United States, yet another group of over sixty exiles was sent into exile. After vehement protests from the foreign press in Japan and the West, they were released at the end of January 1872.[37]

Such was the mood in which the Iwakura mission left Japan. On account of this bad track-record, the mission was rather coldly received in the United States, while in Europe it ran into displays of public indignation in England, France, Belgium and Prussia. The matter was even discussed in the French Assembly. The ill tidings about the treatment of the Japanese Christians preceded the embassy wherever it went. The outcry in France did not fail to spread to Belgium. In Brussels, a large crowd purportedly lined the streets where the carriages of the envoys were passing through, protesting against the persecution and clamouring for the release of the Japanese Christians.[38]

The Catholic newspaper *Le Bien Public* of Sunday 23 February 1873, wrote:

> The newspapers of Brussels have reported on the latest ball at the Court, which, rumour has it, has been most sumptuous and lively. Even if we have to ruffle the self-infatuation of the fairest half of the attendance, we nevertheless have to note that it was the Japanese ambassadors who reaped the honours of the evening. These *magots* [small figurines], packed up more or less elegantly in European jackets, embroidered with raised satin stitch, have been entertained, coddled, adulated, and one has noticed that his Majesty has deigned to converse at length with Mister Iwakura, head of the embassy. No doubt, when seeing this glittering society, these bedecked uniforms and splendid dresses, these ladies decked out in low-necked dresses, M. Iwakura will have regretted to be unable to strike a few telling blows with his sword. That individual is indeed one of the main promoters of the persecution that erupted last year against the Christians and in which, according to the British newspapers, more than 2000 victims have perished.
>
> One has to admit that we push tolerance really to the limit by receiving that bloodthirsty individual with the honours and respect due an ambassador. Let us hope that his Majesty the King, a minister

> or an influential person will have taken the opportunity to drop a word in his ear and recall him to humanity. That the liberals show themselves to be insensitive to the fate of the Japanese Christians, we can perfectly understand, they have been so with regard to the Church martyrs of the Commune. What we fail to understand is that a Catholic minister showed himself indifferent to a just cause and did not avail himself of the opportunity of the presence of the Japanese ambassadors to plead with these individuals the cause of our hapless co-religionists. Moreover, it is possible that there are Belgian missionaries and Catholics in Japan, and Belgium owes it to itself to protect them against persecution.

Since the fall of 1872 Catholic circles in France had been voicing their protest against the persecution of the Christians at Urakami.[39] The Lyons weekly *Les Missions Catholiques* had run letters denouncing the ongoing harassment of Christians. Léon Pagès had published his memorandum on *La persécution des chrétiens au Japon et l'ambassade Japonaise en Europe*, addressed to the members of the National Assembly. At its session on 7 December 1872, a deputy, by the name of le comte Desbassayns de Richemont, had made a pathetic appeal for an intervention to put a halt to 'the odious and inhumane' persecution that had been going on for six years.[40]

Le Bien Public of 25 February, as well as the *Journal d'Anvers* of 25-26 February, both Catholic newspapers, rather belatedly ran extracts of a letter that had been sent from Japan and published in the aforementioned *Les Missions Catholiques* of 27 September 1872. The letter blamed Iwakura and his company for the edicts that ordered the persecution of the Christians. The two newspapers also claimed to have received a letter from Rome, which confirmed Iwakura's responsibility in the persecution. At the time they were publishing these letters, the Japanese government was notifying the Western representatives in Tokyo its intention to halt the arrests and repeal the edicts (*kōsatsu*).[41] However, the Japanese authorities had given similar assurances in the past, but they had remained a dead letter. Catholic public opinion in Europe, therefore, remained very cautious. Finally, on 14 March, the Japanese government abrogated the anti-Christian decrees, and the deported Christians were returned to their home villages.[42]

Even when they were not taking the Japanese to task over their treatment of the Christians, the Catholic press stressed the queer and curious:

> Several among them appear to belong to a temperance society and they do not drink liquor. Apart from that, these gentlemen and their companions have in their way of living nothing austere nor Catonian

(. . .). The public regrets that it cannot see them dressed in their rich and brilliant silk garments with floral designs in gold. They feel with reason that the old hats and simple overcoats in which they have rigged themselves out do not lend them a very engaging appearance. In the matter of arms, the Japanese who are reputed to have such splendid ones, have not so far displayed anything but huge toothpicks which they carefully tuck away in their pockets after having used them. As one can see, Japan is outwitting the West: it was the first to invent the perpetual toothpick. Notice to the disciples of Brillat-Savarin. Seen from fifteen steps away, the Japanese diplomats look young; from close by, they display tired miens, grooved by wrinkles. In brief, they are far from being Antinoüs and they have nothing of what is needed to be called 'lions'. They take a lot of notes, do not talk much and greet even less [salvent moins encore] (. . .). Several of those abject valets [i.e. the liberal press] even push Japanophilie to the point of qualifying the envoys of his Majesty Mutsuhito as 'illustrious'. Let us add, for the sake of completeness, that that ultra-oriental majesty, in an effort to assimilate him to the level of modern progress, is thinking of creating an Order. The ribbon will have the colour of blood and the jewel will be very brilliant. The insignia, they say, will feature a pagan strangling a Christian.[43]

VISITS TO INDUSTRIAL SITES

On 21 February, the party visited the area of Liège and Seraing, the industrial heartland of the country. They were shown around the metallurgical factories and engineering works of the *Sociéte anonyme John Cockerill*, the biggest of its kind on the European continent. They also paid a visit to the glassworks of *La Cristallerie de Val-Saint-Lambert*, which sold a good deal of its fine production on the Parisian market.

William Cockerill had moved from Lancashire to Verviers in 1799. He had been invited by industrialists of that city to build spinning jennies. In 1807 he moved his factory to Liège, and expanded his product range to include steam engines. In 1814, after the death of William, the brothers Charles-James and John Cockerill bought the palace of the former Prince Bishop of Liège in Seraing, on the east bank of the Meuse river.[44] With the support of King Willem I they built one of the most modern, vast and integrated metallurgical plants to be found on the continent. In 1823 Charles-James retired from the company and John became the sole owner.

In 1819 they started up a machine construction factory, followed by a foundry in 1820-2. Subsequently, they added 'une fabrique de fer à l'anglaise', and in 1826, the expansion was crowned with the first coke furnaces.[45] In the same period the company also acquired a number of coal mines.[46]

In 1825 the state of the Netherlands became owner of half the shares of the company. Thus *John Cockerill & Cie* was established on 1 July 1825 'pour objet la fabrication de toutes espèces de machines, . . . l'exploitation de mines de houille et de fer'.[47] Mortgaging his half of the plant at Seraing, Cockerill succeeded in securing a loan from the *Société Générale*, which grudgingly acceded under pressure from King Willem I, and invested the money in expanding and developing the ventures he had acquired in earlier years. In the end the company over-extended itself and in 1831 it had to stop all payments. It had lost its powerful ally, the state of the Netherlands. In 1834 the Belgian state took over the relay and baled him out. Henceforth the company concentrated on building heavy machinery, first textile machines, later on heavy steam engines (100 to 250 hp) for furnaces, foundries, pumping installations, locomotives and ship engines.[48] Again Cockerill over-extended himself, and when he died in 1840 without direct heir, the company was liquidated. Since there was no one to buy it, it was re-started as the *Société Anonyme John Cockerill*, with the Belgian state taking an important stake in the venture.[49]

In 1861 the company was experimenting with a Bessemer converter[50] and in 1864 it was the first to adopt the Bessemer process.[51] From 1871 the company embarked upon a major investment programme to build six Bessemer converters and two furnaces. The complex had just been completed in 1873. When the mission visited the plant, the seven-ton converters were already in operation. The site covered a surface of 192 acres and included two coal mines, coke furnaces, an ironworks, a steelworks, a forging plant and locomotive assembly and boiler manufacturing plant. The finished and half-finished products were moved by cranes that hung from the ceiling, and over railways that ran criss-cross through the premises. The company also made pig iron and steel cannon, but this was not a major section of its activities.[52] It was at one time the biggest steel mill on the continent. It had been visited by the Satsuma mission of 1865[53] and the Tokugawa mission of 1865.

In concluding his description of *Cockerill*, Kume expatiates on the merits of iron. All the Westerners he met stressed the importance of iron and coal as sources of the wealth of nations. In what amounts to a short essay on the question why the Far East had not realized the industrial revolution (although he does not use the word), he writes a short history of iron-making in the Far East. True to his Confucian background, he goes back to Chinese antiquity, and argues that already in those remote times the Chinese had mastered the technology of smelting and had cast cauldrons, forged axes, saws, ploughs and blades etc. The Far East was not later than the West in inventing metallurgical technology. In China it was discovered four thousand years ago. Already during the Han period (202 BC-220 AD) politicians had debated about salt and iron. This coincided with the time that the Romans started using iron. In Japan forging was introduced around the time of Emperor Ōjin, still more or less contemporary with the time that the Roman Empire flourished. Yet, during the 'Middle Ages', the Chinese associated technical arts with luxury and condemned it. They did not realize that they are indispensable to increase the material wealth of a country. As a result, they solely relied on human resources and failed to harness the powers of nature. That is why Kume makes a strong argument for the industrialization of Japan. Japan must not limit itself to handicraft manufacturing and exporting, but must follow a course such as Belgium has taken.

He concludes by relating that, when Cockerill set up his factory in Liège, his countrymen loathed him and accused him of lack of patriotism. But it became the foundation of Belgium's wealth, so much so that Belgium became the major producer of iron on the European continent.[54] Interestingly, although Kume describes in great detail the resources and the manpower involved in this kind of industry, he fails to mention the financial background, although capital was equally important for industrialization. This may be attributable to the low level of awareness of financial and monetary matters, which traditionally typified someone with a Confucian upbringing.

Kume's description of the glassworks at Val-Saint-Lambert is equally detailed.[55] He mentions that the company hires daily 1700 men, and that the glass they manufacture is hollow glass: cups, tumblers, wine cups, bottles, flasks and all kinds of tableware. He then describes the oven where the glass is blown and the production process. The oven is circular and is built in bricks.[56] One craftsman and several boys constitute a team. Some of the boys, too, are very skilled. He rightly observes the guild-like system that still prevails in the glass-manufacturing industry. The apprentices of the glass-blowers are trained on the factory floor. To underscore the merits of this apprenticeship he quotes the ancient Chinese philosopher Guanzhi: 'When they learn at a young age, their hearts are at ease.' He also gives a technical description of the raw materials of glass. He distinguishes the two kinds of glass: potash glass and soda glass, and describes their production process.

That Kume shows such keen interest in glass may have more to do with the fact that glass still had something wonderful for many Japanese. They obviously knew it, yet the following anecdote shows how, until a few years before, they had been unfamiliar with the new varieties of completely transparent glass. When the party of Akitake, the Bakufu mission to the Paris Exposition, travelled by train from Suez to Alexandria, they were amazed by the steam locomotive, but even more so by the windows of the carriage. The dresser and hairdresser of the party, called Tsunayoshi, having eaten a peach, threw the stone outside, thinking that it would fly through the window, only to find it bouncing back and hitting a passenger. He could not believe it and stuck his hand through the window, to feel what was between him and the landscape outside that seemed so close. After close inspection he ascertained that it was a transparent windowpane. This *chōnin* obviously did not know glass.[57]

On 22 February they visited the railworks of the *Société Anonyme des laminoirs, hauts-fourneaux, forges, fonderie et usines de la Providence* in the Charleroi area. This company did not belong to the *Société Générale* group, but was an independent company. It started in 1836 as a rolling mill. It became a joint stock company two years later. In 1841 it established a subsidiary in Hautmont in France. In 1842 it started a coke furnace in Marchienne, in 1846 it built its first furnace in Hautmont,[58] thus realizing a complete production range. Both factories specialized in rails, iron plates for ships, and other rolled steel materials.[59] Kume describes H-shaped iron material for construction ordered from South America.[60]

In the same area the party visited the plate glass factory of Courcelles, a recently established company. The factory was planned only five years earlier. Then the money was raised and after three years production was started. And Kume's spokesman confirmed that in only two years progress had exceeded all expectations. Kume takes this opportunity to make a lengthy commentary about the entrepreneurial spirit of Westerners and Japanese. In his eyes they seem completely opposite. When Westerners plan a new company, they make a detailed feasibility study, and if the result is positive, they make a model, and draw a plan (as already shown in chapter 27 about England), write speeches about (the plan), float a company, and collect subscriptions. This is the start. Then they receive a permit, build a temporary shed and install machinery. They then take two to three years to gradually get the business going, striving for development. On the basis of the accounts of the business and the profits, they improve and further complete their buildings and machinery. Before they have established their name, it takes them at least ten years.

The Japanese, on the other hand, before actually having made any profit, think profit will come easily and they at once start planning, immediately set up a company, and start business with precipitation. Before one year has passed they build magnificent buildings. By the time they have dazzled the people, their profits have actually already started dwindling. Some will say that this is attributable to the buoyant and volatile character of the Japanese, but it is actually due to the fact that they do not understand the profit principle.[61] Interestingly, most present-day comparisons take the opposite view. Apart from this East-West comparison, he expatiates once more on the production process for glass. He compares the differences in work organization between England and Belgium.

On 19 February, the emissaries were escorted to the city and environs of Ghent. Here they visited the cotton spinning and weaving factory of *De Hemptinne*, the nurseries of the horticulturist *Linden*,[62] as well as the linen factory *La Lys*. The facilities of *De Hemptinne* were bigger than anything Kume had seen in Great Britain. Interestingly, about the nurseries of *Linden*, which he believes to be the property of *De Hemptinne*, he says that they are not meant as a park in the workers' section of town, but a nursery, Ghent being famous for its botanical nurseries.

In the afternoon they visited *La Lys* (in full *La Société la Lys pour la fabrication du lin, du chanvre et des étoupes*) established in 1838,[63] the biggest flax factory in the world. Flax is much coarser than Japanese hemp, but the superiority of the processing technique means that the end product is far better than the Japanese *nuno*. After Manchester, Ghent was the first city where integrated cotton mills were operated, whereby mechanical spinning and weaving operated under the same management.[64] In order to reduce wage costs, the Ghent cotton barons replaced the men by cheaper women. Kume confirms the high number of women working in the shops.

CONCLUSION

Although at the time of the visit of the Iwakura mission, Belgium and Japan seemed to be promising partners for each other, the subsequent history of the relationship shows that many opportunities were left unexplored. Belgium was eager to export its products and its capital to the Japanese market, but from the eighties onward, it would increasingly focus its attention on other markets, such as Russia, Congo, Egypt, South America and China. Japan, on the other hand, would increasingly emulate the great European powers, and have less use for the experience of a small country. This notwithstanding, Belgium made a contribution in several areas of Japan's modernization, the most notable instance being the Bank of Japan, which was modelled after the Belgian Central Bank.

It is moreover worthy of note that Kume for all his perspicacity, failed to notice the social problems, in particular the predicament of the proletariat in the industrial cities. Neither does he refer to the divisions that existed (and still exist) in Belgian society such as the opposition between Catholics and Liberals or between the Flemings and the French-speaking segments of the population. It is obvious that we cannot lay the responsibility for these oversights at his door alone. His hosts no doubt did everything in their power to show off the best side of their country.

5

GERMANY

7-28 MARCH, 15-17 APRIL, 1-8 MAY 1873

An Encounter Between Two Emerging Countries

Ulrich Wattenberg

ALTHOUGH the Iwakura Mission spent just four weeks in Germany, Kume Kunitake in his work *Bei-O kairan jikki* allocates 10 chapters to this country, indicating the importance given to Germany. This was due to its military, economic strength and its progress in science, but Kume was also responding to the cordial treatment the Japanese mission received during its stay. German newspaper articles indeed reflect the positive attitude towards emerging Japan.

INTRODUCTION

When Japan's 200 years' seclusion ended with the Kanagawa Treaties in 1854, Germany was still trying to find its feet after Napoleon had brought down the old Empire in 1806. A first attempt to follow the example of Commodore Perry with a treaty for Germany was brought forward by the German merchant F.A. Lühdorf in 1855, but it was without any legitimation and failed. In Northern Germany Prussia had begun to unite the neighbouring states against Austria by setting up the 'Zollverein', a tariff association. It had just acquired a coastal strip along the North Sea from Hannover and had started to set up a naval base there, known today as the city of Wilhelmshaven, showing its willingness to become active overseas. After commercial treaties were concluded in 1858 between Japan and the 'Five Powers' (USA, Russia, Britain, France and the Netherlands), Prussia was not idle and sent a small fleet to Japan in 1860, headed by Friedrich Albert Graf von Eulenburg (1815-99).

The mission with its flagship 'Arcona' arrived at Edo in September of that year, meeting a government (the Bakufu), which was not eager to conclude another treaty with foreign powers. In spring of that year, the 'Sakurada Gate Incident' had occurred, in which the chancellor of the Bakufu, Ii Naosuke, had been murdered on his way to the Shogun's residence by samurai, who were upset by the foreign policy of the Bakufu. Therefore the Bakufu tried to avoid more trouble and had just denied a treaty to Switzerland. Nevertheless, von Eulenburg got quarters in the Akabane district of Edo, where today a plate commemorates the fact. Negotiations went on, while winter was approaching and the mission stayed there under not very comfortable conditions. The negotiations were overshadowed by the suicide of a key person on the Japanese side, Hori Oribe no Sho, apparently in protest against the proposed treaty, and by the murder of Heusken, the Dutch interpreter, who had helped the German mission. On 24 January 1861 a treaty was concluded, although von Eulenburg did not succeed in including Prussia's partners within the Zollverein or the independent Hansa cities of Hamburg and Bremen. A member of the mission, Maximilian von Brandt, returned later as first envoy to the Japanese government in Edo.

In 1862 Japan sent a mission to Europe, headed by Takeuchi Yasunori. In the course of its tour it visited Prussia, e.g. Cologne and Berlin, where King Wilhelm I received the mission in the city palace and where the countersigning of the treaty took place. In the following years, Prussia in a series of successful military engagements beat Denmark (1864), Austria (1866) and finally France (1870/71). In 1871, the German Empire was established with King Wilhelm I as German Emperor Wilhelm I.

These changes in Europe were known to the Iwakura Mission, when it left Yokohama at the end of 1871. In August 1870 the Japanese Government had sent a mission including Shinagawa Yajiro, Hayashi Yuzo, Oyama Iwao, Ikeda Shoichi and Arichi Shinojo to monitor the Franco-Prussian War which arrived in Berlin in October. By the time of the arrival, Napoleon III was already defeated, but Paris had not yet surrendered, so there was enough information still to be gathered. The mission returned in May 1871. So facts were known, but weighing up their significance must have been difficult. France had been beaten, but it got due attention by the Iwakura Mission and was visited for more than two months. The schedule for Germany, which the mission had in any case to pass on its tour through Europe, apparently was fixed en route. The stay, originally planned for just one week, was extended to nearly four weeks, which was still half the time France got. The other Great Powers like Russia and Austria were allocated even less.

When the mission returned to Japan, official reports were written and, in addition, as a lucky circumstance, one member of the mission, Kume Kunitake, undertook the formidable task of writing a five-volume work for the general public about the journey, the *Bei-O kairan jikki* – the 'True report on the United States and Europe'.[1] So we know what the mission did and saw in Germany, and we also get hints as to how the mission was treated there. Together with information from other sources (Kido's diaries, German newspaper articles and other mentions) we can reconstruct the visit very well. It adds up to a lively picture of an encounter between two emerging countries.

KUME'S BOOK, THE *KAIRAN JIKKI*

Kume's report on the journey is remarkable in many respects. When we compare the length of stay in the various countries visited with the number of chapters Kume allocates to them, we find a very well balanced redistribution of space. Out of the 100 chapters the United States and Great Britain get most, with 20 chapters each. Germany is third with 10 chapters, followed by France (9 chapters), Italy (7), Russia (5), Austria, Belgium and The Netherlands (3), Sweden and Switzerland (2), Denmark (1), one chapter for Spain and Portugal. Five chapters on Europe and two chapters on the Vienna World Exhibition of 1873 round up that opus. In describing the different countries, Kume uses a mixture of diary entries and background explanations. For the latter he has without doubt used secondary information, most probably English sources. We find articles on German and Prussian history, an account of the relationship between Japan and Germany (where the ship of Lühdorf is mentioned), and articles on German agriculture and forestry. He includes descriptions of all four German kingdoms, the seven grand dukedoms, dukedoms, eight principalities and the three independent Hansa cities of Hamburg, Bremen and Lübeck, correctly described as little republics directly under the emperor. Unfortunately, none of the references has survived. Thus in the Kume Museum (Tokyo) we only find Appleton's European Guide Book, apparently bought on the way, from which he selected illustrations (Cologne and Stolzenfels Castle) to appear as copper engravings in his book. Kume also used notes, taken by himself and by Hatakeyama Yoshinari (1843-76), who had studied in Great Britain and in the USA since 1865 and was ordered to join the mission in the USA. But Kume is careful, stating sources of probable errors: (1) that information was sometimes secret, (2) that persons giving the explanations knew only little due to division of labour, (3) that the noise of machines interfered with explanations, (4) that written information collected and sent en route was lost in a fire in the emperor's palace, (5) that time was short, (6) that explanations were given in a fixed order, so it was difficult to confirm facts stated before, (7) that new technologies were sometimes hard to understand. The whole introduction to the *Kairanjikki* reflects Kume's well established academic attitude.[2] A recent book on Kume's work should be mentioned, the interdisciplinary studies edited by Tanaka and Takada.[3]

Actually, we find very few mistakes or inconsistencies. In Berlin, the visit to a high school took place on Monday, 24 March, not on Sunday the 23rd, as we know from newspaper reports. The copper plate, 'Frankfurt, view of the Main river' is actually a view of Zurich. The figures given for cotton production at Berlin seem to be inconsistent, and there are some inaccuracies in his historical sections. But there is no real misunderstanding, and Kume's report is so accurate that we can look up the trains the mission used in the railway timetables of that time. Kume mentions about 180 place names, including references to places in foreign countries as London (mentioned nine times), Paris (6 x), Manchester (4 x), Philadelphia, Amsterdam, Newcastle, Sheffield, San Francisco, Vincennes, Edo (Tokyo). Kume cites 70 persons, led by Friedrich II of Prussia (12 x) and Napoleon I (12 x). Some brand names are listed, e.g. the rifles made by Chassepot, Mauser and Snider, and there are references to political events, such as the declaration of 'Allgemeines Landrecht' (1794) in Prussia. Most names of persons, places, things and acts are written down as heard in katakana, but spelled well enough in most cases to be reconstructed to the original by the author, but still about 20 items could not be identified exactly. (Sometimes one has to take into account that German names were pronounced in English, because this was the language widely used by those who acted as guides.)

Besides all the facts Kume transmits, he does not forget to include very atmospheric sketches of touching quality, as when he describes the Danish islands seen from a ship on the voyage from Malmö to Lübeck, comparing these flat islands with the woods on them to bonsai plants floating on the sea.

THE VISIT TO GERMANY

The forthcoming arrival of the Japanese Mission was announced in several newspapers.[4] The Iwakura Mission left The Hague on 7 March for Berlin and was greeted on its way at the German border in Bentheim. The mission, which had left Japan more than a year earlier with about 50 members, had become smaller by this point, about 20 having already returned home. Besides the head, Iwakura, the four deputy ambassadors were still with the mission, although news from Japan led them to consider whether some of them should return as early as possible. Kido insisted on seeing Russia, but Okubo left after the visit to Berlin.

In Bentheim, a noteworthy change of plans took place: instead of travelling straight to Berlin, the mission took a roundabout route to Essen, a place which would have been reached more conveniently from The Hague by travelling via Cologne. The detour occurred, because the visit to Krupp's steel factories was included in the programme apparently at the last moment.

Krupp had become famous, not least for providing heavy guns to the German army in recent wars. The mission stayed one night in Essen, one party in Krupp's guest house, the rest in a hotel. Kume was not impressed by the city, which seemed not to be well developed, but he was impressed by the large factories, not overlooking the fact that there were factory guards present, a safety measure usual for factories of this size, as he was informed. After visiting Krupp's new mansion, which was not yet finished, but impressed them (as it still does today) by its mere size, the mission took the night express to Berlin. They arrived there next morning, on Sunday, 9 March 1873 and stayed on until 28 March, leaving for St Petersburg, while Okubo departed, as planned, for Japan via Frankfurt.

After the visit to Russia, the mission returned to Germany on 15 April. Kido left the mission at Kreuz railway station to take a train via Berlin back to Japan, whereas the mission went through northern Prussia and Mecklenburg to reach Hamburg. After one night at Hotel d'Europe, the mission went to Kiel, where it took a boat for Copenhagen and later went on to Stockholm. On the way back from Sweden, the mission split up in Malmö, Iwakura went via Copenhagen to Hamburg, the other part of the mission went by ship to Lübeck and reached Hamburg from there. The mission thus entered Germany a third time on 1 May, staying in Hamburg for two nights at the same hotel as before. It toured the city, including the red light district near the harbour. That appeared to Kume less refined, 'cheaper' than the comparable district in Edo, the Yoshiwara quarters. It was an occasion for Kume to reflect on governmental measures to handle those districts.

The mission left Hamburg on 3 May, crossing the Elbe river on the newly built iron bridge, passed Hannover and stayed at Frankfurt on the Main at the Hotel d'Angleterre for two nights. There the printing shop of C. Naumann was visited, where the mission observed the printing process of the first modern bank notes of Japan, the 'German money'. This had been issued in April 1872 and was printed for a few years. They also saw the delightful Palmengarten of Frankfurt, which still exists today.

The last stop was Munich, where they stayed at Hotel 'Vier Jahreszeiten'. The mission was impressed by the brass monument of 'Bavaria' the goddess representing the state of Bavaria, which had been erected in 1850. They saw the park 'Englischer Garten' and visited the museums of fine art, 'Alte Pinakothek' and 'Neue Pinakothek'. The mission left Germany on 8 May for Italy.

OFFICIAL VISITS AT BERLIN

As stated in the introduction, Germany and Japan had concluded a treaty of commerce, giving the Germans trading rights in Japan. It was one of the 'unequal treaties' between Japan and the West but, after negotiations had failed in Washington, there was nothing to discuss at governmental level in Berlin. But the newly founded German Empire took great care over receiving the Iwakura mission, and on various occasions the mission met Emperor Wilhelm I.

Early on in the visit to Prussia we read in the newspaper: 'The Japanese Mission is expected to arrive in Berlin this morning. Already at The Hague councillor Kanzki had presented himself to the mission. At the Dutch border, at Bentheim, the mission will be greeted by Colonel v. Wright, chief of general staff, VII. army corps, Lieutenant Colonel Roerdansz and L. Kniffler, now in Düsseldorf, former consul at Nagasaki. These gentlemen will act as escort of honour during the whole visit in Prussia. For the travel, saloon cars of the railway companies have been made available, all travel expenses being borne by the Government. From Bentheim, the mission will proceed to Essen to visit the famous Krupp factories. At Berlin, the mission will stay at Hotel de Rome, expenses again being borne by the Government, and will visit Berlin for one week. The members appear in European dress.'[5] The article mentions the ambassadors by name, spelled in a French way: Iwakoura, T. Kido, T. Okoubo, H. Ito and N. Yamagouti. Also mentioned are T. Tanabé, N. Gah, T. Kouzimoto, K. Soughioura, T. Ando, K. Koumé, M. Tanaka, M. Tomita, J. Foukoui as medical doctor, and without giving names the treasurer, interpreters (including a shorthand writer) and service personnel. The newspaper states that the mission was sent to revise the treaties, but that this had been already given up during its stay at Washington. Now the mission was visiting the main courts in Europe in order to explain the changes which had taken place in Japan.

The mission arrived at Berlin, Lehrter Bahnhof on 9 March, a little before 7 am and was welcomed by fellow-countrymen, e.g. the staff of the Japanese legation, led by envoy Sameshima Naonobu (1844-80), who had come from Paris, and several dozen students already in Berlin. Kume mentions the fact that the Japanese students were able to appear at the railway station in large numbers, because the teachers had given them leave. And the teachers did so, because they revered their Emperor and wished to act in the same way as him, greeting the Japanese mission, as Kume remarks. The mission was equally delighted by the way the accommodation was handled. Of course, one of the best hotels of the city, the Grande Hotel de Rome, had been chosen, but it was the additional care during the stay, which pleased them so much that Kume states: 'This was more than we experienced in other countries.'[6]

Two days later, on 11 March, the reception by Emperor Wilhelm I took place. All newspapers[7] brought out official communiqués on the same day or during the next days. The Japanese Mission was collected by carriages drawn by four and six horses. Kido notes: 'I have not seen such a beautiful carriage as the one we had today in any other country.'[8] The reception took place in the 'Weißer Saal' at the Royal Palace, the very place where Emperor Wilhelm already received the Takenouchi Mission in 1862, then as King Wilhelm of Prussia. Besides Emperor Wilhelm, Chancellor Bismarck and other high-ranking officials were present. 'The Emperor received the delegation standing and bareheaded', as the official communiqué says. Addresses were given in Japanese and German, translated by a Japanese, most probably by Aoki Shuzo (1844-1912), one of the able students, who would later become ambassador to Germany and finally minister of foreign affairs. After the reception by the emperor, Empress Augusta, together with the court ladies, met the mission at a separate reception.

The next official event took place, when the mission attended the opening ceremony of the Reichstag session on the following day, 12 March. Kume's description summarizes the event very accurately, when we compare it to the Official Records of the Reichstag.[9] As Kume describes, the members of the parliament went first to church, then assembled in the Weißer Saal of the City Chambers. The government and the Upper House joined together; and then the Emperor entered with the princes, was greeted by applause, took the address from Bismarck and read it, gave a 'speech', as Kume notes, using the English expression. The Official Record states that one of the galleries was reserved for the diplomatic corps, the other was occupied by the Japanese mission. At night, the mission was invited to the Palace, where a dinner was given for them by the Emperor, attended by members of the royal family and 120 civil and military officials, including General Moltke.

In connection with these official visits, we find two lengthy newspaper articles on Iwakura and the Iwakura mission, where the diplomatic relations, dating back to 1861, are explained and also the changes, which had taken place in both countries, the Meiji Restoration of 1868 and the foundation of the German Empire in 1871. 'Japan is learning, buying, copying. It gives an impression of freshness, in which the whole country is involved, quite different from other nations in Asia and Africa. . . . Some day, we will have to learn from Japan. . . . The Mikado encourages studies abroad, even six young ladies are sent to America.' The articles conclude with citations from Ito Hirobumi's speech in San Francisco, where he had said: 'The red disc is no longer a piece to seal an envelope, but it is revived to its original meaning, to be the rising sun, a symbol of dynamism.' The next day the same newspaper explained the personal background of Iwakura.[10]

The next official event was the Emperor's birthday on 23 March, to which the mission was invited. Kume reports on it; and the newspapers also note that the Japanese Mission was among the guests. As an interesting coincidence in German-Japanese relations, the same day, far away in Tokyo, some German diplomats, learned men and businessmen founded the 'Deutsche Gesellschaft für Natur- und Völkerkunde Ostasiens' (OAG), because they felt the need to study Japan and the Far East in more detail, to publish results and to exchange the 'Mittheilungen' with other scientific societies all over the world. The OAG is still active today, together with the 'Asiatic Society', founded a little earlier.

With the royal princes, members of the mission went to see the horse races at the hippodrome (which later had to give way to the railway station 'Berlin Zoologischer Garten'), which the mission enjoyed very much. It reminded Kume of the horse races within the *yashiki* (estates) of the samurai in former days.

The ambassadors saw the Emperor a last time on 25 March, at the 'Große Fischerei-Ausstellung', an event to promote consumption of fish in Berlin. The mission was surprised to see the Emperor and his family at the front of a crowd, entering the exhibition halls. Kume mentions what a newspaper describes in more detail: that among the 'panoramas', set up to show fishery boats and customs from various parts of the world, 'Japanese junks of Dr von Martens, a Japanese fisherman's house and smoking chamber of the Gärtner brothers' could be seen.[11] But he is more concerned with the fact that fishing nets, mechanically woven, were exhibited. Later in his account he even gives the place name in Katakana, something like 'Ikiueyu', a little search revealed that it is the town of 'Itzehoe' (Northern Germany), where indeed the factory which exhibited nets in Berlin can be confirmed.

BISMARCK'S SPEECH

At the Governmental level, Prince Bismarck personally took an interest in the visit and invited the higher ranking members to his place for dinner on 15 March, after having visited them at their hotel the day before. The newspaper reports: 'Chancellor Bismarck is giving today a dinner, honouring the Japanese Mission, to which 30 persons are invited.'[12] We know the persons invited by name, Envoy Sameshima, Graf Eulenburg, now Minister of the Interior, Minister of State Delbrück, the President of the Reichstag (National Assembly) Dr Samson and four members of the National Assembly, and of course the Germans accompanying the mission, like Colonel von Wright, Roerdansz, Kniffler and others. At the table, Bismarck gave a speech of considerable importance. After some remarks on his youth he addressed the Japanese side, saying that all nations of the world treat each other with courtesy, but this was fictitious. In reality the governments of strong countries apply pressure on weak countries. When he, Bismarck, was young, Prussia was weak, and he always wished to change that. The law of nations has the purpose of keeping order between the nations. But if a strong country has differences with another country, it will act according to the law of nations as long as it suits its purposes, otherwise it will use its own power. Weak countries are always at a disadvantage. This was true for Prussia, but Prussia was able to change it, helped by the patriotism of its people. Now foreign countries hate Prussia for the recent wars, but they were fought only to protect Prussia. It is Britain and France which are enlarging their colonial empires, so these countries cannot be trusted, courteous as they may appear. Japan is, he argued, in the same situation as Prussia not long ago, so Prussia and Japan should keep cordial contacts with each other.

How well do we know the contents of this remarkable speech? Kume gives an account as written above, effectively concluding chapter 58 with it.[13] When we check Bismarck's collected writings, speeches, addresses, we indeed find this speech in Vol. 8.[14] But in his introductory remarks the editor writes that it was a member of the Japanese Mission who had taken notes and that a certain Han-Nama (most probably Hatakeyama) had published Bismarck's remarks later. And on the occasion of the visit of one prominent member of the Iwakura Mission, Ito Hirobumi, then premier, to Berlin in December 1901, these remarks, made 28 years before, surfaced and were printed in the German newspapers as a 'new(ly found) speech'. In this way, the speech came to be included in the collection. There is no need to mistrust the correctness of its contents, as confirmed by Japanese sources, but there is apparently no German source as such for it.

Besides Bismarck, Graf Eulenburg gave hospitality to the mission and invited it on 26 March. This is mentioned in the newspapers,[15] but not by Kume. Besides all these official visits, the mission was busy, as we know from Kido's diaries, receiving people from near and far and engaged in discussing the German constitution (1871), which was supposed to be the most modern in Europe.

VISITS TO MILITARY ESTABLISHMENTS AND SOME IRONIC REMARKS

Graf Moltke, the military genius and learned man, is mentioned several times by Kume, who gives an account of a speech by him at the Reichstag.[16] On 16 March the mission was shown the Armoury, a beautiful baroque building, finished about 1701 by Andreas Schlüter, which has survived WWII. Reflecting on this visit, Kume may have been puzzled by the fact that, although European royalty was linked by marriage, so many wars occurred between the states. He formulates an ironical conclusion, when he heard the story of the huge brass lion monument in the inner court of the armoury. Remembering that Napoleon took away the brass quadriga from the Brandenburg Gate in Berlin, that it was brought back from Paris after Napoleon's defeat, remembering that the lion on top of the Waterloo monument was taken away from the French, and hearing that the lion in Berlin was originally cast by the Danish from weapons seized by them after they defeated the Northern Germans in an uprising in 1854, and hearing that this lion was taken away from Denmark, when Prussia won against that country in 1864, Kume wonders whether wars in Europe are waged because it is a kind of sport: to seize the brass lions of other countries. Actually, the lion Kume saw in Berlin was taken back to Denmark after WWII.[17]

While the armoury visited was already mainly used as a military museum, the mission visited two modern military establishments in the southern part of Berlin on 18 March, the Franz Barracks in the morning and the Dragoons' Barracks at Belle-Alliance-Street in the afternoon, as is reported both by Kume and the newspapers. The Franz Barracks were the most modern example of barracks, three large buildings around a square. The older type of barracks, the Dragoons' Barracks, still exist and are used as the bureau of finance of a city ward. The horse stables, however, have been removed in the main.

CITIZENS' INTEREST

On the citizens' level, the newspapers report that a delegation of the German branch of the Evangelical Alliance, led by Graf v. Egloffstein and Preacher of the Court, Dr Hoffmann, visited the mission at its hotel on 19 March, to 'say a word of sympathy and to tell the truth', stating that the good morals and well-being of America and the European countries were based on the gospel and religious freedom, and that the deputation wished the same could be true for Japan. Iwakura answered that Japan differed in tradition, but that it was willing to take into account the good experience the missions had in the West concerning the principle of religious freedom. After that, an address was read by Professor Meißner, stating their wishes in detail. The Japanese side had prepared a written answer, which was signed by Iwakura and the four deputy ambassadors, praising Germany and the West and stating its acceptance of the request of the Evangelical Alliance. A newspaper remarks that there was information from France that the edicts against Christianity had already been removed in Japan on 26 February and, if that could be confirmed, it would be good news, thanks to the earlier advances of the British and French branches of the Evangelical Alliance.[18]

It was the missionary Guido F. Verbeck (1830-98), who had taken part in Japan in the preparations for the mission and had brought up the necessity for the Japanese to study religious matters in the West and to consider lifting the ban on Christianity, after more than 200 years of repression (Jonathan Swift has some lines on this matter in the third book of *Gulliver's Travels*). So the mission was prepared for these questions. And as we can see from Kume's writings (he does not refer to the visit just mentioned), the 'Kirchenkampf' (the fight between Bismarck and the Catholic Church) and other problems within Christianity had not escaped him. He also observed the beginning of people being alienated from the Church, at least in Northern Germany. In academic circles, he notes, that 'Moralphilosophie' (using this German expression) is making progress instead.[19] For the sake of clarity, however,

Kume always states in his report whether the inhabitants of a German state belong to Protestant or Catholic Churches.

Another event got more attention in the newspapers. We read: 'Yesterday the Japanese Mission received a number of persons (learned men, artists, businessmen, reporters) who wanted to express their sympathy with the mission and Japan. Prof. Dr von Holtzendorff addressed the mission, which was dressed according to European style (black cutaway, white necktie, white gloves) in English, because they were able to understand this language.' Holtzendorff stated, 'Our Emperor has received you with honours, and we as his subjects want also to express our pleasure that Japan is making such fast progress. Your countrymen, who are studying here, are so diligent and quick in grasping the essentials that your efforts will be met with success. In this respect, the Japanese Government is doing much better than those of South America. And there will come a time when we will have to learn from you. Germany does not insist on a monopoly in culture; it wants to share its knowledge, to learn from other countries, to promote civilization together.'[20] After a younger member of the mission had translated the speech into Japanese, Iwakura answered that the Emperor of Japan had sent the mission to Berlin to promote mutual understanding, and he, Iwakura, was thankful for the chance to exchange greetings. After that, the visitors were introduced and a lively discussion in English and French took place. One newspaper says that everybody was convinced that there would be increasing good relations between the two countries.

The flattering remark that Germany would have to learn from Japan, may not have been completely divorced from reality at that time. The fast progress the Japanese studying in Berlin had made, had indeed impressed the people. In the representative popular magazine of the latter half of the nineteenth century, the *Gartenlaube*, we find an article in 1873, entitled 'Japan in Berlin'.[21] The author, who signed it 'F.D.', gives many details about their way of living, praising the high motivation of the students and their good examination results. Some names are mentioned, Aoki Shuzo, Prince Fushimi, and Sahami Sato, who arrived at the end of 1869 as one of the first Japanese in Germany. The author estimates the number of Japanese students then in Berlin at 70, a figure which, however, cannot be verified directly. The number of students enrolled at the university was much lower, but apparently there was quite a number of Japanese in Berlin, engaged privately in studies. This is true, for example, for Mushanokoji Saneyo (1851-87), who came with the mission to Berlin, apparently just to report on the new German Empire. Mushanokoji's sons, by the way, inherited his interest in Germany, one (Kintomo) becoming a diplomat, the other (Saneatsu) as writer and artist.

A BUSY SCHEDULE

Kume gives notes on visits which took place almost everyday of their stay. The public institutions visited and described are the Royal Mint, the Royal Printing Office, the Bureau of Telegraphs, the main fire prevention station and the prison of Moabit, where a system of strict separation of prisoners had been introduced, under which everybody had to wear a mask when being together with other prisoners, and seats in the chapel were separated by wooden screens, as Kume correctly observes. Kume thinks that Western law is too severe against persons who inadvertently caused material losses and that the treatment of prisoners – he remembers the prisons visited in the USA – in the West is horrible.[22] The telegraph factories of Siemens were visited and Borsig (steam engines), the Royal Porcelain Manufacture (the manufacturing process is described in detail) and the production site of artificial mineral water by Soltmann. Academic institutions visited include Friedrich-Wilhelm University, the Academy of Fine Arts, the Observatory, the König Wilhelm High School. At the express wish of the Japanese Empress, two representative hospitals were visited and described, the Charité for the general public and the Augusta Hospital for wealthy persons. Kume adds a lengthy passage on modern hospital construction. The visit to the Royal Museum and Mombijou castle is described. More recreational were the visits to the Zoo and to the Aquarium, a private enterprise, showing reptiles. One day was spent viewing the palaces in nearby Potsdam. Kume relates the famous story about Friedrich II, who wanted the noisy windmill nearby to disappear but lost his case in court against the miller. Last stop on this excursion was Babelsberg castle, the small summer residence of Emperor Wilhelm, built by Schinkel in English style. So the days must have flown by until the newspapers report: 'The Japanese mission, 27 persons, left Berlin yesterday from Ostbahnhof station with the courier train proceeding to St Petersburg. Oberst von Wrenl and another higher artillery officer were accompanying them. The Japanese students at Berlin, about 10 to 12, appeared at the station, presenting a lot of oranges to them.'[23]

SUMMARY

Kume's *Kairanjikki* is an important report on Europe of 1872-73 seen by a well educated person, raised in a completely different social and cultural tradition. As for Germany, Kume is impressed by its military and industrial strength and its progress in science and technology. Back at home he studied the German Empire, this complex federation, and explained it quite accurately to the general public.

Kume is less impressed by Western society in general. He observes that in Germany the feudal system is still strongly rooted, the local nobility exploiting their various estates too much while at the same time admiring France and spending their money on French arts and crafts. Only recently, after the victory of 1871, it seems to him, the German upper class started to develop cultural tastes of their own. The city of Berlin, seemed to him less refined as compared to London or Paris, and the manners of the common people appeared to him to be likewise, statements we Germans have to accept.

Germany apparently did its best to honour the Japanese mission, which was appreciated by the Japanese. There are remarkable differences from the visit of the Takenouchi mission, just 11 years earlier. First of all, whereas a huge crowd watched the mission in Berlin in 1862 on several occasions, there was not much public interest in the mission in 1873. The newspapers watched the sojourn and reported the daily movements, but just with a few lines, longer articles being the exception. Berlin had become used to foreign missions, and the Japanese had adapted European customs and clothing and no longer looked as exotic as eleven years before, when they appeared in traditional clothing, the *hakama*, with the hair traditionally made up. Moreover, the mission was, as we can see from Kume's report – with the New Japan in mind – much more serious about collecting information and understanding the West than the earlier missions.

Kume's book is a kind of reversed history book on the West, a really unique book, which cannot be written ever again. Today, our 'pre-knowledge' interferes with the things we observe in other countries. A comparison between Kume's reports on the various countries visited will reveal even more details, how the West was seen by Japan at the beginning of their mutual contacts 125 years ago. The fact that the Iwanami edition of the *Kairanjikki* has had to be reprinted many times since 1977, shows the lasting Japanese interest in this unobstructed view on the West.

6

RUSSIA

29 MARCH-15 APRIL 1873

Ian Nish

THERE WAS NO QUESTION but that the delegates led by Prince Iwakura Tomomi should find time to visit the Russian Empire.[1] Russia was a large country with a population estimated at 72 million (1857) and one with a frontier on the coast of the Pacific Ocean. She was a country with which Japan had many points of tension, mainly frontier disputes and territorial anxieties. On the other hand, the Japanese were not greatly interested in imitating Russia or her institutions. Indeed they had already received rather caustic comments from European statesmen about them. But a visit was nonetheless indispensable. Russia had been on the itinerary of the Bakufu mission to Europe in 1862; and there had been a frequent exchange of missions. Japanese students were attending college there. So Russia was being studied like other European countries, though not on the same scale.

From the start of the nineteenth century Japan had been afraid of Russia. Her early encounters had been with Nikolai Rezanov in 1806-7 who sought to open trade relations especially with the north of the country, though he was probably not authorized to do so by his government.[2] The naval mission of Vice-admiral Evfimii Putyatin in 1853 had delivered a letter from the tsar to the Tokugawa authorities in which Russia tried to open trade through Yezo (Hokkaido). Japan ultimately concluded the treaty of Shimoda with Russia in 1855. Some of the provisions concerned the island of Sakhalin (Karafuto) lying off the coast of the Asian landmass which had been the subject of disputes since the turn of the century. While both countries claimed the territory and were encouraging the immigration of their nationals (in the

Japanese case, the Ainu) annexation had not been attempted by either party. It was agreed that the treaty should provide for Sakhalin to be jointly possessed by both. But the Russians had been weakened by the Crimean war and later argued that they had been bargaining from an inferior position and had been forced into making concessions. That treaty was explicitly confirmed by the new Convention of 1 April 1867 which also provided that all disputes should be settled by the authority nearest at hand, whether Russian or Japanese. This led to considerable encroachment by Russia to the south of the island (Aniwa bay).[3]

There were many views about the proper course for Japan. Kuroda Kiyotaka, who was deputy in the administration of Hokkaido (Hokkaido kaitaku jikan) in 1870 was inclined to abandon Japan's stake in Sakhalin on the ground that it was beyond her resources and she should consolidate her position on Hokkaido. Britain, among others, urged Japan to develop that island lest it came under the shadow of an expanding Russia.

Behind the Sakhalin issue was the broader issue, the lack of a stable frontier between Russia and Japan. The naval and military station for the Russian Far East was transferred from Nikolaievsk 600 miles south to Vladivostok which lay opposite Japan's main island of Honshu. This was naturally a matter of anxiety and constant vigilance for the Japanese, though it was in the view of most contemporary observers not so serious as the Russians did not have the will or the resources to develop Vladivostok into a major naval base straightaway.[4]

There was, therefore, a bitter-sweet relationship between the two countries. Russia and Japan had signed the treaty of Shimoda in 1855. When the bakufu sent the Takenouchi mission to Europe in 1862, it had spent six weeks in Russia. It signed with Russia a protocol postponing the opening of ports, though the talks on Sakhalin had been inconclusive. It is true that the treaty ports in which Russia was interested were different from those of the other powers opening relations with Japan. While their interests were concentrated in Yokohama, Russia was more interested in Hakodate and, to a lesser extent, Nagasaki and Niigata. But Russia had had much experience of dealing with Japanese statesmen on their visits to St Petersburg and, on the whole, had shown cordiality. On the one hand, when the Grand-duke Aleksandr visited Japan at this time, he was met with total courtesy. But, on the other, there was a mood of general uncertainty and mistrust: on Japan's part about Russia's future intentions; and on the part of the tsarist government about where their ambitious frontier commanders (like Admiral Putyatin) might lead them.

MEMBERS

The Iwakura mission, by this time experienced travellers, assembled in Berlin for the rail journey to Russia. It consisted of Okubo Toshiaki and Kido Takasuke (Koin) as joint deputy leaders, Ito Hirobumi and Yamaguchi Naoyoshi as senior members. In addition the young Aoki Shuzo (1844-1914) who had been studying in Germany for two years was anxious to make the journey. The flexibility of the delegation allowed the presence of assistants in this way. In August Aoki had visited his clansman Kido in London and given him a briefing which was continued in Paris. In January 1873 he was appointed acting first secretary in Berlin – effectively the head of the legation – and became a bureaucrat for the first time. One assumes that he insinuated himself into Iwakura's entourage because of his linguistic skill in German. He had an insatiable curiosity and was able to appeal successfully to Kido to join the group.[5]

Okubo was the member most inquisitive about Russia. This comes out clearly from the advance preparations he made through Nishi Tokujiro who had been an outstanding student at Daigaku Nanko and was sent to Russia to report on conditions. Nishi felt that Japan's problems with Russia could only be resolved after study there. He had written a memorandum to this effect which was passed through Kuroda Kiyotaka to Okubo, chief assistant to the foreign minister. Nishi was, therefore, ordered to go to St Petersburg, one of the early overseas experiments in the Meiji period. At a farewell meeting with Okubo and Kuroda, he was presented with a sword.[6]

On 26 July 1870 Nishi sailed from Yokohama via the United States and reached St Petersburg in December. Officially he was a Ministry of Education scholar, studying at the capital's university. Undercover he was reporting home on Russian conditions. The presence of Nishi and other students as *ryugakusei* (students studying abroad) at government expense gave the Iwakura mission an extra excuse for visiting the territory: they had to investigate the progress of these cadets. They also provided a useful reservoir of assistance and know-how to the delegates.

Okubo on 27 January 1973 sent a letter to Nishi from Paris calling on him to investigate the Russian form of government in advance of the mission's arrival. Okubo was looking forward to seeing Russia while his protege, Nishi, was counting the days for his arrival. But by a strange irony, shortly before the delegation was due to leave Berlin, several messages arrived from Sanjo Sanetomi, asking Iwakura to release Okubo and Kido to return without delay. Sanjo as dajo daijin (premier) was struggling to preside over affairs in Japan in the absence of half of those of cabinet rank. A dispute had arisen between the Ministry of Finance and other ministries and, in addition, trouble was brewing mainly over the intended expedition to Taiwan and Korea. When this was discussed, the compromise was reached, not without bitterness, that Okubo would return as he did on 28 March via Frankfurt and Marseille, while Kido, the other deputy leader, insisted on accompanying Iwakura. Initially, it was intended that this would be for the whole European itinerary though Kido also was later instructed to return early in view of the continuing crisis.[7] It was ironic that it should have been Okubo who was most curious to learn about Russia who should be recalled.

Another example of the forethought that went into the Russian visit was that the education expert, Tanaka Fujimaro, visited St Petersburg before the arrival of the mission on instructions from Okubo who felt that Russia was worth studying as what might be called 'a less developed country'. But in the field of education Tanaka was so impressed with the educational provision he had witnessed in the new Germany that he did not rate Russia's progress highly.

TRAVEL

Although deprived of Okubo, the party, consisting of Iwakura, Kido, Ito and Yamaguchi, set off, together with their diligent scribe, Kume Kunitake, for Russia from the Ostbahnhof in Berlin on the evening of 28 March. They called at Koenigsberg and crossed the frontier at the River Neman at Chernyakhovsk (Insterburg). There they were met by Wirsky from the Asia bureau of the Foreign Ministry who was to serve as their escort. They joined the Russian train which had been sent for them. Kido relates in his diary that he had 'not seen such a convenient train since we left America'.[8] Evidently the mission's frequent use of railways in Britain, the home of the railway boom, had not impressed them. The European railway expansion had penetrated to Russia in the 1850s when the Russian Railway Company had built strategic lines from St Petersburg to Warsaw to link up with the European system. On this occasion, the mission used the spur to the main line which joined up with Prussian railways.

As they made their way via Vilna and Pskov to the Russian capital, they were astonished how different was the vista of flat landscape on both sides of the train from that of their own country. Thus, Kido wrote:

> [for most of the route] nothing but a vast plain appeared outside the windows . . . except for a forest which lasted for a few dozen miles. Human habitations were exceedingly rare. The hamlets of the natives,

> which we did see here and there, were all small and poor. I have never seen such impoverished villages, not even in Japan.[9]

This is to be explained partly by the effect of snow covering the ground for four to five months of the year and partly by the poverty and carefree approach of the peasantry.

Before the ambassadors reached St Petersburg, they received the official welcoming party, consisting of senior army officers and Melinikov of the Foreign Ministry. The delegation was entering the Russia of Tsar Aleksandr II (ruled 1855-81). After the defeat of his country during the Crimean War, he had courageously taken the first steps for the emancipation of the serfs in 1961; but these reforms were being implemented only slowly in the teeth of fierce opposition from the landowners. Hence the squalor which the visitors observed. Kume and others found it hard to understand the objectives of this emancipation policy.

ACTIVITIES IN RUSSIA

Iwakura and his colleagues reached St Peterburg at 8pm on 30 March[17] after the forty hours journey from Berlin and were escorted to the Hotel de France where they were visited by the governor of St Petersburg.[10]

Inevitably, their first reactions were those of admiring tourists. Kume wrote that the city streets were broad as government regulations laid down, while the buildings were grand and were indeed outstanding on the European continent.[11] It was the boulevards that were so impressive with their evidence of aristocratic life. Since the French revolution, he alleged, the nobles of Europe had sought a new base (*shintenchi*) here.

Naturally, they were impressed with the Neva river, dividing the city which was still frozen in April. They were impressed by the pleasing prospect of people walking or riding on the ice. Kume, ever the enthusiastic chronicler, collected photographs of the recently completed St Isaac's Cathedral with its golden dome and the baroque of the Winter Palace (later to become the Hermitage Museum).[12]

The Russian royal family went out of their way to offer hospitality to the visitors. They were received by the tsar with the deepest ceremonial at a banquet for 140 persons at the Winter Palace on 3 April (22 March) and later escorted to military manoeuvres. They were entertained with the greatest cordiality by the Grand-dukes Aleksandr and Konstantin at their palaces and by the tsar's younger brother, Nicholas, at his home. Intrigued like most Japanese with ablutions, Kido speaks ecstatically of Nicholas's modern bathhouse: 'in neither America nor Europe have I seen so well-equipped or beautiful a bathhouse [?sauna] as this one'.[13] The delegation was most hospitably received by the royal house. Thus, the Japanese felt that they had fulfilled one of the subsidiary objectives of their mission, to study foreign royalty.

The Russian state, too, organized an interesting programme of visits. With undimmed enthusiasm, the delegation called on departments of government with which they were especially connected. They attended the parades of the armed services and fire services of the capital. As elsewhere in Europe, their inspections covered a broad mixture of cultural and industrial sights. They visited various museums and were clearly intrigued by the cathedrals and churches of the Orthodox faith which they had not previously seen. They were welcomed by aristocrats and industrialists. They inspected the Kolpino naval ordnance factory on 8 April (27 March) and the Obukhov steelworks. Kume makes the perceptive comment that Russia was rich in minerals though many were only to be found in inhospitable parts of the country but the profits from mining were very great.[14] They appear to have been especially impressed by the reputation and achievement of Tsar Peter the Great whose programme of modernization for Russia had some resonance with their own objectives.

They pursued the interest they had shown in other countries in social welfare institutions, notably the home for foundlings and the college for the deaf and dumb. Among the many papers Kume collected, he preserved one, a recently published pamphlet on the origins of the latter entitled 'About the foundation of a school for the deaf and dumb in St Petersburg' by A. Meller.[15] This had been set up under imperial patronage at the turn of the nineteenth century and continued to be regularly visited by the imperial family.

The Iwakura delegation seem to have been especially entertained by the great family of Trepov. Their programme of visits was influenced by suggestions from General Trepov, the chief of police of St Petersburg, who was to be shot by assassins before five years had elapsed.

Their official host was Prince Aleksandr Gorchakov, the long-serving Russian foreign minister (1855-82) and simultaneously chancellor in recent years. It was he who ensured that the Russian government should cover the cost of travel, accommodation, carriages and postage. It is not quite clear what diplomatic negotiation took place between him and Iwakura in return for this. The Japanese had gone to Russia as one of the countries with which Japan had treaties but, as Professor Inou Tentaro writes, it is unlikely that they would try to negotiate with Russia the revision of her treaty (despite their claim that it was due to expire) after the brushoff they had received in Washington and London. Gorchakov asked Japan to set out in writing her fundamental objectives. The Japanese then handed over a memorandum in English, justifying her desire to recover her right to determine import-export tariffs and residence and port regulations independently and to place foreigners under the jurisdiction of Japanese laws and courts. Evidently Gorchakov found this too technical and localized a matter to debate straightaway. Instead he promised to reply formally through his representative in Japan – a tactic of decentralization that other foreign ministers had employed during the delegation's sojourn abroad.[16]

It would have been difficult not to mention Sakhalin and Hokkaido. One journalist in *Golos* (voice or view), sometimes regarded as the mouthpiece of the Russian Foreign Ministry, wrote:

> . . . all the Russian maps I have seen during the last few years, whether official or non-official, represent Sakhalin as Russian territory. Now that Iwakura, the great reformer, has come in person to St Petersburg, it is intended to put the finishing stroke to the business [of acquiring Sakhalin] and legalize an acquisition which is practically already theirs. If the transaction can be completed, it will considerably strengthen the position of Russia in what is beginning to be an important quarter of the world.

The American minister, James L. Orr, who had only recently arrived, was impressed by the volume of speculation on these lines. He had no doubt, for his part, that the Sakhalin question had been raised in discussion:

> Part of this island has for a long time belonged to Russia, has been under her control, and is at present one of her penal colonies. She is now endeavouring to get complete mastery of it; and, it is said, to accomplish this, proposed to cede part of the Coreil Islands [sic] to the empire of Japan. Nothing however has been decided as yet.[17]

But, if the matter was indeed raised, Iwakura left the Russian capital without agreeing or compromising his country's standpoint. Indeed he had no authority to do so.

It would appear that Nishi and his fellow-students had all the while been acting as *annaiyaku* (guides) and interpreters. Before the delegation left, Nishi sought an interview with Kido and handed over his analytical report *(chosasho)* on Russia. Kido thought highly of it and, when he too returned to Japan unexpectedly early via Vienna, Italy and Geneva, he was able to pass it over to Okubo on 23 July.[18]

The Iwakura mission paid its final respects to the tsar and left St Petersburg at 11 am on 14 April, took a meal at Luga and tea at Pskov. It crossed the Neman river again on the following day and the main group made its way to Copenhagen through north Germany. As it passed from Russia into Germany, the diarists recorded the evidence of prosperity on the part of the German farmers and the improved quality of the soil.

CONCLUDING THOUGHTS

How did the Russian trip fit in with the journeyings of the Iwakura Mission as a whole? The mission had conscientiously and attentively examined affairs in the Russian capital. But its tour could not be said to be comprehensive. It had not visited Moscow which, in the view of one historian, Sir Bernard Pares, was the 'heart of the country'. Moreover, their time in Russia – a mere 16 days – was short, in comparison with their long stays in USA, Britain, France, Germany and Austria. The coverage of Russia in Kume's chronicle is much shorter than the account given of the mission's activities elsewhere. Despite all their efforts, the investigators left Russia less well informed about conditions they found there than for other smaller countries which they visited.

The mission had come with an unfavourable impression of the Russian empire which derived from their direct dealings with her in the past. They had also received disparaging accounts from people in Britain and France which were then unfriendly towards Russia. But on the spot they met with great cordiality and kindness. In their reports they gave praise where it was deserved and were balanced in their judgements.

The Russians, for their part, formed a favourable image of the Japanese visitors. The court was evidently impressed; and, while it is difficult to judge private thinking from the evidence of public pronouncements, it appears that friendships developed. Many years later the tsarevich, then twenty-three years of age and later to become Tsar Nicholas II, was sent to Japan on a goodwill mission in 1891. Although cordially received by the Japanese court and government, he was attacked by a policeman in the notorious Otsu affair. This illustrates the undercurrent of tension which persisted between the near neighbours, Japan and Russia.[19]

The tsarist government was interested in Japan but there was no end-product of the Iwakura visit. The press was 'monosyllabic' in its coverage of these events.[20] And subsequent generations of Russian and Soviet historians have tended to disregard the mission as though it were cultural and had no political significance.[21]

The commissioners who were after all to become the leaders of the new Japan were as a result of their journey able to see Russia in a new perspective. In the east, Russia appeared to the Japanese to be a country which was powerful, arrogant, expansionist and interfering. On her home territory Russia was shown to be backward and unstable with a largely illiterate population and a huge gulf between rich and poor. In his concluding chapter, Kume writes that there were five great powers in Europe – Britain, France, Germany, Russia and Austria – and that Britain and France were the most powerful (this in spite of the Franco-Prussian War) while Russia was the least admirable. It is not clear whether the ways of the tsarist autocracy appealed to the visiting Japanese for their own purposes, but the monarchic institution was certainly a matter of intense fascination for them.

When the delegates returned to Japan, the heated arguments over whether to send an invasion force to Korea were at their most intense. Those who had been on the Iwakura mission and had been absent during the earlier stages of the argument came out strongly against the proposal on their return. One of the arguments which they employed to defeat the proposal was that of Kido. If Japan, Kido said, were to find herself involved with another country, it should not be with Korea but with Russia, a country which threatened Japan's own territory in Hokkaido (then Ezo). This indicates the underlying suspicion with which the Japanese delegation had approached their visit to the Russians.[22]

The activities of the Iwakura Mission have to be seen against the background of the everyday diplomacy between the two countries which had to continue while they were abroad. How did the impressions of the commissioners affect Japan's approach to Russia in future? On 12 July 1873 Evgenii Karlovich Biutsov (1837-1904), the temporary Russian minister in Tokyo, presented the tsar's reply to the memorandum (*shuisho*) which had been handed over by Iwakura. It merely stated that Biutsov was authorized to negotiate for the amendment of the commercial treaty. A treaty was signed on 21 August. But this was two months before Iwakura returned to Japan; and there were so many issues of a pressing nature to be dealt with that the fundamental discussions did not take place.[23] Biutsov was transferred back to China.

When things had settled down, Japan appointed Sawa Nobuyoshi, who had earlier served as foreign minister, as minister to Russia. But he died when he was on the point of leaving for his new assignment.[24] Rear-admiral Enomoto Buyo was appointed in his place; and it was he who in 1875 concluded the treaty of St Peterburg whereby possession rights in Sakhalin would be conferred on Russia, while all the islands of the Chishima archipelago to the north of Urup would become Japan's territory. This treaty gave the two countries two decades of peace though it can be said that it frustrated the expansionists in both Japan and Russia and had a bad press.[25]

The Japanese delegates rightly pointed to the contradictions which existed in Russian society: the architectural magnificence of the cities compared to the backwardness of the countryside; the atmosphere of pride, ambition and expansiveness compared to the shortage of resources and lack of industrial development. Their recognition of the negative side of Russian life is reminiscent of *Pictures at an Exhibition*, the pictorial music which Modest Mussorgsky composed – coincidentally in 1873 – especially the trundling ox-cart at the Great Gate of Kiev. This was the symbol of a venerable state, high in culture, large in size but unpredictable in its objectives.

It is 125 years since Prince Iwakura and his colleagues visited St Peterburg but some of their concerns still find a resonance in relations between Japan and Russia today. There were the possibilities of trade and fisheries and the aspiration of reaching a definitive treaty. But Japan still felt unsure about the intentions of her vast and powerful neighbour.

7

SWEDEN

23-30 APRIL 1873

Bert Edström

'SINCE FOUR, five days the temperature has turned to cold and snow. A Japanese embassy, which arrived yesterday, could enjoy Stockholm in winter garb. It consists of three ambassadors whose head is Sionii Tomomi Iwakura; nine secretaries accompany. They will stay five, six days. The King gives a dinner today, after which they end the day at the Innocence Ball.'[1] This entry on 25 April 1873 in the diary of the famous Swedish cartoonist and court noble Fritz von Dardel (1817-1901) recounts an important event in the relations between Sweden and Japan that has gone almost unnoticed. This event was none other than the week-long visit to Sweden by a diplomatic mission dispatched by the Meiji government. The mission's eighteen-month tour of the world was of tremendous importance for the future of Japan and its policies of selective modernization.[2] The visit that Japan's new leaders made to Sweden was a part of this tour of the world whose purpose was to fulfil the promise of the Meiji Emperor's Charter Oath to 'seek wisdom throughout the world in order to strengthen the foundation of imperial rule.' The purpose of the mission was three-fold. Apart from information gathering, the tasks of the mission were to engage in diplomatic negotiations and strengthen the goodwill of the new Japanese state.

Not only the length of the mission, but also its members, comprising as it did almost all members of Japan's new political leadership, made the mission a bold undertaking. 'The scale of the operation was enormous', J. E. Thomas writes. 'Apart from the travelling, the number of countries visited, the range of visits, and discussions in every kind of institution and organization, the speed at which they accumulated and integrated information in the eighteen-month visit, must make the operation one of the most remarkable missions in not only Japanese, but world history.'[3]

By sheer chance, it was an opportune moment for the delegation to visit Sweden. For its purpose of studying industry and society, Sweden was a suitable country since it was undergoing rapid industrialization. As a courtesy call, the moment could not have been better chosen since the king, Oskar II, had ascended the Swedish throne in September 1872. The visit of a high-ranking mission was a way of confirming the good relations between the two countries which had been established when they had initiated diplomatic relations in 1868. The moment was equally suitable for diplomatic discussions. Swedish foreign policy was in the midst of a process of change, and the new king attempted to redirect Swedish foreign policy, as he had strong views in this area. At his disposal were means to have changes implemented. According to the constitution the king had a constitutionally guaranteed possibility to wield personal power over foreign policy, and so the new king was a driving force behind policies pursued.[5]

Since the Iwakura mission is one of the most significant events in the history of Japanese modernization, a substantial amount of research has been done. However, researchers in both Sweden and Japan have almost totally neglected the mission's visit to Sweden. Symptomatic of the state of research is the fact that a significant new addition to research on the Iwakura mission, a collection of articles edited by Tanaka Akira and Takata Seiji published in 1993, does not cover Sweden.[6] The only scholarly report published so far on the mission's visit to Sweden is an article by Okuda Tamaki in which basic facts are presented.[7] Due to the scarcity of documents available to Okuda, her report focuses less on the mission's activities and more on Stockholm as it existed in 1873. Apart from Okuda's study, the mission's stay in Sweden has only been treated rather superficially or figured in popular versions of the official report of the mission.[8]

For any study of the Iwakura mission, the basic material is the official report of the mission written by Kume Kunitake. The report, *Tokumei zenken taishi Bei-Ō kairan jikki* (A true account of the tour in America and Europe of the Special Embassy) was published in five volumes in 1878.[9] It has the format of a diary with frequent essays and interpretative comments.[10] Kume's use of *kairan*, 'travelogue', in the title indicates that he avoided dealing with treaty negotiations and other diplomatic and foreign policy matters.[11] The report has been described by Marlene J. Mayo as an 'extensive introduction of the entire world beyond Japan'.[12] This characterization must be said to be somewhat exaggerated even if the mission travelled widely.[13] In Kume's report, out of one hundred chapters, 20 are on the USA and England, 10 on Germany, 9 on France, 6 on Italy, 5 on Russia, and 10 in all on Belgium, Holland, Switzerland, Denmark, and Sweden, and 13 on Southeast Asia. Two chapters deal with Sweden. The number of countries visited, and the number of volumes issued reflects the attention paid at that time to various countries and regions.[14] The disregard of Asian countries is striking, but, as pointed out by Hirakawa Sukehiro: 'It was only natural for the Meiji Japanese to turn to America and Europe rather than to Asian countries in formulating plans to modernize their nation rapidly, and they were wise to select the strong points of each Western nation to further this process.'[15]

This paper will deal primarily with the mission as a foreign policy event. It is a preliminary study based on materials found in Swedish archives. Despite the fact that the Iwakura mission was the first Japanese delegation to visit Sweden, materials in Swedish archives are not abundant. Not much material on the subject is available in Japan either. In the Kume Museum of Art, which houses the materials collected by the mission as well as other materials relating to it, there is almost no material directly concerned with the mission's stay in Sweden.[16] This is probably the main reason why almost no research dealing with its stay in Sweden has been presented so far, despite the mission's important place in Japan's modern history.

PRELUDE TO VISITING SWEDEN

While the Iwakura mission was visiting the United States, no dispatches dealing with it were sent to the Swedish Foreign Ministry by its representatives there. When it came to Europe, however, the Swedish diplomatic missions in the countries visited reported about its activities. The first report to reach the ministry was sent by the Swedish embassy in London on 21 August 1872, a week after the mission's arrival in Liverpool. The embassy's secretary, Otto Steenbock, had had the opportunity to take a look at the members of the Japanese mission at a dinner hosted by Lord Granville, the foreign secretary. He described the Japanese dignitaries as 'most distinguished personalities who all wore European clothes and in general seemed to have, for Easterners, an unusually high level of culture.'[17] Comments on their clothes was to become a standard theme in subsequent Swedish descriptions. In a second report filed three-and-a-half months later, the Swedish envoy C. F. L. Hochschild informed his home office that five

Japanese ambassadors were going to be received by the Queen but that Lord Granville was going to recognize only one of the five as ambassador.[18] According to Hochschild's next dispatch, the somewhat cool British attitude to the Japanese had become aggravated. The Japanese ambassadors had invited the members of the government and foreign representatives to a dinner but, apart from Hochschild himself, only the prime minister, the foreign minister and the Lord Privy Seal attended the event, along with the Russian, Danish, Italian, Dutch, and Belgian representatives.[19] The Swedish embassy's reports amounted to no more than these three. The meagre reporting was probably influenced by the fact that the mission was not considered as particularly important in British eyes. This confirms W. G. Beasley's conclusion in a recent work that 'one is left with the impression, when reading the diplomatic correspondence, that Japanese missions to Europe no longer had the same curiosity value as in the past'.[20]

The somewhat lukewarm attitude of the British contrasted to the mood in the Netherlands when the Japanese mission visited there. Already some days before the mission arrived, the Swedish minister to The Hague, Carl Burenstam, informed the Swedish foreign ministry that the mission was expected soon and that one of its main purposes was to obtain a revision of the trade treaty with the Netherlands and abolition of the Dutch extraterritorial rights in Japan, something that the Dutch government did not seem to be interested in unless 'most of the other European powers are willing to replace their Japanese treaties'.[21]

In another letter a week later to Prime Minister for Foreign Affairs, Oscar Björnstjerna,[22] Burenstam conveyed more information, this time based on first-hand knowledge since he had had the opportunity to talk with the delegation leader. Burenstam wrote:

> Through an interpreter, His Excellency graciously expressed, among other things, his wish to travel to Petersburg and Stockholm after the visit in Berlin, where the delegation will head for in a few days – in what order seemed yet not decided. On a map I pointed out the routes to Stockholm from Berlin and Petersburg. . .[23]

In a later letter to Björnstjerna, Burenstam indicated that it was still uncertain whether the mission would visit Sweden. He informed Björnstjerna that the Dutch government would pay for the Japanese mission's travel costs and hotel expenses, but not meals. Burenstam gave a detailed description of how the delegation was received in the Hague for the benefit of his home office in case the mission decided to go to Stockholm.[24]

Obviously, the mission was judged as important by Prime Minister

Björnstjerna. The same day that he received Burenstam's letter of 28 February, Björnstjerna replied in a telegram indicating Sweden's willingness to receive the foreign guests: 'If the Japanese ambassadors express their intention to come here, reply that the government would see it with pleasure.'[25] Burenstam did not get an opportunity to extend the invitation to the mission to visit Sweden, however, despite the fact that he met one of the highest-ranking members of the Japanese delegation, Itō Hirobumi, at a dinner on 5 March.[26] The reason seems to be that he wanted to hand over the invitation to the highest-ranking Japanese, Iwakura.

The uncertainty continued whether the Japanese would come to Sweden or not. During the mission's stay in Berlin, the Swedish minister there, F. Due, informed the Swedish foreign minister that he had inquired into the travel plans of the mission and had been informed that the Japanese planned to go from Berlin to Petersburg and then probably to Vienna. Whether the embassy would come to Stockholm later in the summer was still uncertain.[27]

A telegram dated 11 April from the Swedish chargé d'affaires in Petersburg, L. Reuterskiöld, obviated this uncertainty. He had been approached by the Japanese delegation which had expressed its wish to visit Stockholm 'si agréable au Roi'.[28] The prime minister replied positively in a telegram two days later.[29] In a letter the same day Reuterskiöld informed Björnstjerna that he had conveyed this message to Iwakura 'who expressed his satisfaction and gratefulness'.[30] According to Reuterskiöld the mission would arrive in Copenhagen around 17 April and stay in Denmark about a week. Iwakura had mentioned to him that the Japanese intended to stay in Sweden five days. Reuterskiöld emphasized that the purpose of the mission was not to sign treaties or deal with matters of a political character but only to get acquainted with different civilized countries in order to contribute to the enhancement of its own country. Reuterskiöld went on to describe the mission's reception in Russia. They had been met at the border by a Foreign Ministry official who accompanied them while in the country, and had been received by the tsar who had given a dinner for 140 persons, and also received the delegation for a farewell audience. The Russian foreign minister had also given a dinner for the mission representatives. The Russian government covered all costs of travel, accommodation, carriages, mail and telegram correspondence, etc.:

> In all these [European] countries the governments have paid both its travel expenses as well as accommodation. Only in Holland has an exception been made, in that only costs for travel by train have been paid by the government, but [the mission] must itself pay all other

> costs. Even if the embassy is very satisfied with the courteous way it has been received in other countries, it has expressed its dissatisfaction with its stay in Holland which has made a disagreeable impression.
>
> Since it would be of importance for our coming trade relations with Japan that the Embassy retains a pleasant memory of its stay in Sweden, I have thought it better to submit this information which I have received from the Head of the Asian Bureau of the Imperial Ministry of Foreign Affairs. Mr Stremoukhov explained that he was convinced that the embassy with its Oriental character carefully observed the greater or lesser degree of attention and generosity shown to it, and thought it to be in the interest of each country visited, for the future profit that could be harvested, to accept the costs related to the visit.
>
> I may add that the Danish Minister here, as a result of the reception of the mission in other countries, has encouraged his Government to take measures so that the embassy will be received in a similar way in Denmark.[31]

When Björnstjerna received the telegram from Reuterskiöld informing him that the Japanese mission had asked for permission to visit Sweden, he wrote to the Swedish Minister in Copenhagen, Lave Beck-Friis, inquiring as to how the Danish government intended to treat the Japanese mission.[32] Beck-Fries answered in a telegram and a letter to Björnstjerna on 17 April. In the telegram he mentioned that the mission would be met by a Foreign Ministry official at the border. Twenty-one rooms had been booked at Hotel Royal. Travel and accommodation would be covered by the Danish government.[33]

Beck-Friis gave further details in his letter. The stay in Denmark was estimated to last four or five days. Denmark was going to show the foreign guests 'a rather extraordinary hospitality'. The reason was that the Danes had the impression that other European governments, with the exception of the one in the Hague, had treated them in a similar way, which would make such treatment seem natural to the Japanese. 'Under these circumstances, I am afraid that it will be very difficult, if not impossible, for His Majesty's Government not to pay the mission's travel and accommodation.' He advised Björnstjerna as to the costs that bothered his home office: 'To keep them in Sweden until the coronation would in this way be too costly and much more expensive than to arrange a couple of dinners especially for the mission.' Beck-Friis further stated that the Danish diplomat Julius Frederick Sick, who knew some of the members of the mission from his stay in Japan, would accompany the delegation during its stay in Denmark.[34]

The unanimous advice from the Swedish representatives in the Hague, Petersburg, and Copenhagen made it 'probably necessary', as Björnstjerna wrote to Beck-Friis, to accept the costs. Björnstjerna instructed Beck-Friis to 'welcome them now since the visit will not extend over the coronation'.[35] The next day Beck-Friis informed Stockholm that the Japanese would leave Copenhagen on the 23rd but that the length of the visit to Sweden was still uncertain, probably 'around five days'.[36]

Meanwhile, the Swedish government had appointed Carl Lewenhaupt, the head of the trade and consular bureau of the Foreign Ministry, and Count C. E. de Champs, Lieutenant of the Coastal Fleet, as attendants to the Japanese delegation.[37] The under-secretary of state for foreign affairs, H. H. Essen, informed Beck-Friis that Lewenhaupt had gone to Copenhagen to welcome the Japanese and that a special train for the Japanese was departing from Malmö on the 24th.[38] Beck-Friis soon had the opportunity to meet Iwakura and conveyed the information to him. The information pleased Iwakura and he asked Beck-Friis to convey his warmest thanks. According to Burenstam, it was not to be decided whether presents would be bestowed upon the Japanese until information of Petersburg's action in this regard was known but in his view it would not be necessary to give any gifts.[39] In a telegram the next day he confirmed that neither decorations nor gifts would be given to the Japanese.[40]

THE MISSION IN SWEDEN

The Swedish government had prepared as best as it could for the Japanese visit. It had not been easy since it was not known whether the mission would actually visit Sweden or not, and even when this was known, the date of arrival and the length of the stay were still unknown. Details were not clear until the last minute, because of the rather ad hoc, flexible, planning of the Japanese mission. It arrived in Stockholm by special train on 24 April at 4.23 pm. The *Dagens Nyheter* reported that Director-General Carl Oscar Troilius, Police Superintendent Semmy Rubenson and Lieutenant de Champs were waiting for the mission at the central station.[41] Advance reports in the press of the visit had aroused interest among the public and a large crowd had assembled at the central station to take a look at the Japanese.[42] From the station they were taken to Hotel Rydberg, where 21 rooms were reserved for the mission, the same number of rooms as in Copenhagen.[43] Later in the day, the mission paid a visit to Prime Minister Björnstjerna, a visit which he repaid the same day.[44] The mission was also visited by Chief Master of Ceremonies Count Philip von Saltza, who informed it that the king would receive the mission in an audience at 2 pm the following day.[45]

The next day the weather was 'more like January or February' with a temperature of four or five degrees below zero.[46] Kume noted in his travel report that it snowed.[47] Before the audience with the king, the mission squeezed in a visit to the Royal Swedish Academy of Sciences, at the suggestion of the Swedish attendants.[48] As was his habit, Kume gave the Academy exhibition a fairly extensive description.[49] Museums were one of Kume's greatest discoveries and delights in the West and he immensely enjoyed going through them.[50]

After lunch the mission was taken from the hotel to the audience with the king in five state coaches. Despite the cold weather, a large number of people had assembled outside the hotel and in the courtyard of the castle to have a look at the Japanese.[51] And what they saw should have pleased not only the public but also the status-conscious Japanese. Iwakura, the highest-ranking Japanese, was placed in the fourth carriage together with Chief Master of Ceremonies von Saltza. It was drawn by six black horses, the other carriages by four brown horses. Court lackeys paraded on both sides of the carriages. The Japanese were dressed in uniforms 'rather similar to the court uniforms used here', a newspaper noted.[52]

At two o'clock the mission was received by the king and queen at a public audience and Iwakura, accompanied by Itō and Yamaguchi, presented the mission's credentials.[53] The letter was delivered both in Japanese and in French translation.[54] Prime Minister Björnstjerna noted later in his diary: 'Solemn presentation to Their Majesties of three Ambassadors from Japan with suite.'[55] At five o'clock, the king hosted a dinner.[56] Apart from the Japanese guests, twenty-two other guests participated in the dinner, among them the three prime ministers, Axel Adlercreutz, the prime minister for justice, Oscar Björnstjerna, the prime minister for foreign affairs, and Richard Kierulf, the Norwegian prime minister. In the seating-list prepared by the court, three of the Japanese – Iwakura, Yamaguchi, and Itō – were indiscriminately called 'Japanese ambassador' and the other eight invariably 'secretary to the embassy'. Only two of the Japanese were mentioned by name in the seating – Iwakura, who had the place of honour to the right of the queen, and Itō – while the others were called only 'Japanese'.[57] This must be taken as an indication that the court was not certain of the ranking order of the foreign guests, since seating at a royal table was strictly regulated. It can be noted that the seating comprises eight Japanese guests, while the seating-list mentions nine. Since Iwakura, Yamaguchi, and Itō were the three members of the mission who had been presented as ambassadors, the fact that Yamaguchi's name is not found in the sketch of the seating may mean that he was not present at the dinner and that it was not clear until the last minute that this was the case.

Five members of the mission attended a ball in the evening called the Innocence Ball. It was a biannual ball given by Ljusets orden (The Order of Light), founded 1765, and a great event in the social life of Stockholm of the time. Iwakura was absent, but the Japanese who did attend wore European-style uniforms. In press reports it was noted that the Japanese caught particular attention among the participants.[58]

DIPLOMATIC INTERMISSION

The Japanese mission met Prime Minister Björnstjerna on a number of occasions, apart from the courtesy call he made on the day of their arrival. The prime minister was present at the audience with the king and participated in the ball in the evening, and also hosted a dinner for the Japanese the next day after which he noted in his diary: 'Large dinner for the Japanese hosted by me in my banqueting rooms. 34 persons.'[59] He also paid a farewell visit on the day of their departure.[60]

A meeting with the prime minister on the 27th focused on diplomacy. The Japanese wished to renegotiate the 1868 treaty since it was patterned on treaties concluded with other Western countries and thus unequal; it was actually among the last unequal treaties that Japan entered into.[61] According to Kume's travel report, the mission explained to Björnstjerna the details of the purposes of the mission on the day of arrival.[62] In Japanese sources it is noted that no negotiations took place since Sweden-Norway conveyed its intention to entrust negotiations to the Dutch representatives in Japan.[63] In his recent report on Swedish-Japanese treaty negotiations between 1868 and 1896, Ingemar Ottosson mentions the mission only in passing.[64] Nevertheless, Prime Minister Björnstjerna's diary, which is overlooked by Ottosson, indicates that negotiations did take place, since he notes in his diary on 27 April: 'Negotiations with the Japanese.'[65] He does not mention the contents of the negotiations but to do so would diverge from the customary lapidary style of his diary notes.[66] It is reasonable to think – based on Björnstjerna's diary – that some negotiations or exchange of views took place but that they did not result in any changes but only a confirmation of past positions. This is not surprising. The Swedish-Japanese treaty had been concluded only some few years earlier, and Sweden had no intention of going it alone but wanted to coordinate negotiations with Japan with those of other Western treaty powers. The Western countries had made it clear to the Japanese that they were not interested in giving up the advantages they had secured through the existing treaties.[67]

STUDY ACTIVITIES

From 26 April the mission started an intensive study programme. Acting on the suggestion of the Swedish attendant, the first industrial site visited was a naval yard.[68] It is not known which naval yard it was but it was probably Stockholms örlogsvarv (Stockholm Naval Dockyard) on Skeppsholmen.[69] The tour proceeded to the Scandinavian Museum (now the National Museum), which was given an almost two-page long description in Kume's report.[70] On the way back from the museum to the hotel, the mission paid a visit to what Kume describes as an 'exhibition place', *tenranjo*. Okuda has been unable to identify it but press reports show that it was Svenska industrimagasinets utställning (The Swedish Industrial Warehouse Exhibition) at Brunkebergstorg.[71]

Snow continued to fall on 27 April when the mission boarded the Sköldmön, 'the Valkyria', a boat which would take them on Lake Mälaren to Drottningholm, a royal castle outside of Stockholm. In his travel report, Kume gives a fairly detailed description of the scenery and the surroundings that met the mission. On its way back to the hotel a hospital and a military training school were visited as well.[72] Which institutions were visited on the way from Drottningholm to the hotel is unknown. There were three hospitals that they could have visited, the Conradsberg Hospital, the Serafimer General Hospital and the Garrison Hospital; and two military schools, Marieberg and Karlberg. Okuda surmises that the hospital was Conradsberg and the military school Marieberg.[73]

In the evening the delegation had been invited by the king to enjoy *Den stumma från Portici* (The mute from Portici), an opera performed at the Kungliga Stora Teatern (Royal Great Theatre, i.e. the Opera House).[74] A weekly commented later that the theatre audience observed the foreigners more intently than the performance.[75] The Japanese did not miss an opportunity to enrich their knowledge of Western technology: according to a report in a newspaper, during one of the breaks, the Japanese left their seats and went onto the stage to study the theatre facilities.[76]

The delegation's diligent studies of Swedish industry continued the next day with a full programme. Before the visits to industrial sites began, an experience well-known to the Japanese by now was repeated, however; in other Western countries, the delegation had been hounded by delegations from evangelical alliances or temperance unions with petitions for religious freedom in Japan.[77] Such a 'hounding' took place also in Stockholm when representatives of the Evangelical Alliance, accompanied by interested citizens – priests, businessmen, and parliamentarians – came to the delegation at half past nine in the morning. The leader of the delegation was Chief Court Chaplain Fritiof Grafström. The Alliance's Swedish secretary, Erik Nyström, a missionary, read a message. It is to be noted that the report in the *Aftonbladet* from this meeting is the longest of all its reports on events around the Japanese mission, due to the fact that the newspaper quoted *in extenso* an answer to the petition prepared by the Japanese delegation that was read in Japanese by Iwakura and in English translation by another member of the mission. This was a result of the fact that the mission had been informed in advance of the deputation and its message.[78]

The mission then proceeded with its study programme. Kume names few of the companies in his report but they seem to have been representative of Sweden which was at this time going through a rapid industrialization. At ten o'clock in the morning, the party left the hotel to study a textile factory, which was interesting in that its workers consisted (at least partially) of prisoners, both male and female. The mission continued to the naval yard of 'Berugusansu Co', identified by Okuda as the Bergsunds Mekaniska Verkstad.[79] A factory belonging to the 'Rikumen Co' was also visited, a company which still is not identified. It is described as a wood industry company.[80] The delegation then visited a match factory. Such a visit was not unexpected since safety matches had recently been invented by a Swede and had become a major export product.[81] Okuda was not able to identify the company.[82] Press reports show, however, that it was Stockholms nya tndsticksfabrik (Stockholm New Match Factory) situated at Igeldammarna on Kungsholmen. In the Swedish press it was noted that the Japanese were very interested in the production methods used by the factory, which had opened just one year prior to their visit and used the most modern production technology available. Later, the press quoted the Japanese as stating that this factory was the most interesting of those they had seen in Sweden.[83] Another company well representing modern industry, Bolinders mekaniska verkstad (Bolinder Iron Works Co), was then visited; after the round tour in the factory the Japanese were invited by one of the owners to his private home.[84]

In the evening, the seemingly indefatigable Japanese went on to watch the opera *Villars dragoner* (Villar's dragoons).[85]

The factory visits were not over yet. It is not certain when they did so, but it was probably the following day that they visited what Kume describes as a 'cheese factory'. According to Okuda, it is unknown which one.[86] It was, however, Mälareprovinsens mejeriaktiebolag (The Mälaren Province Dairy Co). According to articles in the press, the Japanese informed themselves with unflagging interest about the production of butter and other dairy products.[87] The choice of this particular factory was probably due to the fact that it was situated at the Clara Vestra Kyrkogata and thus close to a school that the mission visited, Klara folkskola (Klara Elementary School), invited by C. J. Meijerberg, the chief inspector for education in Stockholm, whose intention was to present the Japanese a display of drills by the pupils.[88] The *Dagens Nyheter* filed a report:

> The embassy came at about half past ten to Klara elementary school and was met by some of the members of the Supreme Board and the School Council. The strangers busied themselves during somewhat more than one hour in the school, in particular looking at the excellent school materials, which are found here, and listening to the lively songs which the pupils struck up, in honour of the visitors. A group of uniformed boy pupils were in the school yard to march past the guests, but due to bad weather, that came to nothing but the boys in one of the classrooms burst out in a 'Long live the embassy'and gave three cheers.[89]

In Kume's lengthy description of this school visit he mentions that the number of pupils, comprising both boys and girls of five-six to fourteen-fifteen years of age, as 10,000.[90] Researchers have deduced that this figure referred to the number of pupils in this particular school.[91] But Kume must have been citing a figure for the number of pupils in Stockholm schools since the total number of pupils of Klara parish, which had more than one school, was around 950.[92] It was characteristic of the never-ending energy of the Japanese that the school visit took place in the morning of the day they left Stockholm.

CONCLUDING REMARKS

The visit of the Iwakura mission was an illustrious event which caught the imagination of Swedes. Never before had official representatives from this 'exotic' country come to Sweden. One can sense a certain disappointment in the reports filed by diplomats and journalists at the appearance of the strangers, since they did not exhibit 'anything particularly special'.[93] Already the first diplomatic dispatch to reach the Foreign Ministry, from the Swedish minister in the Hague, pointed out the ordinary look of the Japanese. Three of the newspapers reporting their arrival at the Central Station noted in almost identical phrasings: 'Their look was quite ordinary apart from a somewhat darker complexion, since everyone wore European-style clothes and behaved as normal travellers.'[94] A weekly commented afterwards:

> Persons who met members of the Japanese delegation during their recent stay in our capital could not praise the men from the faraway East enough for their intelligent and pleasant bearing, but despite their close knowledge of European thought, their way of speaking revealed something strange and old-worldly, like some ghost from the age of chivalry just emerging among us, and just breathing the air of the new age long enough to obtain modern clothes and cursorily orient themselves in the most peculiar differences of the new age from their own.[95]

The ordinary looks and behaviour that surprised the Swedes should not have done so. From the mission's stay in the US, Charles Lanman reported that most of the mission's members had never been outside of Japan which 'naturally provided a series of comical mistakes and blunders, and [were] often the objects of laughter by the populace'.[96] By the time the mission came to Sweden, the Japanese had become experienced and were conscious of the necessity 'to behave properly while abroad and avoid disgracing Japan'.[97]

The fact that Japan was seen as an exotic country was certainly one reason why Prime Minister Björnstjerna wanted to find out how the mission was treated in other European countries and questioned the Swedish diplomatic representatives in Copenhagen, Paris and Petersburg about this matter, despite the fact that the Swedish ministers to both London and The Hague had already submitted such information. It must have been a bit worrisome for Björnstjerna when he was informed that the other European governments treated the Japanese representatives lavishly, since this indicated that the costs linked to a visit in Sweden would be exorbitant; one of the problems in the government's relationship with the parliament was costs incurred by the foreign service which the parliament regularly wanted to cut.[98] It was thus not easy for Björnstjerna to accept costs on behalf of the government and it was therefore natural for him to be cautious. His worries were well-founded, for after the mission had left and costs could be tallied, they amounted to no less than 7,831:90 riksdaler, or equal to four months' salary of the very well-paid prime minister.[99] The Japanese did pay some costs in Sweden, however. As seems to have been common, the delegation paid out a gratuity to be distributed among the attendant staff.[100]

For the Swedish diplomatic service the visit had been a success. The Japanese proposals for renegotiating the bilateral treaty had been thwarted and future trade had been promoted. It was therefore probably with satisfaction that the prime minister read a letter which arrived some weeks after the delegation had left Sweden.[101] The letter is crowned with the Japanese imperial chrysanthemum and reads:

Roma, May 19th 1873.

Sir,

Agreeably to promise, I avail myself of the earliest opportunity to enclose you my photograph. We take constant satisfaction in recalling the many pleasant incidents of our visit to your hospitable country and deeply appreciate the friendly attentions so kindly bestowed upon our party.

With renewed assurances of distinguished consideration,

I have the honor to remain,
Yours most respectfully,
Hirobumie Ito
Associate Ambassador Extraordinary of Japan

To
His Excellency,
Major-General, Baron Oscar M. De Bjœrnstjerna,
Minister of State and Foreign Affairs,
of H. M. the King of Sweden

BIBLIOGRAPHY

Primary Sources

The National Archives (Riksarkivet)
Björnstjernska familjearkivet, O.M.F. Björnstjernas arkiv
- Dagbok 1839-1905
- Brev from kungliga, furstliga och enskilda

Utrikesdepartementet, 1902 års dossiersystem
- 103A2: Underhandl: om revision af 1868 års traktat med Japan 1871-87

Kabinettet, UD, Huvudarkivet
- Kabinettet för utrikes brevväxlingen
  - BiB:615, Koncept, 1873, Svenska beskickningar: Aten-Köpenhamn
  - C2CE:1, Diarium för Notifikationsskivelser från utländska hov, 1840-1899
  - E2D:86, Depescher från beskickningen i Berlin, 1873
  - E2D:184, Depescher från beskickningen i Haag och Bryssel, 1873-1874
  - E2D:347, Depescher från beskickningen i Köpenhamn, 1873
  - E2D:460, Depescher från beskickningen i London, 1872
  - E2D:747, Depescher från beskickningen i Petersburg, 1873-1874
  - E2JA:23, Notifikationer 1870-1874
- Utrikesdep:ts kameralavdelning – personal och räkenskapsavdelning

G2AB:2. Räkenskaper. Tredje huvudtiteln och norska diplom. anslagen. Koncepthuvudboken, 1870-1879

The Archives of Stockholm Castle (Slottsarkivet)

Handlingar och räkenskaper avseende fester, vol 8, 1872-1875, Middagar och Soupeer hos DD HH Konungen och Drottningen 1872 8/10-1875 12/1

Hovet, Gratifikationer, 1838-1890

Hovförtäringsrkenskaperna fr.o.m. Karl XIV Johans tid, Oscar II, 1873, ID:51

The Archives of Stockholm City (Stockholms stadsarkiv)

Evangeliska Alliansens Svenska Avdelning, Protokoll. Huv. Serie 1854-1980: AI

Secondary Sources

Aftonbladet 24, 26, 28 and 29 April 1873.

Beasley, W. G., *Japan Encounters the Barbarians: Japanese Travellers in America and Europe*. New Haven & London: Yale University Press, 1995.

Bæckström, Anton, *Ett besök i Japan och Kina jemte bilder från vägen dit öfver Goda-Hopp-sudden, Bourbon, Nya Kaledonien, Manilla och Kochinkina. Anteckningar och minnen från en treårig tjenstgöring i franska flottan*. Stockholm 1871.

Cortazzi, Hugh, *The Japanese Achievement*. London: Sidgwick and Jackson; and New York: St. Martin's Press, 1990.

Dagens Nyheter 21, 25, 26 and 30 April 1873.

Dardel, Fritz von, *Dagboksanteckningar 1873-1876*. Stockholm 1916.

Duus, Peter, 'Introduction', in Peter Duus, ed., *Cambridge History of Japan*, vol. 5. Cambridge: Cambridge University Press, 1988, pp. 1-52.

Emanuelson, Kjell, *Den svensk-norska utrikesförvaltningen 1870-1905: Dess organisations- och verksamhetsförändring*. Diss. Bibliotheca Historica Lundensis XLVIII. Lund: CWK Gleerups, 1980.

Hedin, Einar, 'Sverige-Norges utrikespolitik i början av Oskar II:s regering'. *Historisk Tidskrift* 1946, pp. 229-60.

Herlitz, Nils, *Grundragen i det svenska statsskickets historia*. 6th ed. Stockholm 1967.

Hirakawa Sukehiro, 'Japan's turn to the West', in Peter Duus, ed., *Cambridge History of Japan*, vol. 5. Cambridge: Cambridge University Press, 1988, pp. 432-98.

Ishii Takashi, *Meiji shoki no kokusai kankei*. Tokyo: Yoshikawa kbunkan kank, 1977.

Izumi Saburō, '*Bei-Ō kairan' hyakunijūnen no tabi: Iwakura shisetsudan no ashiato o ōtte*. Tokyo: Tosho shuppansha, 1993.

Kume Kunitake, *Bei-Ō kairan jikki*. Tokyo 1878. Reprint ed. edited by Tanaka Akira, Tokyo: Iwanami shoten, 1978-82.

Lanman, Charles, *Leaders of the Meiji Restoration in America*. Re-edited by Y. Okamura. Tokyo 1931.

Larsson, Jan, *Diplomati och industriellt genombrott: Svenska exportsträvanden på Kina 1906-1916*. Diss. Studia Historica Upsaliensia 96. Uppsala 1977.

Lindberg, Folke, *Kunglig utrikespolitik: Studier i svensk utrikespolitik under Oskar II och fram till borggårdskrisen*. Stockholm 1966.

Mayo, Marlene J., 'The Western Education of Kume Kunitake, 1871-6', *Monumenta Nipponica*, vol. 28, no. 1, Spring 1973, pp. 3-67.

Nagashima Yōichi, 'Denmāku ni okeru Iwakura shisetsudan', in Tanaka Akira and Takata Seiji, eds, *Bei-Ō kairan jikki no gakusaiteki kenkyū*. Sapporo: Hokkaidō daigaku tosho kankōkai, 1993, pp. 163-81.

Nya Dagligt Allehanda 24, 25, 28 and 30 April 1873.

Ōkubo Toshiaki, 'Iwakura shisetsu haken no kenkyū' (Research on the dispatch of the Iwakura mission), in *Ōkubo Toshiaki rekishi chōsakushū*, 2. Tokyo: Yoshikawa kō bunkan, 1986, pp. 1-170.

Okuda Tamaki, 'Iwakura shisetsudan ga mita Suēden – 'Bei-Ō kairan jikki' dai 68/dai 69 ken 'Suēdenkoku no ki jo/ge' o yomu'. Kawamura gakuen joshi daigaku kenkyū kiyō, vol. 6, no. 1, 1995, pp. 29-67.

—, 'Meiji seifu no Suēden hōmon – Iwakura shisetsudan to 'Bei-Ō kairan jikki''. *Hoku-Ō shi kenkyū*, vol. 6, no. 13, 1996, p. 146-52.

Ottosson, Ingemar, 'Svensk frihandelsimperialism: Det ojämlika fördraget med Japan 1868-1896'. *Historisk tidskrift*, no. 2, 1997, pp. 199-223.

Samtiden, veckoskrift för politik och literatur. Utgifven af C. F. Bergstedt, no. 20, 17 May 1873.

Spetze, Gudrun, *Stockholms folkskolor 1842-1882: Ambition och verklighet*. Årsböcker i svensk undervisningshistoria, 72. Uppsala 1992.

Stockholms Dagblad 25, 26, 28 and 30 April 1873.

Svalan, weckotidning för familiekretsar, utgifven af Lea, no 18, 2 May 1873.

Tanaka Akira, *'Datsu-A' no Meiji ishin: Iwakura shisetsudan o ou tabi kara*. Tokyo: Nihon hōsō shuppan kyōkai, 1984.

—, *Kaikoku*. Nihon kindai shisō taikei, vol. 1. Tokyo: Iwanami shoten, 1991.

—, *Iwakura shisetsudan Bei-Ō kairan jikki*. Tokyo: Iwanami shoten, 1994.

— and Takata Seiji, eds, *Bei-Ō kairan jikki no gakusaiteki kenkyū*. Sapporo: Hokkaidō daigaku tosho kankōkai, 1993.

Thomas, J. E., *Modern Japan: A Social History since 1868*. London and New York: Longman, 1996.

Tominaga Shigeki, 'Hoku-Ō de mita koto, Nan-Ō ni tsuite kīta koto', in Nishikawa Nagao and Matsumiya Hideharu, eds, *'Bei-Ō kairan jikki' o yomu-1870 nendai no sekai to Nihon*, Tokyo: Hōritsu bunkasha, 1995, pp. 321-38.

Wingren, G., *Svensk dramatisk litteratur under åren 1840-1913*. Uppsala 1914.

Personal communications

Christina Nilsson, Curator, Stockholm County Council, 30 July 1997.

Takata Seiji, Professor, Kume Museum of Art, 12 July 1995.

Christer Wijkström, Librarian, Center for History of Science, The Royal Swedish Academy of Sciences, 22 July 1997.

Margareta Östergren, Senior Archivist, Military Records Office, 13 August 1997.

8

ITALY

9 MAY-3 JUNE 1873

Silvana de Maio

THE EXHIBITION entitled 'Japan discovers the West: A diplomatic mission, 1871-1873' held at the Japanese Cultural Institute in Rome from 25 May-30 June 1994 provided an opportunity to study the Iwakura mission in Italy more closely, the result of which has been published in the catalogue accompanying the exhibition.[1] The catalogue, prepared by Prof. Iwakura Shōko, has recently been translated into Japanese under the title *Iwakura shisetsudan to Itaria.*[2]

This essay will deal with the visit of the Iwakura mission to Italy, beginning with the treaty signed between Italy and Japan in 1866, and with reference to archive documents in the Ministry for Foreign Affairs it will describe how much news about Japan was reported in Italy during that period.

The key player in the relations between the two countries at the time was Count Fè d'Ostiani, appointed minister plenipotentiary for China and Japan in 1870, just over a year before the Iwakura mission set out for the Western world. The count was later to return to Italy to accompany the members of the mission during their visit there from 8 May to 3 June 1873.

One of the most important sources of information regarding this visit was books 73-78 of the *Tokumei zenken taishi Beiō kairan jikki* by Kume Kunitake. In addition, articles on the Iwakura mission in Italy published in the local press proved equally valuable, and some of these have been included here in the Appendix.

OFFICIAL RELATIONS BETWEEN ITALY AND JAPAN

Diplomatic relations between Italy and Japan were formally established with the signing of the friendship, trade and navigation agreement[3] between 'His Majesty the King of Italy and His Majesty the Tycoon of Japan'[4] on 25 August 1866 at Edo by Commander Vittorio Arminjon of the Pirocorvette *Magenta*.[5] Under the terms of the agreements a diplomat and a commercial *attaché* were to settle in Tokyo and Yokohama from 1 January 1867 onwards. At that time it was Foreign Minister Visconti Venosta who appointed Vittorio Sallier de La Tour as official envoy and plenipotentiary minister, and Cristoforo Robecchi as consul in Yokohama. Both arrived in Japan in the summer of 1867.[6]

De La Tour remained in Japan until April 1870, performing a highly delicate task given the nature of the transition the country was undergoing at that time.[7] He knew how to move very wisely in the subtle game of the new equilibrium just created: at first, he would sit back and observe all of the variables involved before laying solid foundations to ensure that Italian silk worm egg breeders could do business profitably.[8] In fact it was the spread of pebrine which had spurred Italian silk breeders to look for silk worm eggs in countries such as China and Japan.[9]

Alessandro Fè d'Ostiani was born in Brescia on 13 June 1825. He graduated from the Law Faculty of the University of Vienna in 1847[10] and by the following year he held several military posts under the King of Sardinia as well as being in the employment of the Foreign Affairs Ministry in Piedmont. From 1849 to 1870 he held a variety of positions in Italian legations abroad and on 7 March 1870 he was appointed Special Envoy and Plenipotentiary Minister and sent to China and Japan. On 22 May he arrived in Shanghai and immediately began an inspection of the most important areas where Chinese silk was produced.[11]

Although Japanese archive sources state that the Count arrived in Yokohama on 10 October[12] to replace Count Vittorio Sallier de La Tour it would appear that he arrived in Yokohama on 10 October and presented his credentials to the Tenno on 8 November.[13]

He dined that evening at the invitation of the Minister of Foreign Affairs 'in the delightful Sea Palace (a gift from the Tenno to the Duke of Edinburgh during his stay in Tokyo). Throughout the entire day the utmost cordiality was shown to both me and my retinue'.[14]

PREPARATIONS FOR THE IWAKURA MISSION

The next year, following a period of absence from the Italian Legation in Yokohama during which he had been living in China, the count returned to Japan where preparations were underway for the mission to the Western world. The *America*, with the members of the mission on board, sailed from Yokohama on the 23rd December.[15] Count Fè, who as we will see further on, was to accompany the mission during its entire stay in Italy, wrote the following letter about one month before the mission left:

> The Italian Legation in Japan, to His Excellency Visconti Venosta, Minister of Foreign Affairs of His Majesty the King of Italy in Rome.
>
> Tokio, 22.11.1871
>
> The Japanese Government, with the aim of coming to an agreement with the main foreign powers with respect to the preliminary stages of the new treaties, for which the conferences have long since been arranged for 1 July 1872, has decided to send to America and Europe an embassy comprising the Chief Minister for Foreign Affairs, the Chief Minister for Finance and another Chief Minister as well as a group of high-ranking officials and interpreters.
>
> The embassy will depart from Yokohama on 22 December next and will reach America via the Pacific. It will be accompanied as far as Washington by the American Minister Plenipotentiary accredited here, Mr De Long.
>
> In Japan, much importance is being given to this mission and from what can be seen here in the move towards progress and the new European Legislation it is believed that the embassy has instructions to obtain information regarding the foreign laws and regulations which may be applicable to this country.
>
> I was informed of this unofficially yesterday by the Minister of Foreign Affairs who will let me know at a later date when exactly the mission will reach Italy via England and France.
>
> The wish of the Imperial Government regarding all of the imminent reforms as expressed to the Diplomatic Corps so that it exerts a favourable influence over the opinions of the Japanese princes, has at the same time encouraged the latter to establish relations with the diplomats and now that most of the princes live in Tokyo, many have sent their visiting cards to the Legations. Through interpreters they are finding out when it is possible and convenient to meet the Ministers personally.
>
> This new state of affairs makes it all the more urgent to prepare the premises of the Legations as fittingly as possible and it is for this reason that I again urge your Excellency to consult what I had the honour to outline in the accounts report (no. 8) and political report (no.15).[16]

We can presume that Fè d'Ostiani was not aware of the document *Brief Sketch* drawn up by Guido Verbeck and handed over in 1869 to

Ōkuma Shigenobu who, at the time, was Deputy Minister for Finance. Verbeck (1830-1898) had arrived in Nagasaki in 1859 and had been a professor of politics, jurisprudence and other subjects, as well as the tutor of Ōkuma (1838-1922) and other future illustrious statesmen such as Itō Hirobumi (1841-1909) and Ōkubo Toshimichi (1830-1878). In his *Brief Sketch* Verbeck suggested setting up a mission which would travel through the United States and Europe and would provide its members with the occasion to find satisfactory answers to the many queries they had about Western life and society, given that the simple reports foreigners resident in Japan had been asked to give proved unenlightening. Count Fè d'Ostiani may not have been aware of the document but we can see from his letter quoted above that he summarizes perfectly the aims of the mission. Although the revision of the unequal treaties drawn up during the *bakumatsu* constituted the mainstay of the mission, it was of no less importance that the embassy should obtain information on 'those foreign laws and regulations which may be applied to this country'.

A few days later the Count sent a further report to Rome in which he listed the names of those who were to participate in the mission:

> The Italian Legation in Japan to His Excellency Visconti Venosta, Minister of Foreign Affairs of His Majesty the King of Italy in Rome.
>
> Tokio, 30.11.1871
>
> It would seem that Iwakura (Kugné [*sic*] – rank of princes) will maintain his position as Chief Minister for Foreign Affairs and will leave with the full credentials of ambassador. He will be joined by Their Excellencies Okubo, Chief Minister for Finance, Ito, Second Minister for Public Works, Iamaguci, Third Minister for Foreign Affairs and Mr Kido, who has held the position of Minister for Finance several times. All of these officials will travel as ambassadors given that the Imperial Government declared that His Majesty the Tenno had intended to confer upon all five of them the highest rank within the diplomatic corps. It is believed that there will be a fairly large number of staff travelling with the Mission.[17]

During the first year of the mission's journey, which actually lasted much longer than the ten months originally planned, Count Fè d'Ostiani continued his work in Japan and only left in February 1873 along with Sano Tsunetami, who was appointed by the Japanese government as 'Envoy' for the two new legations in Europe (one in Rome and one in Vienna) as well as Vice President of the Commission for the Exhibition of Vienna which was to be inaugurated in May of the same year.[18]

During Fè d'Ostiani's absence from Japan, the Italian Consul in Yokohama, De Barillis, took over his work at the legation. He wrote a very detailed and flattering report about the welcome given to Fè by the Japanese court on 22 February on the occasion of the envoy's official farewell visit to the Emperor.[19] Count Balzarino Litta did not arrive in Tokyo until the beginning of May to take over from Fè at the Italian diplomatic seat.

On 9 May 1873 Fè d'Ostiani welcomed the Iwakura mission to Florence after it had passed through the Customs at Ala the day before. It was to remain in Italy until 3 June and he was to accompany it throughout its visit.

REPORTING THE MISSION

The presence of the Iwakura mission in Italy was followed with much interest by the national and local daily newspapers,[20] and we have included the most important of these in the Appendix. It should be mentioned that although the visit by the Japanese mission never made front page news, the articles printed on the second or third page – often alongside national or local news stories – showed much curiosity and contained important information regarding the major transformations already made to Japan: articles were published on the institutional organization of the country,[21] on their calendar,[22] on the latest agreements reached by the Japanese and Italian governments thanks to the mediation of Count Fè d'Ostiani.[23]

A close study of the reports in the Italian press also makes it possible to draw some conclusions on the attitude of the Vatican towards the mission. The *Osservatore Romano*[24] only gave it brief mention in passing: '(. . .) A Japanese embassy has arrived in Italy for business negotiations (. . .).' The fact that there was no official visit to the Pontiff envisaged by the mission was probably due not only to the illness of Pope Pius IX but also because in all likelihood the Vatican did not request it because of the uncertain future of Catholicism in Japan.

The Italian press reports were a vital source of information on the itinerary taken by the mission, as Iwakura[25] insisted that Kume Kunitake's *Tokumei zenken taishi Beiō Kairan jikki* was not completely reliable. Indeed, since this was an official report of the mission it did not include any mention of the unofficial visits made, e.g. those to Brescia, Milan, and Turin, the programme of which was published in detail in *Il Secolo*[26] including news on when and where some members of the mission went accompanied by Count Fè d'Ostiani.

Analysing the chapters of the *Tokumei zenken taishi Beiō kairan jikki* on the mission's stay in Italy we come across the report on the visit to a porcelain factory near Florence[27] and to the glass factories in Venice[28] from which we can deduce that their interest in Italy was mainly directed towards production at an artisan and not an industrial level. Besides, it is well known that when speaking about Europe, Kume himself makes a distinction between the industrious northern countries and the considerably more backward southern areas,[29] thus indicating that his powers of analysis were particularly good despite the fact that the Italian itinerary had actually excluded – at least officially – the more industrially advanced areas such as Milan and Turin.

In any case, he proved to have an extremely keen eye for observing several aspects of modernization in Italy, such as the development of the railway network, for example, which in Japan was still totally inadequate[30] even though the first rail link had been opened between Tokyo and Yokohama in 1872. Kume reports data on the length of the entire Italian railway network built by three companies: one in the south, one in the midlands and one in the north. The government intervened in these projects by issuing debentures which were proportionately linked to the kilometres of railtrack laid.[31]

However, it is necessary to point out that there are several incongruences in the figures given by Kume in that the total number of kilometres of railtrack laid[32] exceeds the individual totals quoted for each of the three construction companies. In the light of this it is important to remember that Kume did not compile the report during the trip but only made notes in notebooks – which are still preserved in the *Kume bijutsukan* in Tokyo – where we can see that the chronological order of the visits is not even respected. Furthermore, even though Kume had asked for help from experts in various sectors before the work was published, we cannot exclude that errors of this kind depended also on the local guides who did not always provide correct information.[33]

In reality, the itinerary of the visit to Italy[34] had been arranged in order to visit the origins of European civilization, classical antiquity and the art of the Renaissance. As was mentioned earlier, Kume was a man of culture but presumably he did not have any great knowledge of the fine arts and even less of Western painting. When speaking of his brief stay in Florence he relates in detail his impressions of the grandeur of the Cathedral, which he describes as one of the largest and most spacious churches in Europe.[35] Although he pays particular attention to architecture Kume also mentions his visit to the Uffizi Gallery where he was struck by the number of people there who were reproducing the art works;[36] he talks mainly about the sculptures he saw there and only makes brief general references to the paintings.[37]

The visit to Rome, which had just been made the capital of Italy two years earlier in 1871,[38] was centred around the meeting with the King Vittorio Emanuele II[39] during which the credentials were presented and an official lunch was given in honour of the embassy. The members of the mission also visited the Basilica of St Peter, the Vatican Museums[40] as well as many monuments of ancient Rome such as the Colosseum and the Spa Baths of Caracalla.[41]

Still accompanied by Fè d'Ostiani, the delegation left Rome for Caserta, where Charles of Bourbon had commissioned the Neapolitan architect, L. Vanvitelli, to build a palace for the royals to hold court during spring and autumn. Vanvitelli laid it out in such a way that the palace atrium, when seen from the tree-lined avenue leading to Naples, formed a picturesque frame for the cascade situated at the end of the park, and this was much admired by the Japanese.[42]

On the evening of the same day they arrived in Naples from where they left to visit the ruins at Pompeii.[43] This fascinating city, founded more than two thousand years ago, had conserved people, objects, buildings and roads exactly as they were before the eruption, and somewhat puzzled the Japanese as they had not expected to find that in Roman times the Western world already had roads with lanes for both carriages and pedestrians.

On the way back from Pompeii the mission stopped at Herculaneum[44] where the Japanese visited the excavation area, which was made even more charming by the dim lighting there.[45]

The mission returned to Rome and after the official visit to King Vittorio Emanuele II in the Quirinal and to the Minister for Foreign Affairs, as well as excursions in and around the city, left for Venice where it was to visit the Basilica of St Mark, the splendid bell tower and the spectacular view over the lagoon.[46] The next day some of the members of the mission visited the State Archives[47] which preserve the documents relating to the visit of the first Japanese embassy in Europe in 1585 and the second in 1615.[48]

Thanks to the reports printed in newspaper articles we can have access to news of what the other members of the mission, including Itō Hirobumi, did along with Count Fè in Brescia and Milan, as the information given in Kume Kunitake's work only concerns official visits.

The local press provides us with many details on the visit to Brescia where the city's dignitaries and the silk worm egg breeders of the various sericultural firms in Brescia were introduced to the members of the mission. After lunch at Count Fè's house the latter visited the Town Hall and the Patrio Museum before carrying on to Milan.[49] This coincided with the funeral of Alessandro Manzoni, which was given exclusive coverage by the press as it was an event of national importance. On 2 June this party returned to Venice and together with those who had stayed there left by train for Vienna.

Count Fè d'Ostiani and the officer from the Royal Navy assigned to the Embassy accompanied them to the border where they were met by the Austrian minister for Japan, the Japanese minister resident in Vienna, Mr Sano and an officer of the Imperial Navy.

As was noted several times by scholars who studied the Iwakura mission, it could mistakenly be considered a failure on a diplomatic level given that despite every effort none of the unequal treaties were amended. Although Japan had made considerable progress in renewing the country in the years immediately following the Meiji restoration, it was still premature to recognize it on an equal footing with other advanced countries.[50] In any case, it should be pointed out that one of the outcomes of the mission was that Japan saw what steps it had to take in order to request that amendments be made to the inequitable treaties. Fè, in report no. 150 written a year after the return of the mission from abroad, has this to say about the amendments: '(. . .) In any case the Imperial government is showing no signs whatsoever of wishing to hurry and given the current state of affairs it is wiser to wait than to make rash decisions (. . .).'

The foundations laid down during the mission abroad were to produce positive results over the next few years. In 1875 and 1876, during which time Italian business interests in Japan were on the wane, relations between the two countries were strengthened by the hiring of Italian experts by the Japanese government. Edoardo Chiossone[51] arrived in Tokyo in January 1875 and took over the management of the state printing works. The following year he was joined by the architect Giovanni Vincenzo Cappelletti, the sculptor Vincenzo Ragusa and the painter Antonio Fontanesi[52] who were to take up teaching posts at the *Kōbubijutsugakkō* (School of Fine Art).[53] The school had been set up on the express wishes of Ito Hirobumi (who at the time was the head of the Ministry for Public Works, the *kōbushō*) upon the suggestion of Fè d'Ostiani, but it was not a successful venture and was closed down in 1883. On the other hand, young Japanese came to study in Italy at the International College in Turin.

APPENDIX

Selected extracts from the Italian Press[54]

FLORENCE

'At 2.40 am last night the Japanese Embassy arrived in Florence from Stockholm via the Brenner Pass. The delegation comprises the two ambassadors Saonii-Herouboumi-Jwakura and Jushu-Herouboumi-Ho and the secretaries: Taubé, Kowrimoto, Ando, Kommé, Fuikui, Brooks, Jomita Songigama and Kawage and is accompanied by four servants including one European.

As His Worship the Mayor is currently in Rome, the diplomats were greeted at the station by Marquis Garzoni, the Chief of Police and Mr Cesari, the secretary representing the owner of the Grand Hotel *La Pace* where the delegation will be staying.

Travelling in four carriages belonging to the Hotel they were met at the entrance by the owner, who personally accompanied them to their spacious apartments along with Count Fè d'Ostiani, the special envoy and Italy's minister plenipotentiary to Japan.

The ambassadors, secretaries and servants are all dressed in European clothes, speak English and French fluently, eat European food and greet people they meet by folding their arms in front of their chests and bowing low. This feature and their olive-coloured complexion are the only visible differences between the delegation and Europeans. They had such a large quantity of luggage with them that it was necessary to call upon the services of the shipping agent Mantellini to transport it from the station to the hotel. They will shortly be leaving for Rome.

Yesterday morning they toured the city in four *landau* coaches accompanied by Count Fè d'Ostiani. They visited local Galleries and Monuments and in the afternoon strolled in the nearby countryside.'

La Nazione, 10 May 1873

* * *

'Last Saturday the Japanese ambassador visited Doccia where he cast an attentive eye over everything that Marquis Ginori was able to show him, although the one-and-a-half hours available were not sufficient to allow a tour of the whole factory. Count Fè d'Ostiani and Mr Cristoforo Negri were also in the group accompanying the ambassador.

In addition to the visitors' book, the ambassador also signed a ceramic plate in coloured paint. This plate will be an elegant souvenir for the Doccia factory to treasure.'

La Nazione, 13 May 1873

* * *

ROME

'At 6.45 this morning the Japanese Embassy arrived in Rome from Florence. The delegation comprises the two ambassadors Saonii-Herouboumi-Jwakura and Jushu-Herouboumi-Ho and the secretaries: Taubé, Kewrimoto, Ando, Kommé, Fuikui, Brooks, Jomita, Songigama and Kawage and is accompanied by four servants including one European.

The Mission, which is accompanied by Count Fè d'Ostiani Italy's minister plenipotentiary to Japan, is staying at the Costanzi hotel. . .

The ambassadors and the secretaries all have the appearance of perfect gentlemen. Today we will probably see them travelling by carriage along the Corso and tomorrow at the latest they will be received by His Majesty the King at the Quirinal.'

La Libertà, 12 May 1873

* * *

'At 10 o'clock this morning the Japanese Embassy was granted an audience by His Majesty the King at the Quirinal Palace.

Six lavishly embellished Court carriages with outriders took the ambassadors from the *Costanzi Hotel* to the Royal Palace where they spoke at length with His Majesty the King before being introduced to His Royal Highness Prince Umberto.

The ambassadors were dressed in European-style clothes and were accompanied by one of His Majesty's aides-de-camp on both the outward and the homeward journeys.

An army regiment was on parade in the Quirinal Palace courtyard and played the national anthem on the arrival of the procession.

Inside the palace Royal Cuirassiers in dress uniform acted as guard of honour.'

L'Opinione, 14 May 1873

'As I reported, at the Quirinal Palace yesterday evening a gala evening was held in honour of the Japanese Embassy.

His Majesty The King entered the dining hall in his general's uniform accompanied by Her Royal Highness Princess Margherita wearing an extremely elegant and lavishly embellished pale pink gown and superb diamonds.

After a brief introduction to the Ambassadors, His Majesty the King took his seat at the centre of the dining table.[. . .]

After the banquet the guests held informal conversations in the large yellow hall. The Japanese ambassadors wore their official diplomatic uniforms but sported no decorations although they had received them in Sweden and other countries. They speak excellent English, with the exception of the most senior diplomat, who spoke to His Majesty the King and the other members of the royal family through an interpreter.

The Japanese diplomats spoke at considerable length with Princess Margherita and her ladies-in-waiting who are all accomplished English speakers. The ambassadors are enchanted by Italy and take every opportunity to sing its praises and express their admiration. They will remain in Rome for a few days and await the arrival of the Empress of Russia.'

La Libertà, 16 May 1873

* * *

'Here are the latest details on the banquet offered in honour of the Japanese Embassy at the Quirinal Palace.

As I have already reported, Her Royal Highness Princess Margherita was seated next to Ambassador Iwakura. A stool had been placed between them and set slightly back, on which sat Mr Yoshida, the Japanese interpreter of Italy's delegation to Japan. He translated both sides of the animated conversation between the Princess and the Ambassador throughout the banquet.

Iwakura belongs to the second rank of nobility (in Japan there are nine ranks, each subdivided into two grades). He is a gentleman of approximately 50 years of age, short in height but stocky and was a sort of infantry officer in the army. He was born in Yamakiro but has lived in Yeddo for several years now with his wife and eight children.

An unusual feature is that the Japanese diplomats do not wear a uniform typical of their country but rather the same apparel as European diplomats, including the sword and gloves.

They are staying at the *Costanzi hotel* where they have occupied twenty rooms. They have three meals a day: coffee and milk for breakfast, a large lunch at midday and dinner at 6.30 p.m.

They do not seem to have been instructed to pay a visit to the Holy Father and they will be leaving for Naples in about 10 days time.'

La Libertà, 17 May 1873

* * *

CASERTA AND NAPLES

'The members of the Japanese Embassy arrived, as already announced, in Caserta from Rome at 6 am this morning.

Waiting for them at the railway station were the Court footmen in full livery and four carriages.

They got out of the carriages at the Royal palace and were shown into the apartments on the ground floor where they were received by Mr Sacco and Mr Gargano who offered them coffee.

At 1 pm luncheon was served in the delightful Castelluccio pagoda in the Old Wood.

Needless to say, the Japanese diplomats were clearly amazed by the grandeur of the Caserta Palace, the park, the fish ponds, the cascade and the English Garden.'

Il Pungolo, 20 May 1873

* * *

'The Japanese Embassy arrived in our city yesterday morning. Court carriages were waiting for them at the railway station to take them to the Royal Palace where they were welcomed by stewards of the Royal Household who showed them to their apartments on the ground floor. Count Fè d'Ostiani who is accompanying the Embassy on their trip to Italy is being accommodated at the *Hotel d'Angleterre*. As is well-known, the Lombardy-born Count Fè d'Ostiani is the Italian Minister Plenipotentiary in Yokohama where he was transferred from Buenos Aires to replace Count Barbolani who was transferred to the diplomatic seat in Constantinople.

Yesterday evening, one of the members of the Embassy, wearing European-style dress, attended a show, watching from the 3rd court box at the Politeama Theatre.'

La Gazzetta di Napoli, 21 May 1873

ROME

'In the halls of the Ministry for Foreign Affairs a conference has taken place over the past few days between the Minister Visconti Venosta and two worthy Japanese Ambassadors Messrs Iwakura and Yamaguchi. The meeting was attended by numerous functionaries of the Ministry in addition to Count Fè d'Ostiani, the Royal Minister Plenipotentiary to Japan, currently on leave, two secretaries of the Japanese Embassy and one of the interpreters from the Royal Embassy in Tokyo.

The Japanese ambassadors, who – as is well known – have no other mission to perform than that of sounding out the various governments' opinions regarding the reviewing of treaties, asked the Ministry for Foreign Affairs a number of questions which allowed the Minister to state the Italian government's desire to improve and advance trade relationships between the two countries and, above all, to mention the strong need of Italians in Japan who are deeply committed in the silk industry for free movement in the inland provinces.'

La Gazzetta di Milano, 28 May 1873

* * *

VENICE

'As was announced, yesterday the Japanese ambassadors arrived in Venice. Two royal *salon* coaches had been provided for their journey directly from Rome, during which they were accompanied by His Excellency the Minister Plenipotentiary, Count Fè d'Ostiani, and the Navy Officer Mr Carini.

Waiting to greet them at the station were the Japanese Consul General, the delegated Councillor from the Prefecture and the Chief of Police. They left in six gondolas, all flying the Japanese flag, and entered their apartments in the *Hotel New York*. It is thought that they will leave again tomorrow morning for Milan, although the first ambassador, His Excellency Mr J. Iwakura, who is not feeling in the best of health, may well remain a few days in Venice. He is one of Japan's most eminent politicians, having already held the position of Supreme President of the State Council.

Count Fè d'Ostiani is staying at the *La Luna* hotel. He will accompany the Embassy to the border before returning to join the Japanese silkworm breeders' Commission for inspections and studies of silkworm farms and silk factories in Northern Italy.'

La Gazzetta di Venezia, 28 May 1873

* * *

'With the 7 am international train this morning, two ambassadors and their secretaries and aides left for Milan, accompanied by Count Fè d'Ostiani, the Minister Plenipotentiary to Japan. It is thought that they will return to Venice in a few days' time before departing once again for Vienna. His Excellency the first ambassador Mr Iwakura has remained in Venice with three secretaries, two interpreters and his private physician.

Yesterday the Japanese ambassadors, accompanied by the Consul General who resides in Venice, visited the Doge's Palace and the Temple of St. Mark, climbed the large tower to get a view of this unique city and visited the city gardens. They received a visit from the Chief of Police and they made a similar visit themselves.

This morning they went to see the Frari's general archives and the portico of the Seminary, where the ambassadors examined with great interest the Japanese memoires conserved here. As we have already reported once, the documents in the Frari archives state that in 1585 the first embassy to Europe under Mr Ito Mantio came to Venice from Rome, and was subsequently followed by another mission in 1615 under the ambassador Mr Nasekura. The documentation regarding these embassies was published in part and we are informed that the current embassy has commissioned the complete collection.

In the portico of the Seminary there stands a marble stone with an inscription dated 1585 commemorating the first Japanese embassy to visit the Confraternity of Charity.

La Gazzetta di Venezia, 29 May 1873

9

ENGINEERING EDUCATION IN JAPAN AFTER THE IWAKURA MISSION

Silvana de Maio

IN THE LAST FEW YEARS great attention has been paid to engineering education in Japan. In March 1997 the 'Henry Dyer Symposium' was held in Tokyo organized jointly by Tokyo University and the University of Strathclyde, Glasgow. During the inauguration, Professor Yoshikawa Hiroyuki, President of Tokyo University, suggested:

> Engineering education at universities should be reexamined, revised, and reconstructed. It is not just a matter of curriculum and courses, but of the whole system of engineering education. To this end, Henry Dyer, who invented a revolutionary educational system and exercised it in young modernizing Japan, could be a good starting point for discussion to seek a new model of engineering education.[1]

Furthermore during the spring of the same year, the Tokyo Station Gallery mounted a comprehensive exhibition entitled 'Josiah Conder: A Victorian Architect in Japan'[2] which confirmed the recent interest in the two Professors of Tokyo's Imperial College of Engineering, founded in 1873.

The origins of the Iwakura mission have been well discussed and researched[3] so I will only mention here that as early as 1869, Guido Verbeck (1830-98) suggested to Ōkuma Shigenobu (1838-1922), who had been his pupil in Nagasaki, to organize a mission to visit America and Europe. Verbeck set out the programme and the aims of this mission in a paper, titled *Brief Sketch*.[4]

> A commission of three Officers and a Secretary [should be sent to Western countries] to examine the various systems of national and high schools, the laws in regard to popular education, the manner of establishing and supporting public schools, school regulations and branches of learning, school examinations and diplomas. The Officers of this commission ought to visit and see in full operation Universities, Public and Private schools as well as Special schools, such as Polytechnics and Commercial schools.[5]

So a commission of investigation[6] for learning about the education system existing in Western countries was one of the important tasks of the Iwakura mission.[7] Its members paid particular attention to 'the sources of the West's wealth and strength[8] such as science and technology,[9] especially to their military and industrial applications as well as the political and economic background.

Actually a technical education system had already been initiated in Japan during the *bakumatsu* period as military technical education which aimed to promote Western military knowledge in Japan;[10] later it was expanded to many different fields but it is certain that modern industrial education developed from the cultural tradition which had been accumulated up to the Meiji Restoration.[11] The chief object of the education was to enable the Japanese to meet the conditions of a modern country and therefore it paid great attention to practical life.[12]

Some scholars such as Brock[13] and Checkland[14] have pointed out how engineering education developed in Japan as a result of the contacts that Itō Hirobumi made in Great Britain, especially in Scotland,[15] during the Iwakura mission. On the other hand, Professor Miyoshi Nobuhiro[16] of Hiroshima University has studied in detail the engineering education in Japan while Professor Kita Masami of Sōka University has analysed Japan's relations with Great Britain, in particular with Scotland, in commercial and educational fields as well.[17]

Here I would like to examine as a case study how engineering education developed in a short span of time, before and after the Iwakura mission. During the *bakumatsu* and early Meiji periods some dockyards were constructed and a few technical schools were established. Furthermore, in some cases, as in the Takashima pioneering mine, we can recognize the attempt to spread mining technical knowledge among those coming from many parts of Japan to study modern mining structures.[18] It goes without saying that the introduction of new technology into Japan involved not only the use of new tools and new machinery, but also a change in people's life, their way of thinking and values.[19]

First of all, I will look at two technical schools formed prior to the Iwakura mission, namely the *seitetsujo Kōsha* (ironworks school) in Yokosuka dockyard and the *Shūgikō* (school to master technique) in Yokohama which was attached to the *Tōdairyō*, the Department of Lighthouses. Next, I will consider the *kōgakuryō* (the Imperial College of Engineering), founded in August 1873 when some of the members of the Iwakura mission were already back in Japan. Finally, I will highlight the novelties of the *kōgakuryō* in technical education and how its development is connected with the social changes of the early Meiji period.

□

In 1865 the shogunate founded the Yokosuka ironworks (*Yokosuka seitetsujo*), later called Yokosuka dockyard (*Yokosuka zōsenjo*) where Françoise Verny (1837-1908, in Japan from 1865 to 1876) two years later established a shipbuilding school (*zōsen gakkō*, known as *Kōsha*).[20] The idea was presented to the *bakufu* by the French minister in Japan, Léon Roches (1809-1901).[21]

The initial intention in Yokosuka was that in a few years French technicians would have left the work to Japanese so that, from the beginning, the Japanese were urged to learn French as soon as possible.[22] The school had two main courses: the technical (*gijutsu denshūjo*) and the workmen's (*shokkō denshūjo*). In the former students were admitted after having graduated from the Yokohama French school and having passed an examination in elementary subjects. In the latter pupils were sons of the peasants of the Yokosuka neighbourhood who had no knowledge of French and technical subjects, so that they were taught from the rudiments.[23]

A first proposal for the curriculum of the technical course was drafted by Verny himself as follows: Year One – mathematics, geometry, cartography, physics, geography, French, drawing. Year Two – mathematics, geometry, mechanics, physics, chemistry, zoology, French, drawing. Year Three – physics and strength of materials, chemistry, naval architecture.[24] Subjects taught in the school changed slightly during the following years but I will not go into any further details here.

On the other hand, in the workman's course the following subjects were taught in Year One: arithmetic, geometry, algebra, cartography and French. Year Two: geometrical description, trigonometric function, elementary physics, elementary chemistry, cartography and French. Year Three – mechanics, instruments, advanced physics, advanced chemistry, cartography and French. Year Four – naval architecture, steam mechanics, sail manufacture, hygiene, cartography and French.[25]

Three years after the foundation of Yokosuka's *Kōsha*, the Shūgikō was founded in Yokohama as a project of the Scottish engineer Richard Henry Brunton (1841-1901), who arrived in Japan in 1868, to construct lighthouses around the Japanese coast. Before leaving for Japan, Brunton had had a training period and learnt about the construction of lighthouses from the Stevensons, at that time highly esteemed engineers who were active in Scotland. Yet what has to be emphasized here is that he did not get a school degree, but worked as an apprentice. As a result he gained practical experience in Great Britain before undertaking construction of more than thirty lighthouses in Japan.

The British minister, Sir Harry Parkes (1828-1885), pressed the Japanese government to construct the lighthouses[26] as early as possible to ensure safe landing for British merchants and, consequently, broader trade.[27] In this period Parkes was allowed to develop his diplomatic policies towards Japan on his own initiative not only because communications between Great Britain and Japan were slow and difficult, but also because Japan was actually not considered to be of primary importance to Victorian Britain.[28]

During his work in Japan, Brunton awakened the Japanese to the necessity of attaining the knowledge to carry out the projects by themselves. Since it was not possible to do so without any preparatory education, in 1870 the Japanese resolved to form a regular school, the *Shūgikō*, under the supervision of the Ministry of Public Works for mathematics and other related subjects. A large building was erected close to Brunton's office in Yokohama and 'educated men as could be found in the ports in Japan or China were engaged as teachers'. Pupils, young men of the samurai class, devoted themselves to studying English; some practised mechanical drawing and alike, some learned navigation from Captain Brown, some devoted themselves to the simple study of mathematics.[29] The Meiji government strove to have young Japanese trained to carry out surveys and projects by themselves as soon as possible.[30]

Different classes were formed depending on the level of students. The subjects offered were: construction, surveying, drawing, instruments, trigonometry, measurements, algebra, arithmetic, square and grass characters (writing), English.[31]

In August 1873, when some members of the Iwakura mission were already back in Japan, the Imperial College of Engineering, the *kōgakuryō*[32] (from 1877 called *kōbu daigakkō*) was founded in Tokyo with the cooperation of Henry Dyer (1848-1918).[33] Dyer, who took his degree at Glasgow University, became the Principal of the College and Professor of Civil and Mechanical Engineering in the same institution from 1873 to 1883.[34] One year after the foundation of the College, in 1874, the *Shūgikō* merged with it.[35]

But, how did Dyer and other professors of the Imperial College of Engineering take up employment in Japan and what were their contributions towards Japanese modernization?

As early as 1863 five young students of the *han* of Chōshū[36] left Japan secretly. They were: Itō Hirobumi (1841-1909), Inoue Kaoru (1835-1915), Endō Kinsuke (1836-93), Inoue Masaru (1843-1910) and Yamao Yōzō (1837-1917).[37] Yamao, who had attended the evening course in Anderson College in Glasgow as Dyer himself did in the same period,[38] thought that even if there was no industry at that time in Japan, an educated force was the first step to the establishment of industry itself.[39] So he actively carried out Itō Hirobumi's programme for the College of Engineering.[40]

In fact, it was Itō Hirobumi who, during the Iwakura Mission, asked H.M. Matheson,[41] a British businessman active between Great Britain and Japan, to find him a person suitable to organize a higher technical college in Tokyo. Matheson introduced him to Lewis Dunbar Brodie Gordon (1815-6), Professor at the University of Glasgow who, in his turn, introduced to Itō, Macquorn Rankine (1820-72), a very esteemed Professor of mechanical engineering of the same university. It was Rankine who finally selected Henry Dyer (1848-1918) as Principal of the new technical institution to be founded in Tokyo. In spring 1873 Dyer,[42] W. E. Ayrton (natural philosophy), D. H. Marshall (mathematics), Edmund Divers (chemistry), Edmund F. Mondy (technical drawing), William Craigie iEnglish language jand three assistants, George Cawley, Robert Clark and Archibald King left Southampton for Japan.[43] Some years later, other professors among whom were Milne[44] and Conder[45] arrived in Tokyo to teach at the College.[46]

The subjects available on the syllabus were as follows: English, Drawing, Mathematics, Natural Philosophy, Chemistry, Surveying and Levelling, Construction, Hydraulic Engineering, Machinery, Principles in Naval Architecture, Workshop Construction, Telegraphic

Engineering, Architecture, Mineralogy, Geology, Mining and Metallurgy.[47]

As early as 1875 a controversy published in *The Japan Weekly Mail* arose between Dyer who had organized the Imperial College of Engineering, and Brunton whose *Shūgikō* had been absorbed there. Brunton wrote that he was far from criticizing the organization of Imperial College in any way, but he emphasized:

> . . . that the profession of civil engineering, by which a person is enabled to design and direct the execution of works, is one, in which proficiency can only be gained by practical experience, and that no book learning or theoretical knowledge will be of any value without this.[48]

Dyer, on the other hand, answered this letter saying that he could gather from Brunton's article that the only fault which was found with the teaching programme at the college was that too much time was taken up with theoretical studies to the detriment of the practical part of the students' education. Yet Dyer had received letters from men who stood high in the profession, and without exception, they agreed with the arrangement which he had made. He wrote:

> I will shortly mention an engineer, celebrated for building light-houses, Robert Stevenson of Edinburgh, of whom 'R.H.B.' may have heard. If so, is he aware that this Robert Stevenson, when building the Cumbrae Light-house, spent every spare moment he had in going to Glasgow to obtain instruction in mathematics and mechanics at the Andersonian University? (. . .) I have no doubt 'R.H.B.' thinks this time was sadly mis-spent, or at least would have been spent to greater advantage in practical work; but Stevenson thought otherwise, and I am very much inclined to agree with him.[49]

Apart from the strict content of the controversy which arose between Dyer and Brunton in Japan, what I would like to point out is that it reflects the approach to engineering education at that time in Great Britain where discussion about the relative importance of theory and practice in technical education had not been resolved. Dyer himself, back in Glasgow in 1883, devoted a considerable amount of time to research about engineering education, pointing out the important social role of engineers. Some years later he wrote:

> It has been truly said that the engineer is the real revolutionist. His work has shrunk the world into small dimensions, and has brought into action forces against which the efforts of statesmen are vain, and even the action of armies and navies is of little avail, since ultimately economic conditions determine the fates of nations.[50]

Anyway, Dyer was since the time of his appointment as Principal of the Imperial College of Engineering quite aware of the position that the graduate students of the College, mainly of samurai origin, would have had in the changing society of the time. In fact the College, established under the orders of the Ministry of Public Works (*kōbushō*),[52] was organized so that the course would have allowed them to get a suitable training in order to be active as soon as possible in construction works. As we can read in the *Calendar* of 1876 written out by Dyer, the course of training extended over six years. The first two years were spent wholly at college. During the next two years, six months of each year were spent at college, and six months in the practice of that particular branch which the student had selected. By this alternation of theory and practice the students were able during each working half year to make practical application of the principles acquired in the previous half year. The last two years of the course were devoted wholly to practical work. The system of instruction was partly what is usually termed professorial and partly tutorial, consisting in the delivery of lectures and in direction and assistance being given to the students in their work.[53]

It has been said that Dyer realized his own programme for the college and that there was not such a college in any other part of the world that balanced theory and practice in this way, the former being preferred in French and German engineering education, the latter in British tradition. Some scholars suggest that the idea may have come to Dyer from the Zurich Polytechnic[54] but, whatever was the origin of Dyer's project, it was a suitable response to Japanese expectations. In fact, after the Iwakura mission, Japanese attitudes towards foreign employees, the *oyatoi gaikokujin*, had changed: Japanese were now more self-reliant and more conscious of the priorities in the modernization of their country. In time, the services of foreign advisers were no longer required as the Japanese did the jobs themselves.[55] Furthermore, they were much more conscious of the necessity of improving technical education and the Iwakura mission represented a good chance to lay the foundation of a new institution like the Imperial College of Engineering. Its creation was possible because, during the first years of modernization, the Japanese had not simply added to their national culture certain elements from the West but they had also absorbed them and, as a result, they had improved the qualities which they already possessed.[56] In about ten years, most of the instruction at the Imperial College of Engineering was given by Japanese professors and teachers, and almost all the text-books had been translated into Japanese.[57]

In 1885 the Ministry of Public Works was abolished and the Imperial College of Engineering was put under the control of the Ministry of Education. In March 1886 the *Teikoku Daigaku* (Imperial University) was organized and the Imperial College of Engineering merged with the new institution.[58]

Finally, I would like to discuss the impact that the college had on the changing society of the time.

The Imperial College of Engineering was established when the Korean crisis was at its peak. Soejima Taneomi (1828-1905), at that time foreign minister, had just returned from China where, he said, he had received *carte blanche* regarding war with Korea. As a result, the Council agreed to arm. In fact, since the establishment of prefectures in place of feudal domains in 1871, the samurai had become a menace to the internal security of Japan and the war with Korea seemed a way of releasing the tension.[59]

At the Imperial College of Engineering, the students were mainly of samurai origin.[60] Initially, considerable effort went into the study of English. The results were truly impressive when one examines their undergraduate theses written in near-perfect English. It is interesting to note that in each thesis of the first round of graduates[61] in mechanical engineering, there is always a chapter about 'The History of . . .' which demonstrates that they had a literary background and political and historical interests.[62]

In December 1871, the new government permitted the samurai and the peerage to pursue any occupation they desired which for centuries had been denied to them.[63] Of course, Japanese at that time were still not familiar with new infrastructures such as railways, telegraphs and, in general, with Western engineering technology.[64] Yet, at the same time, there was an urgency to rehabilitate the samurai class. One could, therefore, say that the College of Engineering could be seen as a link between the members of the Iwakura mission returning from Europe and America with new ideas and projects and the imperative of finding a solution for employing the samurai class in the speedily changing society of the time.

10

THE SOCIAL WHIRL OF 'WHITE' YOKOHAMA AFTER IWAKURA'S RETURN

Olavi K. Fält

THE RETURN of Iwakura's mission in 1873 from its two-year journey to Europe and the United States marked the dawn of a new era in Japan. The mission's report laid emphasis on the backwardness of Japan and its need to learn from the West, and the intention was to obtain this new information by inviting Western experts to Japan and by sending Japanese students to Europe and the United States. It was also possible for Japanese to observe Western culture and social models and practises on their home territory, however, as, from 1859 onwards, Westerners had been allowed to settle in certain 'treaty ports', of which Yokohama had rapidly become the most significant.

The period in question, the 1870s, is recognized as a time when the globalization process began to advance at an ever-accelerating rate, when the influence of Western culture and the various forms of local reaction to this throughout the world formed the principal trend distinguishable in world history. The aim in this paper will be to examine what model Yokohama furnished for the Japanese of the way Westerners spent their leisure time on working days and holidays. It will also be apposite to consider, if at all possible, whether Yokohama really served as a model in this respect. The year selected for evaluation is 1874, that which immediately followed the return of Iwakura's mission, since it represents the point of departure from which the Japanese set out to develop their country in accordance with the impressions gained by the mission. The source material consists primarily of newspapers published by Westerners in Japan, which allow us to create a fairly reliable picture of what the Western community of Yokohama was engaged in at that time, as the community's own press faithfully recorded both the joys and sorrows of that community.

Yokohama was opened as a port for foreign trade on 1 July 1859, the new area being divided into two parts, that inhabited by the Japanese and that reserved for foreigners.[1] As foreign trade continued, both settlements gradually began to prosper and their population grew. Thus there were as many as 2411 foreigners in Yokohama by 1874, about half of whom were Chinese, working as money changers, porters etc. About half of those working in a commercial capacity were British and a fourth American, with the Germans and French forming the next largest groups. There were also some Swiss, Italians, Australians, Portuguese, Dutch, Russians, Belgians and Austrians.[2] Life in Yokohama became more lively as the settlement grew in population and affluence, one token of which is the fact that there were three newspapers being published there by 1874, one magazine and one satirical paper.

Both the chroniclers of the time and later writers divide the early history of Yokohama into two periods, the boundary between which is provided by the fire that destroyed a large part of the settlement in 1866. In the opinion of W.E. Griffis, an American who visited there in the early 1870s and has gone down in history as an authority on Japan, the fire proved a turning point in a moral, as well as a civic and economic, sense.[3] His reference to morals may well be connected with the fact that life in Yokohama in the early days was said to have been easy but restricted and monotonous. Contacts with the outside world were few and far between, as the parcel post, for example, came only once a month. Life was all the more trying as respectable Western ladies, or indeed any Western womenfolk, were a rarity. It was on account of the lack of young ladies, for instance, that the first dance to be arranged there was held only in 1866.[4]

In order to enliven the Western males' existence, the friendly Japanese had built a large, enclosed amusement park, Miyosaki, better known as Gankiro after its tea-rooms. Opened in 1859, the purpose of this amenity was to make Yokohama more attractive to Westerners. The Gankiro tea-rooms, for instance, had 300 pretty Japanese girls waiting on their visitors.[5]

Even more than Gankiro, however, the traveller from Victorian Britain may have been disturbed at the arrangement or way of life known as the 'Butterfly Game', a system under which the Japanese authorities would help lonely Western men to acquire a temporary Japanese wife. Arrangements of this kind were available in all the ports that had been opened to Westerners. Although it aroused much disapproval, there were many who regarded it as a good thing in a society which had insufficient unmarried Western girls and in which social pressures and economic considerations frequently prevented a young man from marrying properly until he had achieved a certain financial and social status. One young Japanese girl caught up in the 'Butterfly Game' became famous worldwide as the Madame Chrysanthème immortalized by a French naval officer, who wrote under the name of Pierre Loti, although admittedly Loti's adventures in the hot, intoxicating summer of 1885 took place in Nagasaki rather than Yokohama.[6]

The situation in Yokohama as far as morality was concerned had altered substantially by 1870, when more of the men were able to bring their families with them, and this improvement was universally welcomed in principle, as the port served as an example of the Western life-style and it was thought desirable that it should also convey the essential respectability of this way of life.[7]

Although the way of life of the early settlers in Yokohama may have been criticized by their successors, there was undoubtedly a certain attraction in it. They could spend their leisure-time riding, sailing, hunting, practising athletics, going for picnics or taking longer walks into the surrounding countryside, as far as the territorial agreements allowed. Foreigners were permitted to travel up to 24 miles from their treaty port, but any longer journey required a special permit from the authorities. Further colour was added to life in Yokohama by the garrisons that arrived in 1864 to protect the foreign population. The last of these left in 1875. Similarly, Yokohama was a favourite port of call for Western ships, which brought many social benefits, including the fact that the ships' orchestras would frequently entertain the local inhabitants with open-air concerts.[8]

A traveller arriving at Yokohama in 1870 would have found a very different settlement from that of the early 1860s. It had been rebuilt after the fire of 1866, its town plan was clearly defined, and the increased affluence meant that the buildings owned by the Westerners were quite impressive. The standard of the hotels had also greatly improved. as in all the ports in the East, the dominant culture in terms of manners, dress and other features was that of the British.[9] The general style of life, of course, was a leisurely one. Offices opened late and closed early, and there was a lunch hour in the middle of the day when everyone went home to eat. Most offices were empty by 4.30 in the afternoon, after which the older gentlemen usually went to their clubs and the younger ones went off riding or sailing.[10]

The focal point for entertainments was the Gaiety Theatre, opened in 1870, and musical evenings were also arranged in the hall of the Grand Hotel. Another prominent place of entertainment was the public park, also opened in 1870. Griffis paints a particularly attractive picture of the atmosphere on a summer's evening, when the unbearable heat and humidity of midday had given way to a milky-warm darkness. Ships' orchestras, or even the first Western-style Japanese orchestra, would play in the park and the people of Yokohama would sit or stand under the dark green leaves of the trees, listening to popular Western tunes. One could then crown this pleasant evening with a delicious meal, as a good dinner was regarded as the event of the day, the highest form of social intercourse and enjoyment.[11]

What else was there for the people of Yokohama to do in 1874? The following details are based on the 1875 edition of the *Hong List and Directory*, a yearbook containing a large amount of information on the Western community. This volume records that Yokohama had 10 religious organizations, mostly engaged in missionary work, an enthusiastic response to the decision taken in 1873 to permit overseas missionaries in Japan. The organizations were the following: the American Baptist Missionary Union, the Independent Baptist Mission, the American Methodist Episcopal Church Mission, the American Presbyterian Mission, the American Reformed Church Mission, the American Women's Union Mission, the Christian Church, the Union church and the Roman Catholic Mission.[12]

The actual clubs and societies operating in Yokohama at the time were the Chamber of Commerce (founded 1865), the Amateur Athletic Association of Yokohama, the Art Union of London, the Race Club (founded 1866), the Yokohama United Club (founded 1863), Club Germania (founded 1863), the Eastern Club, the Cricket Club, the Racquets Club, the Yokohama Rowing Club, the Yokohama Rifle Association (founded 1865), the Swiss Rifle Club, the Public Hall Committee, the Temperance Hall (founded 1873), the Independent Order of Good Templars, the Literary Society of Yokohama, the Choral Society of Yokohama, the Cemetery Committee, the Asiatic Society of Japan (founded 1872) and the Masonic Lodge (functioning regularly from 1866).[13]

In addition to these, the Japan Total Abstinence Society, which had been responsible for opening the Temperance Hall, and a Ladies Benevolent Society had been founded in 1873. Mention should also be made of the community's three voluntary fire-fighting services, the Victoria Steam fire Engine Company, the American Fire Brigade and the Private Fire Hook & Ladder Company.[14]

The list for the following year, 1876, already contained a number of new entries, the Yokohama Football Association, the Amateur Dramatic Club, the St Andrew's Society of Japan and the Young Men's Christian Association, together with two new voluntary fire brigades, or at least, two new names, the Relief Steam Fire Brigade and the Yokohama Fire Brigade.[15] The Dramatic Society, at least, did not represent a new pastime in the community, as the 1872 edition of the Directory had mentioned a Yokohama Amateur Dramatic Corps.[16]

One outstanding feature of this array of clubs and societies which tells us something of the variety of activities taking place in Yokohama is the wide range of sports on offer. This is no surprise, since the British made up a large proportion of the Western population, and Britain was undoubtedly the cradle of Western sport in the nineteenth century, from where the custom spread throughout the world, accelerated by the belief held in other countries that one of the pillars of British might was the prominent part played by sport in the nation's upbringing.[17] The middle classes in Britain had been eager participants in team sports since the 1850s, and also in other sports such as tennis; and the upper classes had been amusing themselves with hunting, shooting and cricket for centuries. It was the spread of sport to the middle classes in particular that led to the proliferation of sports clubs of all kinds.[18] Why should this British middle class affection for sport not have spread to Yokohama along with the British settlers? The sports activities mentioned are indeed those most typical of the British worship of bodily health: gymnastics, riding, tennis and rowing.

A list of clubs and societies does not suffice, however, to illustrate the active lives pursued by the inhabitants. We must also ask how enthusiastically people took part in these activities. If we exclude the religious organizations, fire brigades and freemasons, the list of people in charge of these clubs and societies numbers 78. (Admittedly, the information available varies from one organization to another, some naming a chairman, secretary and treasurer, some only one or two officials, and some far more.) Among these 78 there were 17 people who were involved in more than on organization, 13 in two, 2 in three and 2 in four,[19] so that there were evidently plenty of active, interested people available, and the societies were by no means reliant on just a handful of active members.

The organization of such activities was greatly facilitated in practice by the fact that under the general treaty between Japan and the Western powers all this could take place in accordance with Western legislation. The extraterritorial rights granted to these communities meant that Japanese law did not extend to them and therefore did not restrict their lives in any way.

EXAMPLES OF LEISURE-TIME ACTIVITIES

Let us look now at a few examples to illustrate the nature of the leisure-time activities that took place in Yokohama. One of the most active of the clubs and societies was the Asiatic Society of Japan, each monthly meeting of which featured a usually very well-informed talk on some topic connected with Japan. As these talks were usually published verbatim in the local press afterwards, they were in principle accessible to the whole Western community. In 1874, the society had 168 members and its first meeting of the year, on 14 January, was opened by the chairman, J.C.Hepburn, and heard a talk by Capt. S.T.Bridgford on 'Yezo, a description of the Ishi-kari River and the new capital, Satsporo'. Indeed, looked at in retrospect, the range of speakers for the year was a most impressive one, as it included Ernest Satow, on 'Shinto shrines of Ise', W.E. Griffis on 'The games and sports of Japanese children', in which he exalted Japan as a paradise for children and those of like mind, W.G.Aston on 'Has Japanese an affinity with the Aryan languages?' and J.C.Hepburn, presenting 'Meteorological tables from observations made in Yokohama from 1863 to 1869 inclusive'. The last talk of the year was given by Henry Gribble on 'The preparation of vegetable wax in Japan'.[20]

Literature had its own active group of devotees. A literary evening held at the Grand Hotel in January, for instance, heard George Paunceford read Dickens' Christmas story 'Dr Marigold', following by the Irish 'Bad Ballad'. There was also piano music. The press account of the event praised the performers but suspected that the audience may not have returned home in an entirely happy frame of mind as the choice of works had not come up to expectations. The range of topics dealt with in the course of the year was certainly broad enough, as later talks were concerned with such matters as 'Identity of the Mikado, Miya and Kuge Sama && with the ten lost tribes of Israel' and 'The rise and progress of the system of banking carried on in the east'.[21]

A significant step forward was achieved in the theatrical life of Yokohama in February 1874, with an amateur performance of a drama 'Still waters run deep', written by Tom Taylor and directed by George Paunceford, as their repertoire up to that time had consisted entirely of farces. Amateur theatre also formed an important part of the activities of the Club Germania, with at least eight plays produced in the course of the year. In February, for instance, they performed a double bill 'Wer zuletzt lacht' and 'Sachsen in Preussen'.[22]

Life was reasonably rewarding for those interested in music as well. A concert was held in April 1874, for example, at which a Mr Marsh played the piano, but the critic from the *Japan Weekly Mail* was not satisfied with his choice of pieces. More space was devoted to the songs performed by a Mr Black, while songs by the Misses Miles, a duet for flute and piano by Messrs. Marsh and Wagner and songs by M. Jaquemot were passed over with just a brief mention. The critic noted in his assessment of a concert of religious music in May that the soloist was the only person east of the Cape of Good Hope who was capable of singing Bach correctly.[23]

People naturally had many opportunities to meet together apart from at the theatre or concerts. Slightly less formal but no doubt very amusing and exciting for all concerned were the series of evenings arranged by the bachelors of Yokohama for the young ladies of the community in spring 1874. There were also various celebrations held by national groups, such as the St Andrew's Dinner arranged by the Scottish Committee at the Grand Hotel and the party organized by the British community for the Queen's Birthday. Temperance was a cause that attracted many followers at that time, as indicated by the fact that its society had a membership of 200 and the opening of the Temperance Hall attracted about 220 guests. The indisputable highlight of the year as far as entertainment for the whole family was concerned was the visit of Chiarini's Circus in September-October, to the extent that a performance held at the beginning of October in aid of the General Hospital was reported in the press to have attracted more people than any event ever held in Yokohama previously.[24]

Sport was also a source of great interest, the most popular sports in terms of coverage by the *Japan Weekly Mail* being athletics (9 times), horse racing (9 times), shooting (4 times), cricket (3 times), sailing (once), croquet (once), chess (once) and skating (once). This latter was intended for the general public and not as a competition, as the sports club had the idea in January of creating an ice rink and covering the land rent, equipment and other costs by charging an entrance fee. No mention can be found of how successful this novel idea proved to be. Athletics was a fairly popular pastime, and the Amateur Athletics Association had a total of 60 members and 28 honorary members. Very respectable results were achieved at its meetings too, e.g. 11.4 sec for the 100 yards, 150 cm in the high jump, 533 cm in the long jump and 211 cm in the pole vault. Of the more esoteric events, mention should be made of the 150 yards handicap race for married men, the 200 yards for ex-soldiers and the consolation race for non-winners.[25]

THE ROLE OF WOMEN IN RECREATION

As is obvious from the above, there were enough active men for all these events and pastimes, but what was the role of the womenfolk in all this? Miss Pat Barr deduces that their lives must have been somewhat dull, as the majority of the clubs, sports and committees were the provinces of their husbands and fathers. At the same time the majority of the families had Japanese or Chinese servants who took care of the housework. There were also very few shops in Yokohama, so that shopping was not a pleasure that the Western women could enjoy. They were visible in the community to some extent, however. Their names appeared in the births and deaths columns of the newspapers, they baked cakes for various events, held bible classes for the girls, attended church and various competitions, filled the seats at the theatre, took walks in the park and met their other lady friends. They also kept up a routine of minor intrigues and flirtations with their numerous admirers.[26]

Apart from the fact that those whose father or husband was in an influential position were called on regularly to present the prizes at sports competitions, the majority of their time was spent waiting. They waited for their husbands to come home from work or from their sports or other activities, they waited for their children to be brought by their nanny to be kissed goodnight, they waited for the mail boat to arrive with news from their distant but greatly missed native land, they waited for the servant to announce that dinner was ready, and they waited for the hot, sweaty summer weather to be over.[27]

Nevertheless, the inhabitants of Yokohama were in the long run very active people who brought many aspects of Western culture to Japan and tried to involve themselves in them and maintain them in this new, utterly strange environment, for the sake of their own comfort in life and their own sanity. In this way Yokohama served as a showcase for the Japanese in this aspect of life as in others, as they had a chance to acquaint themselves at first hand with the leisure-time pursuits of the newly-emancipated Western middle classes, and even to adopt some of the customs.

Finally, we should ask what was the outcome of all this. Did the Japanese come to model their lives on those of the Westerners? The material available for the present purpose allows only a very brief, cautious estimate to be made on this point. There are clear indications that the Westerners hoped that Yokohama would really serve as a model for the Japanese in matters of leisure-time activities as well and indeed felt that it did so. In the opinion of Griffis, who visited Japan at that time, it was the task of Yokohama, regardless of any changes that the future might bring, to continue to serve as a master instructor and example to Japan in all that was good and bad in the Christian culture.[28] Discussions in the *Japan Weekly Mail* on the future of the Westerners' park contained the hope that it could be opened to Japanese and foreigners alike,[29] and active participation by the Japanese in many Western activities was gradually becoming more common. One of the first indications of this in the material studied here was the occurrence of a Captain Murata and a Mr Tasae in the list of results of a shooting competition, the former having taken part in six events and the latter in three.[30] Thus it can be claimed, at least with certain reservations, that the familiarity with western culture regarded as so important by Iwakura's mission was acquired to some extent on the spot in Japan, in the sense that the 'treaty ports', with Yokohama at their head, served as a showcase in this respect.

11

KUME KUNITAKE AS A HISTORIOGRAPHER

Iwakura and After

Shigekazu Kondo

KUME KUNITAKE, the author of the *Bei-Ō Kairan Jikki* (a true account of the tour of the Special Embassy to the US and Europe), is also well known as one of the first professors of history at the Imperial University who was forced to resign because of his article, 'Shinto wa saiten no kozoku' (Shintoism is a Primitive Custom of Heaven Worship). The so-called Kume Affair is regarded as a conflict between science of history and politics or ethics.[1]

In this paper I shall shed light on Kume's view of history. The question is where his historical view came from.

Related to Kume's work I shall refer to the historiographical project in modern Japan. Margaret Mehl gave a paper about this project at the EAJS conference in 1991 in Berlin titled 'Tradition as Justification for Change: The Predecessor of the *Tokyo daigaku Shiryo hensanjo* (Historiographical Institute)'. She also wrote a book in German on this subject titled *Eine Vergangenheit für die japanische Nation* (A Past for the Japanese Nation). This paper owes a lot to her study.

THE LIFE OF KUME KUNITAKE

Kume Kunitake was born in 1839 in Saga. His father served in Saga *han* as a samurai. Kunitake studied from 1854 to 1859 at the *han* school, *Kō dōkan*, and from 1863 to 1864 at the school of the shogunate, *Shōheizaka gakumonjo*, in Edo. While he studied at the *Kōdōkan*, he got to know Ōkuma Shigenobu, who later became the prime minister and founded the Waseda University.

Kume served in Saga *han* during the Meiji Restoration. After the abolition of the feudal domains and the establishment of the prefectures (*haihan chiken*) in 1871, he became an official at the *Dajōkan* (Central Government Office). He was ordered to join the Iwakura Mission to the US and Europe which left Japan in the same year and came back in 1873. After the return of the mission, Kume was engaged in writing the official report of the mission, which was named *Bei-Ō Kairan Jikki*. It was published in 1878.

In 1879 Kume took a new post at the *Shūshikan* (House of Historiography). The House was under the control of the *Dajōkan* and had the project of compiling the official national history. After the establishment of the cabinet system in 1885 the House was reorganized as the Temporary Office of Historiography (*Rinji Shūshikyoku*) under the control of the cabinet. The project of compiling the official national history was transferred from the cabinet to the Imperial University in 1888. The Temporary Office of Historiography became the Temporary Department for the Compilation of a Chronological History (*Rinji Hennenshi Hensan Kakari*), which was renamed the Department for the Compilation of History and Topography (*Shishi hensan Kakari*) in 1891. With the transfer of the project, Kume became a professor of the College of Literature at the Imperial University with his colleague, Shigeno Yasutsugu and Hoshino Hisashi. They gave lectures at the Department of National History, and at the same time held responsibilities as members of the Department for the Compilation of a Chronological History.

Kume's article, 'Shinto wa saiten no kozoku', caused him his resignation from the Imperial University in 1892. He took a new post in the *Tokyo senmon gakkō* (Tokyo Vocational College), which was founded by Ōkuma Shigenobu. It was renamed later as Waseda University. He gave lectures about historical sources, ancient history and histories of the Nara Period and the period of Northern and Southern Dynasties. The University Press published his lectures. Kume retired from Waseda University after Ōkuma's death in 1922. Kume died at the age of 91 in 1931.

BEI-Ō KAIRAN JIKKI

The *Tokumei Zenken Taishi Bei-Ō Kairan Jikki* (a true account of the tour of the Special Embassy to the US and Europe), which is usually abbreviated as *Bei-Ō Kairan Jikki*, was Kume's first work as a historiographer. But it was issued with the authority of the *Dajōkan*. It was Verbeck's suggestion that the records of the Iwakura Mission's inspection tour should be compiled and published. Guido Herman Friedrich Verbeck (1830-98), an adviser of the new Meiji government, suggested to send abroad an Embassy to Europe and America in 1869. In his suggestion he wrote: 'Let all the Officers of the Embassy, and especially the Secretaries, be commanded to write a detailed account of all they see and hear, and obtain in writing or print all possible information about their respective branches, so that on their return home the government may, if it choose to do so, compile and publish all the results of the mission for the general benefit and enlightenment of the nation'.[2] He wrote another paper about how to write the mission's experience, in which he showed ten points.[3]

1. No member of the mission should personally publish the record of his experience.
2. Every member of the mission should note down what he has read, heard and seen. He should also record the date, the place, and his name on the notes, so that they may be compiled afterwards.
3. Any documents, tables or maps that may be useful for the nation should not be lost.
4. Every member should consistently hand these notes and documents to the official who is in charge during the inspection tour and upon return.
5. Upon return, the government should appoint a veteran historiographer to compile the records. The records should be compiled chronologically. Each chapter should contain one topic. The records should be supplemented with documents and tables.
6. The historiographer who is in charge should have the right to summon and ask questions to anyone who has offered his notes or documents.
7. The historiographer should be assisted by translators and painters.
8. The prose of the record should be written in an elegant but simple style. The published work should be sold at a low price so that even poor people can afford to buy it. The objective is to have as many people read it.
9. Purely official affairs which people take no interest in should not be included in the publication. One of the executives of the mission should edit the draft before publication.
10. The following points should be inspected during the tour: Architecture, cities and villages, stores, famous landscapes, mountains

and rivers, climate, weather, roads and streets, conveyance, manners, customs, rites and festivals, entertainment, theater, food, plants, expositions, night scene and day scene of the streets, acquaintances, man-woman relationships, conditions of children, accounting, conditions of people, education and religion, schools, inventions, newspapers and magazines, paintings, libraries, accounts of an imperial audiences, kind treatments that the mission received, addresses at the audiences, officially or personally exchanged letters, accounts of an official or personal banquet, finance and national loans, agriculture, industry and commerce, welfare and hospitals, national character, the result of religious oppression, beggars and the poor, constitution of the government, national projects, quality of laws, municipal government and prisons, assembly and court, system and strength of the navy and army, fortresses and armoury, ports, and so on.

Bei-Ō Kairan Jikki, a five-volume account of the journey in a diary form, was the realization of Verbeck's plan. It was published for the general benefit and enlightenment of the nation. It was an official publication, and not Kume's personal work. Kume devoted his time to editing the notes taken by himself and other members of the mission. He distinguished the objective experience and the subjective view while he wrote. Even when he wrote the subjective view, it was not his personal view but a so-called 'official view'. In the preface of *Bei-Ō Kairan Jikki* he wrote he did not hesitate to quote another person's view as if it were his own view. This is proof that he believed he could write in an 'official' capacity. This was the belief of an official historiographer which he was to follow consistently in later life.

OFFICIAL NATIONAL HISTORIOGRAPHY

I would now like to survey the project of the official national historiography which Kume was engaged in after the publication of the *Bei-Ō Kairan Jikki*.

The compilation of national history was very important in order to legitimate the imperial rule on the basis of the Confucianism. Six national histories (*Rikkokushi*) were compiled in the classical age between 7c. and 9c. After the Meiji Restoration in 1868 the new government, whose motto was the revival of the imperial rule, planned to restart the project of compiling the official national history, and thus established the *Shiryō Henshū Kokushi Kosei Kyoku* (Office for the Collection of Historical Materials and the Revision of National History), which was soon renamed *Kokushi Henshū Kyoku* (Office for the Compilation of National History). Emperor Meiji appointed Sanjō

Sanetomi as the president of the project, since the president was expected to be a high-ranking person in the *Dajōkan*. However, the *Kokushi Henshū Kyoku* was closed in the same year because of a conflict at the *Daigakkō* (great house of education) which controlled the office.

In 1872 the *Rekishika* (Department of History) was established within the *Dajōkan*. At the same time the Ministry of Education had made a three-year plan in 1873 for the compilation of a national history and ordered Kawada Takeshi to carry it out. The project was eventually transferred from the Ministry of Education to the *Rekishika* in the following year. The *Rekishika* ordered Kawada to compile the national history from the reign of Emperor Gokomatsu (1382-1412) at his private home. We must notice that the starting point of the historiography was the reign of Emperor Gokomatsu. This meant that there was a change of plan. According to the old plan, the new national history had to begin where the *Rikkokushi* ended, at the reign of Emperor Kōkō (884-887). According to the new plan, however, it picked up where the *Dainihonshi* (the great Japanese history) ended, at the reign of Emperor Gokomatsu. This was because the Dainihonshi of Mito *han* was treated as the official national history.

In 1875 the *Rekishika* was renamed as *Shūshikyoku* (Office of Historiography). The office, receiving a new member, Shigeno Yasutsugu, as the vice-director, started to carry out the project. The work was divided between Kawada and his colleague who worked with the age of Ashikaga, Oda and Toyotomi (1392-1613) and Shigeno and his colleague who worked with the age of Tokugawa (1614-1867). As a preliminary work for the historiography, they compiled materials based upon the form of the *Shiryō* (Materials). The Compilation of the *Shiryō* was planned by Hanawa Hokiichi (1746-1821) and was carried out from 1806 to 1861 by the *Wagaku Kodansho* (Institute of Japanese Studies). They compiled 430 volumes, which carried on the work of *Rikkokushi* and ended at 1024. Various materials were chopped and arranged under proper headings in a chronological order. This was the style of the *Shiryō*, which was followed by the Office of Historiography. The materials compiled by the Office were also called *Shiryō*.

In 1877 the *Shūshikyoku* was renamed *Shūshikan* (House of Historiography). Two years later Kume became a member of the office and worked under Shigeno with the Tokugawa Period. Shigeno had a plan of writing an official chronological history, but Kawada and his colleagues were against the plan. In 1881 Shigeno excluded Kawada and his colleagues from the House and reformed it. First, members of the House were divided into two groups, one that compiled *Shiryō* and another that wrote an official chronological history. Shigeno, Kume and Hoshino belonged to the latter. Later the official chronological history was named *Dainihon hennenshi* (Great Japanese Chronological History). Secondly, Kume replaced Kawada and began to work with the Ashikaga Period. Kume proposed that the starting point of the historiography should be 1318, the year when Emperor Godaigo acceded to the throne. According to his opinion, they needed to rewrite the history of the period of Northern and Southern Dynasties (1318-1392) with new materials, because the *Dainihonshi* was full of holes as far as this period was concerned.

The work of compiling materials and writing a chronological history continued, while the office of the project was renamed to *Rinji Shūshikyoku*, *Rinji Hennenshi Hensan Kakari*, and *Shishi Hensan Kakari*.

The so-called Kume Affair, which was brought about by his article, 'Shinto wa saiten no kozoku' (Shintoism is a Primitive Custom of Heaven Worship), made the historiographical project a target of criticism. In 1893 Inoue Kowashi, the Minister of Education, ordered the Imperial University to stop the historiographical project. Two years later in order to restart the project, the *Shiryō Hensan Kakari* (Department for the Compilation of Historical Materials) was established in the College of Literature at the Imperial University. The newly begun project, however, only consisted of the compilation of historical materials, and not the writing of a chronological history. The work was divided into sixteen sections according to periods. The compilation of all sections did not begin at one time; only three were begun at this time. The first product of their work, named *Dai Nippon Shiryō* (Great Japanese Compilation of Historical Materials), was published in 1901.

KUME'S METHODOLOGY OF HISTORY

In 1889, the year when the Department of National History was established in the Imperial University, the *Shigakkai* (Historical Society of Japan) was also established and the journal of the society, named *Shigakkai Zasshi* (later renamed as *Shigaku Zasshi*), was issued. We can find Kume's contribution in each issue of the magazine.

One of the important articles printed in the *Shigaku Zasshi* was 'Taiheiki wa shigaku ni eki nashi' (The *Taiheiki* Does Not Contribute to Historical Studies). The *Taiheiki* is a chronicle about the civil war caused by the rivalry between the Northern and Southern Dynasties in the fourteenth century. Kume emphasized the usefulness of documents at first, and then argued the uselessness of the *Taiheiki* as a historical source, showing several cases of fabrication in it.

Kume's criticism about the *Taiheiki* was closely related to his work of writing a chronological history. As I have mentioned before, Kume proposed moving the starting point of the historiography to 1318. Since his proposal was accepted, the historiography overlapped with the *Dainihonshi* that ended at the reign of Emperor Gokomatsu (1382-1412). This naturally meant that the quality of the *Dainihonshi* would be examined.

The period of Northern and Southern Dynasties was one of the most important parts in the *Dainihonshi*, which was written from the standpoint of Confucian morality. According to this moral, there should never be two dynasties in a land. The Southern Dynasty fought against the shogunate, while the Northern Dynasty was supported by it. The *Dainihonshi* regarded the former as legitimate, and as a result, did not adopt the diaries or the documents of the Northern Dynasty's side, but adopted the *Taiheiki* that stood on the side of the Southern Dynasty. However, it became clear that the *Taiheiki* had many mistakes and fabrications, when it was compared with other materials that the *Dainihonshi* did not adopt.

We shall now look into the case where the text of the *Dainihon hennenshi* was revised through critique of the sources. Take the case of Kojima Takanori, for example. According to the *Taiheiki*, when Emperor Godaigo was banished to Oki Island for treason against the shogunate, Takanori tried to rescue the emperor on his way and failed. He crept into the lodge where the emperor stayed. He could not meet the emperor, but left a Chinese poem on a cherry tree in the garden. In the poem he compared Godaigo to an emperor of ancient China and himself to his loyal subject. It was the message revealing his loyalty. The *Dainihonshi* provided his biography in order to praise his loyalty. In the first manuscript of the *Dainihon hennenshi* Kume adopted the episode about Kojima Takanori. However, in the second manuscript, he excluded the episode from the body and only mentioned it in the note.[4] This was because neither his colleague nor he could find any source referring to Kojima Takanori except the *Taiheiki*. The official view of the historiographical project, therefore, was that the episode about Kojima Takanori in the *Taiheiki* was a fabrication.

Shigeno, Kume's boss, relied on the *Dainihonshi* at first. Before the Meiji Restoration in Kagoshima, he engaged in the project of reorganizing the *Dainihonshi* into a chronological order. He thought they could easily make a chronological history of the period of Northern and Southern Dynasty on the basis of the manuscript of the chronological *Dainihonshi*. However, as their project progressed, he had to realize that the *Taiheiki* was most inconsistent with other sources. He respected facts. He did not hesitate to change his opinion if the facts ordered him to do so.[5] In 1886 Shigeno gave a lecture at the Tokyo

Academy about the fabrications of facts in the *Taiheiki* and criticized the *Dainihonshi* because of its disproportion of sources.[6] In 1890 he took up Kojima Takanori in his lecture at the Historical Society of Japan. He said that Kojima Takanori was a fictitious character, named after the author of the *Taiheiki*, Kojima Hōshi.[7]

The first three professors of national history, Shigeno, Kume and Hoshino, were justly official historiographers. Their views about history were based on their historiographical project. They respected sources and eradicated historical episodes that had no evidence in sources. Many of them, however, had supported the national morality. Kojima Takanori, especially, had been one of the important characters who supported the ideology of the Emperor system or *Kokutai*. But the most important motto of the official historiographers was the independence of history from morality. Kume gave a lecture in this sense in 1893, in which he stated that they should never twist the truth for morality.[8] But the motto itself became a target of criticism. Shigeno was called Dr Eradicator ('Massatsu Hakase'). He was blamed as if he had eradicated not only some historical episodes but also national morality itself. This became the reason of the suspension of the historiographical project after the so-called Kume Affair.

BACKGROUND OF THE HISTORIOGRAPHICAL METHODOLOGY

Shigeno, Kume and Hoshino were influenced by the tradition of the Textual Criticism School, which originally came from Confucianism. However, Kume said that textual critique method was also found in Motoori Norinaga's study and that it was similar to the European inductive method. Kume and his colleagues were oriented towards a universal method. Thus they intended to accept European methods as well.

In the document of the *Shūshikyoku* in 1875 and in the lecture at the Tokyo Academy in 1879 Shigeno talked about European historiography and especially emphasized the usefulness of tables and statistics.[9]

In 1878 the Shūshikan requested Suematsu Kenchō, who was assigned to the Japanese legation to the United Kingdom, to seek for an opportunity to learn the European method of historiography. Suematsu sought for a historian who could answer the request and succeeded. George Gustavus Zerffi, a Hungarian who was exiled after the revolution in 1848, immediately published *The Science of History.* 200 copies of this book were printed and 100 copies were sent to Japan. It was translated by Nakamura Masanao and Saga Shōsaku and named *Shigaku* in Japanese (Numata 1963). In 1887 Shigeno and Kume revised the Japanese translation. Shigeno made a memorandum about the *Shigaku*.[10] These efforts prove that they intended to make use of European methods for the historiography.

We must not forget a German historian Ludwig Rieß. He taught as a lecturer of history between 1887 and 1902 at the Imperial University. He contributed towards the establishment of several institutions for history, two departments of history and national history, the historical society of Japan and the journal of the society (*Shigakkai Zasshi*, later *Shigaku Zasshi*). He emphasized that the historical research or teaching at a university and the official historiography should cooperate with each other. In the article published in the *Shigaku Zasshi* in 1890 he referred to the compilation of historical materials in Germany, Monumenta Germaniae Historica. He wrote that the Japanese historians must also have Monumenta Japoniae Historica.[11]

Having learned the European methodology, the earliest Japanese historians in the modern times found nothing different from their own methodology. What they found was rather a universality of methodology.[12]

It is a natural question to ask whether Kume's long sojourn with the Iwakura mission affected his view of the methodology of history. He had been a conscientious student while he was overseas and had picked up Western ideas. This affected his thinking as he assembled material and prepared his narrative for the *Bei-Ō Kairan Jikki*. This certainly had a beneficial effect on his career as a historiographer.

CONCLUSION

As an official historiographer Kume believed he could write an 'official view' as the 'official subject'. This belief was consistent from the *Bei-Ō Kairan Jikki* to the *Dainihon hennenshi*.

Though his article got him into trouble, Kume had no intention of criticizing the *Kokutai*, or national morality that supported the Emperor system. He only intended to make the facts clear. From this we can deduce his view that the morality should be based on sure facts. He believed that historians should not twist the facts in order to protect morality; if morality were to collapse because of the collapse of the facts, it could not be helped. As far as he tolerated the possibility of the collapse of the morality that could not survive a crisis, he could be considered radical. Such an attitude, however, was one that originated from his respect for facts as a historiographer.

AFTERMATH AND ASSESSMENT

Ian Nish

IT IS OFTEN SAID how remarkable it was that so many top Japanese statesmen could be spared to go overseas at the same time. What is more remarkable is that, considering the difficulties which beset Japan in their absence, they were able to stay away for such an extended period. By and large, the main party presided over by Prince Iwakura followed a leisurely itinerary, which enabled them to do intensive study of institutions and environments abroad. Though the deputy leaders of the delegation, Okubo and Kido, were in effect recalled on political grounds, even they were both able to complete an abbreviated programme of visits in Europe. Many inspectors who were conducting special investigations were also called back early because of the mounting costs of the mission and the financial crisis at home.

Even the journey home afforded further opportunities for study. Thus, Fukuchi Genichiro, who held the rank of first secretary and was primarily an English specialist, was instructed in Paris in February 1873 to go home early but to spend time in the Middle East. He travelled by way of the Ottoman Empire, including a sojourn in Jerusalem. The focus of his study was to be the court system in Egypt which came under the Khedive in the declining days of Ottoman power. The Egyptians were facing problems similar to the knotty problem of extraterritorial rights, with which the Japanese leaders had been struggling, and had devised a system of mixed courts to cope with such legal-diplomatic difficulties. When Fukuchi returned to Japan after a stay of two months, he presented a report on 17 July in which he commended the 'mixed court' system whereby cases involving foreigners resident in Egypt were tried in civil cases in courts made up of both Egyptians and foreigners. He recommended its adoption in Japan, even on a more extended basis covering criminal cases. This is a good illustration of the spirit of serious-minded enquiry which inspired the Iwakura mission. It also shows that the Japanese were seeking practical solutions outside Europe to realistic problems, in this case those connected with the judicial aspects of their foreign treaties.

Fukuchi's mentor, Kido, who also returned early, added the Middle East to his zones of enquiry. He left the ship at Port Said to visit the business area. As elsewhere on the trip, he was a sharp observer of the local scene, pointing out the large number of Europeans living there and the unrefined and impoverished native people. By contrast, he hardly comments on the proud achievement of the canal itself, opened just four years earlier. The absence of reference to the trade it was carrying east is particularly striking.

In various diverse groupings, the members of the large Iwakura mission found their way back to Japan to face the music. The main party travelled by way of Suez and stopped off at Aden and Galle in Ceylon (Sri Lanka), the principal port of call for vessels sailing between Aden and Southeast Asia. They were unable to disembark at Singapore because of a cholera epidemic but they visited Saigon, Hongkong (where they met the Governor and were entertained by the Oriental Bank) and Shanghai (where they were entertained by Governor Chen) before they eventually berthed in Nagasaki. The journey was instructive because the commissioners were able to see at first hand the extent of the overseas influence of the Western world.

Okubo had returned to Japan on 23 May 1873 and left for Satsuma whence he surveyed the Tokyo scene. Kido reached Yokohama on 23 July and, by contrast, found himself embroiled in politics straightaway. But 13 September was the day of celebration when the main party returned to Yokohama and made its onward progress to Edo. The members had taken part in a vast enterprise. They were very numerous; but, when one considers the areas they covered, it might have required an even larger delegation today.

Like other such ventures the report stage was difficult. Immense data had to be moulded into a coherent report. This task rested with Kume Kunitake (1839-1931) to which two essays are devoted in this volume. He had accompanied the main party as secretary to Iwakura and kept a diary. On return to Japan he compiled a record of the journey which was eventually published in five volumes in 1878 with the title *Bei-O kairan jikki*. This has been the major source of many studies of the Iwakura mission. Monumental as was the work of Kume in chronicling the journey and the discoveries of the mission which has been praised by all the contributors, it still fell short of the amount of material which the investigators had accumulated. Many of the subsidiary reports were not completed, while much of the material had to remain on file. At one level there was a sort of administrative indigestion. But at the all-important level the commissioners carried forward their own findings as part of their life experience and were to use them automatically in their future careers.

The problems they encountered on their arrival in Edo were financial and strategic. The serious problem on the financial side was that Inoue Kaoru as minister and Shibusawa Shigekazu (later Eiichi) as vice-minister who were left in charge of the Treasury in the absence of Okubo, had resigned from their posts and claimed that the national finances were in a state of great disorder. In May they had been replaced by Okuma Shigenobu. It is not for us to go into the merits and demerits of the case they made, except to say that the Treasury was the former responsibility of Okubo and a subject in which he took a deep interest. But this was only one of a number of domestic issues which did not please the returning ambassadors.

A much more telling point was that on 17 August the council under the court noble, Sanjo Sanetomi, agreed to send Saigo Takamori of Satsuma to Korea, an action which was likely to provoke war with Korea and the sending of an expeditionary force to the peninsula. It was subsequently agreed to defer the implementation of this edict until Iwakura's return. When the main party did return, Iwakura immediately addressed the issue and stated that it would be inadvisable to attack Korea in view of Japan's global weakness. The members of the overseas embassy, therefore, began to form the nucleus of a peace party and, in doing so, could not fail to antagonize the Satsuma clan, which was the main promoter of the invasion of Korea. In spite of his Satsuma origins, Okubo was tempted back to the centre of affairs. In a series of council meetings the pendulum swung away from a military solution to the Korean problem. Prime Minister Sanjo was forced by ill-health into resigning and on 23 October Saigo's assignment to go to Korea was put on hold. The Emperor agreed and Saigo returned to Kagoshima outmanoeuvred. Iwakura took over the reins of office and the new council was augmented by the admission of several members of the overseas mission, notably Okubo, Ito Hirobumi and Terashima Munenori, who had been minister in London during the mission's time there. Tanaka Fujimaro who had been the education specialist on the mission and had studied foreign education systems became vice-minister for education and (from May 1874 to 1880) minister.

It might be thought that tranquillity and peace would return after the serious clash over policies had been resolved. But in fact one-third of the officers in the newly formed army resigned because of their 'defeat' over Korea. This manifested itself in an assassination attempt on Iwakura's life early in the new year. This was doubly surprising because his reputation as *udaijin* had been considerably enhanced after the success of his leadership role overseas. Six men were accused of the plot. They were thought to have Satsuma connections and to have been hoping by this act to draw attention to the need for war with Korea. The government was temporarily paralysed but it stuck fast to its line that a costly war at that moment would cripple the nation and retard its progress.[1]

This temporary setback did not detract from the fact that it was the rump of the Iwakura mission which took over control of Japanese politics in the difficult days of the 1870s. Their policies were influenced by their experiences abroad and especially their feelings about the backwardness of Japan and her need to learn from the West. But they did not return to high office merely as evangelists for the West. Indeed, when they took over the administration, they disagreed not only over the handling of the Korean question but also over many of the reforms which had been introduced by their predecessors too fast. Even Kido on his return was despondent that so many recent government decisions had gone contrary to his wishes.[2] They slowed down the pace of modernization which, they claimed, should not be adopted until the people could understand the need for it.

There were of course international advantages in having the new administration consisting of so many of those who had recently taken part in a lengthy and comprehensive sojourn in America and Europe. Statesmen in the Western world would be able to identify Japanese leaders. Unfortunately this did not last long: Kido died in 1877; Okubo by assassination in the following year; and Prince Iwakura in 1883. But Ito Hirobumi survived and served at the helm of affairs right up to his death in 1909. This was unquestionably a great advantage for the statesmen of America and Europe who in the Victorian period tended to make policy on East Asia without any first-hand knowledge of the countries or their statesmen.

EASTERN PROJECTIONS

In trying to make some assessment of the Iwakura mission's achievement, let us begin by quoting a contemporary view in the leading treaty port newspaper in Japan, the *Japan Mail*

> The distinguished men who headed [the Iwakura mission]. . . . entertain grateful feelings towards those who spared neither pains, nor marks of respect, nor expense, to please. . . Rarely have men ever been received with more truly cordial warmth, or entertained with more lavish hospitality. Kings and Queens opened their palaces to them, nobles and corporations feted them, the populace followed and ran after them. Whatever was to be seen in America or among the nations of Europe of magnificence or beauty, of ingenious industry, of peaceful effort or warlike preparation, was exhibited to them with the kindliest readiness; and had they been royal princes visiting nations where every door flies open before exalted rank, they could not have been met with more warmth, more interest, or with a greater readiness to serve them.[3]

On the basis of such a reception, the mission could not be judged other than a resounding success. From the accounts given in this collection of essays, these assertions appear to be broadly accurate. All our contributors are agreed that the nations visited, whether in government or commercial circles, put themselves out to entertain and inform and honour the delegates. Sometimes, as is shown in Bert Edström's paper, some caustic remarks were made about the stinginess of the reception they were given, notably in Britain. But this is unfair. The red carpet was put out everywhere in accordance with the usual conventions of traditional hospitality to visitors. And considerations of race and colour were not evident. Certainly some people were curious about 'orientals' and may have perturbed or irritated the visitors. But their interest was friendly in intention.

On the other hand, the *Japan Mail* saw also the down-side of the embassy. The editorial continues:

> . . . it was observed with equal surprize and regret that on their return they made no haste to assure those who had been instrumental in securing to them this flattering reception, of their appreciation of or gratitude for it. . . The truth is that the Mission was bitterly disappointed. Its leading members had left for the Western world with sanguine hopes that their appearance there would at once settle, or lead to the settlement of, a question on which their cherished hopes were fixed – the darling project of Japanese statesmen, and the highest pinnacle of Japanese ambition. This was the question of jurisdiction over foreigners. But the Ministers charged with the direction of the Foreign Affairs of European nations visited by this Embassy though cordial in their welcome of the Ambassadors at once relegated this question to the decision of their respective Representatives in Japan. The Ambassadors knew only too well the opinions held upon it by

the Foreign Representatives in Japan. From that time the Embassy travelled with heavy hearts.[4]

This view seems to find some support in the testimony of R.H. Brunton, a British national who accompanied some members of the mission in Britain and described the mood within it as 'exceedingly dissatisfied'.[5]

How does one explain the paradox inherent in the above editorial that the mission was a success but also a failure? It is not our concern to debate here whether the Japanese expressed their thanks adequately on their return to Tokyo; that could merely be explained by the fact that they were plunged on return into a serious government crisis. The more serious contention is whether the mission was a success and how far its objectives were achieved.

Perhaps three initial points should be made:

1. the mandate for the mission was vaguely defined and could be interpreted in contrary directions. The mission consisted of strong-minded individualists who had in some respects different agendas;

2. the delegates were fairly naïve when they left Japan and there was a large measure of wishful thinking which only receded when they reached the USA. But, as they journeyed, they developed shrewdness and perceptiveness and generally grew in wisdom;

3. the mission was secret and not much about it leaked out to the general public or the journalists. At the Tokyo end, Japan was, in the apt description of the *Japan Mail*, an 'as yet only half-unveiled country'.[6] Abroad, the members of the delegation (apart, that is, from Mori Arinori) were notable for their extreme reticence. The result was that there was much ill-informed speculation circulating at the time in Japan and abroad about the motives and achievements of the ambassadors.

In assessing the question of success or failure, one has to study the objectives with which they set out. It is generally agreed that the objects of the mission were to have preliminary talks for revision of the treaties; to investigate the systems of modernization in foreign states and study Western culture and civilization; and to improve Japan's image overseas. Some rated the objective of Treaty Revision more highly than others. But, since progress could not be made over it, they had little choice but to concentrate on the other two objectives.

Outside the delegation, contemporaries tended to interpret success narrowly in terms of Treaty Revision. In other words, they thought that Japan wanted to remove foreign jurisdiction within Japan's shores and substitute the application of Japanese jurisdiction over foreigners. Perhaps it was the easiest aspect for the treaty port press to grasp because it was something that they feared most. But, if success is interpreted more widely, the mission can be viewed as quite a success.

Let us look at the most authoritative statement of objectives as given by Prince Iwakura to the British foreign secretary, Lord Granville, on 22 November. Iwakura explained the nature of the political changes (opening to foreign trade, abolition of the feudal system the centralization of government) that had taken place in the past five years. He adds:

> Under these altered circumstances, it had become the policy of the Mikado and his Government to endeavour to assimilate Japan as far as possible to the enlightened states of the West, and the present Embassy had, therefore, been sent to England in order to study her institutions and to observe all that constitutes English civilization so as to adopt on their return to Japan whatever they may think suitable to their own country. The time had now arrived for the revision of the Treaty betweeen Japan and England, and he was charged by his Government to ascertain the view of the British Government on this subject. . . Iwakura said that he was not charged with the expression of views of the Japanese Government on this subject, but only to ascertain the views held on it by the British Government.[7]

Granville, we may hasten to add, was no more ready to show his hand than was Iwakura at this point on his journey. The prince was quite correct in the line he took, namely to state that the time was now ripe for Treaty Revision without embarking on negotiations. The studies in this volume suggest that he took a similar position with other governments. They in turn had no ready-made solutions but sought to initiate discussion of the issue through their representatives in Tokyo after the delegation returned there. On the evidence in these essays, it would have to be concluded that the Iwakura commissioners were prepared to solicit opinions about Treaty Revision but not to negotiate. This suggests that the treaty issue was a secondary object of their travels.

Once one has put into perspective the question of the treaties, one has to make reference to the other objectives which Iwakura described. They were, as Alistair Swale writes, in pursuit of enlightenment or civilization. 'Bummeikoku', as the Japanese would say. One should not underestimate the perceptiveness with which the delegates pursued that task and the positive initiatives that they took abroad. It was they who insisted on the need for foreign teachers and, with the help of Tanaka Fujimaro of the Education Department, recruited many. The same qualities which had taken the Japanese towards modernization in the 60s were visible also as they grappled with the next stage of modernization after the Iwakura mission.

WESTERN REACTIONS

The other objective was to inform the rest of the world about Japan and project a favourable image of Japan abroad. Actually the West already knew a lot about Japan and generally had a favourable impression of the country. Thus the London *Times* wrote:

> The members of the [Japanese] Embassy are not only great officials and great nobles in a kingdom more ancient than our own, they are also statesmen who, with their lives in their hands, have worked out an immense and most beneficent revolution in their own country. The power they wield is more potent for good or evil than we can easily realise. . . Upon the relations we cultivate with men of this spirit, intelligence, and power must depend, to an incalculable degree, the prospects of English enterprise in Japan, and even of Japanese civilisation. . . While the Ambassadors deserve at least as much respect as the representatives of most European kingdoms, it should be remembered that their habits induce them to expect even more. . . The feeling of the English people is one of profound interest in one of the most remarkable races of the Old World [Japan], and we trust our Government will not fail to give due expression to this sentiment.

As this comment suggests, Japan was highly regarded as a country which had set herself on the course of modernization – or Westernization, as some preferred to say. The ambassadors presented the characteristics of their country effectively to foreign governments, while others simultaneously exhibited Japanese art objects and goods at the Vienna International Exposition. There is, in most of the countries visited, little evidence of animus or jealousy against Japan or the Japanese. And there is little evidence of Gilbertian humour aimed at the delegates who were portrayed as earnest men, conscientiously trying to better their country. This was the sort of attitude which their hosts respected. With the self-confidence of the early Victorian period, they were ready to give the next generation of Japanese leaders a sort of university course in modernization and industrialization. There were those who were sycophantic towards the Japanese visitors. There were, indeed, those like the chairman of the Manchester Chamber of Commerce who defended the Japanese against unscrupulous Western merchants in the treaty ports and said that the attitude of Europeans in Japan had been with few exceptions aggressive and even dictatorial.

Needless to say, his views irritated the latter very much.[8] But there were very few voices of criticism of the Japanese performance except perhaps for minor faults like reticence or secretiveness.

On a personal level, of course, members of Iwakura's delegation were inclined to be described as quaint. There was much preoccupation with their dress or their hair-styles. From San Francisco to Washington Iwakura's party in public commonly wore Japanese court dress as the members of the 1862 mission had done. This made them conspicuous; but from Washington onwards they amassed a wardrobe of Western dress, which, according to one observer, helped their inconspicuousness but 'did not improve their appearance in dignity or elegance'. Their deportment was much commended; their diligence was praised; and 'the gravity of their dusky visages commanded respect'.[9]

These studies were intended to convey some impression of how the Iwakura mission was received. It is relevant to remember that there were jealousies between the powers in their relationship with Japan where they were competitors. Consider this rather grandiloquent editorial from *The Times* of London which greeted the arrival of Iwakura and his party in that city:

> At length the Japanese Ambassadors have exchanged the profuse hospitality of our American cousins for a less demonstrative, but in no wise less sincere, reception on our shores. The time chosen for their arrival is unfortunate. Six weeks ago they would have found London full of life, gaiety, and display; now it is a desert. The upper classes of society have one and all betaken themselves to the moors and streams; the pavements are empty; omnibuses, cabs, and vans are the sole remaining representatives of the countless carriages which but the other day crowded the streets, and the public offices are tenanted only by those unfortunate clerks whose juniority dooms them to work and toil in London during the months of August and September. The contrast thus afforded to the stirring bustle of New York will be striking but superficial, and by none will its true bearings be better understood than by the Japanese Ambassadors.[10]

This is quoted to illustrate the underlying feeling in Europe that the United States was seeking to establish a special relationship with the Japanese.

Foreign governments each had a distinct set of problems with Japan. The approach to the mission in each country was different. Russia was to some extent regarded by Japan as an enemy, perhaps unique among the powers visited during their round-the-world trip. Britain and France may have been looked at with suspicion because of the military garrisons they maintained in Yokohama. The United States was perhaps viewed most favourably. The Japanese visitors, moreover, had historical characters in each that they greatly admired. Giuseppi Garibaldi in Italy was one such person who was still alive.[11] The visitors also respected Peter the Great whose rule in Russia, though separated by a century and a half, seemed to have done for his country what the new team was trying to do in Japan. Some like Ito Hirobumi developed a great admiration for Bismarck, while others respected William Ewart Gladstone, then still early in his prime ministerial career. Hence each European country was being examined from a different perspective in the search for different qualities.

There seems to be a broad agreement among the contributors about foreign press coverage of the mission. Most found a situation similar to that which Silvana De Maio reports, namely that, while Iwakura's activities did not reach the front pages of the Italian press, there was often considerable coverage in pages 2 and 3. In most countries it was brief and factual. But in Italy she goes on to say that journalists showed much curiosity and included much important information regarding the transformation already made in Japan. Since the delegation was more important politically in the eyes of the Japanese than it was in the Western world, it was unrealistic to expect more detailed treatment than it received.

But mainstream opinion had criticisms over Japan's treatment of Christians. Whether it was Protestant countries like the United States and Britain or Catholic countries like France and Belgium, the authors point out the strong representations that were made to Japan's mission. Iwakura's round-the-world trip coincided with a great Protestant missionary upsurge in US and Europe. It would have been difficult for foreign governments not to have been influenced by one or other of the most potent lobbies of the time, the Christian missionary lobbies, and not to have felt compelled to take up the Christian cause with the visitors. Thus, Lord Granville in Britain in advance of his discussions with Iwakura and his colleagues received a typical submission from the United Presbyterian Church:

> While public opinion is undergoing an entire transformation in that country [Japan], the letter of the law in reference to the teaching and profession of Christianity remains unchanged.[12]

Granville was under compunction to lodge a protest. One after another, the French, Belgian and German ministers, according to our contributors, protested and called for tolerance.

The Western world had collaborated with Iwakura and his colleagues in fulfilling the injunction of the Charter Oath of 1868 to acquire information, knowledge and wisdom. Their capacity to accumulate data had caused wonderment among their hosts. They had also used influence to achieve practical things. Through Tanaka Fujimaro of the Education Department they had recruited teachers, among others David Murray from Rutgers College and Henry Dyer from Glasgow.[13] Through R.H. Brunton, Japan's expert on lighthouses, they had completed various 'commissions'.

In Japan there is no doubt about the importance of the work of Iwakura and his colleagues. They were impressive during their journey and equally dynamic when they returned to grasp power and steer their country through a major crisis. For the countries visited the Iwakura mission was a matter of lesser importance. While it was one of many such visits, it was a visit from a country which was much admired. Their leaders dedicated a lot of effort to it for Japan was recognized as an up-and-coming country. For all the imperialist attitudes which prevailed at the time and the 'hang-up' that these governments had over Treaty Revision, they showed great respect for their visitors and remarkable goodwill in sharing their knowledge and experiences.

APPENDIX

THE KUME MUSEUM OF ART (TOKYO)

Ito Fumiko (Curator) and Takata Seiji (Research Staff)

THE MUSEUM was established in 1982 in commemoration of Kume Kunitake (1839-1931), the historian, and his son, Kume Keiichiro (1866-1934), the artist.

Below, we describe our activities with the emphasis on the historical side, namely on the historian, Kume Kunitake, and his accomplishments. For that purpose, we divide our activities into two: the Historical Division and the Art Division. The former will be treated in detail here. The Art Division of course deals with items such as paintings, the croquis, the sculptures, the manuscripts, the diaries etc. of Kume Keiichiro, the artist.

Kume the historian was born on 11 July 1839 and died on 24 February 1931. He was born in Hachimankōji in Saga (now the main city of Saga prefecture) as one of the former Saga clansmen. In his infancy, he studied at the Kōdōkan of Saga *han* and then, in 1863, went to Yedo (now Tokyo) to study at the Shōheikō, the shogunal academy. Returning in 1864, Kume became a retainer to Nabeshima Kansō, the former daimyo of Saga *han*, and later in 1868, became a teacher at the Kōdō kan.

From 1871 to 1873, he joined the mission, headed by Iwakura Tomomi, to the United States and Europe to observe up-to-date matters, particularly the cultural and industrial activities of the Western nations. On the way, while the mission was staying in London, Kume was selected as one of its two recording secretaries. When the mission returned to Japan in September 1873, Kume continued to be employed for about five years, first in the mission's bureau and then in the recording section of the government. During this period, Kume completed the five-volume account of the journey, *Tokumei Zenken Taishi, Bei-ō Kairan Jikki* (1878). This title is expressed in English either as 'A True Account of the Tour of the Special Embassy to America and Europe' or as 'The Iwakura Mission's Itinerary'. The details of the original and later editions of this book will be shown afterwards; see 6.(a) below.

From 1879 onwards, Kume became engaged in editing Japanese histories at the Shūshikan and the Shūshikyoku, the national offices for history compilation. Together with his senior colleagues, he began compiling the Japanese authentic and strictly critical chronology in Chinese composition, the manuscripts of which are partly preserved in the Museum. This project was unfortunately stopped later in 1893 by government intervention.

These historians, however, completed in 1890, the *History of Japan in view of the Regime Changes* in the Japanese language, the manuscripts of which are also preserved in the Museum.

Kume also endeavoured to search for historical materials in a wide variety of local regions, for example, the Tōkai, Tōsan and Chinzei areas, and summarized the itineraries of these search travels.

In 1888, he was appointed professor in the Faculty of Literature of Tokyo Imperial University. He and his colleagues made efforts to organize a new society for historical research and succeeded in doing so. The Society launched its own historical journal (*Shigaku-kai Zassi*, later *Shigaku Zassi*).

Shortly after, Kume contributed to this journal an article entitled 'Shintoism is an Outmoded Custom of Worshipping Heaven' (1891, reprinted in another magazine with slight revision in the following year). The journal and this important manuscript are preserved in the Museum.

As this article was severely criticized by conservative Shintoists and nationalists, he was forced to leave the service of the university in 1892. Even after his resignation from the Imperial University, he continued writing articles on Japanese and East-Asian history, most of which, together with the manuscripts, are preserved in the Museum.

In parallel, he began in 1899 to give lectures on archival science at Tokyo Senmon Gakkō (known from 1902 onwards as Waseda University) and published monographs on archival science, ancient Japanese history and the detailed biography of Nabeshima Kansō mentioned above. In 1909, he received the degree of Doctor of Literature from Waseda University.

In sum, Kume was the founder of modern historical science in Japan, who took the initiative in pursuing rational and realistic research into history.

The site of the Memorial Museum is at Kume Building, 8F, 2-25-5, Kamiōsaki, Shinagawa-ku, 〒141-0021, Tokyo, Japan. (Close by the west exit of the Meguro Station, Yamanote Line, Japan Railways.) Closed on Wednesdays.

TEL 03-1491-1510, FAX 03-3491-6617, e-mail ricca @ t3. rim. or. jp.

ACTIVITIES OF THE HISTORY DIVISION OF THE MUSEUM

Exhibitions

We have organized the following exhibitions:
Kume Kunitake and *Bei-ō Kairan Jikki*
Kume Kunitake, the Historian
The US and Europe in the Eyes of the Iwakura Mission
Copper Plates from *Bei-ō Kairan Jikki* – geographic and thematic display
The Roundtrip of the Iwakura Mission – showpieces for the young

We have also cooperated in such exhibitions as 'Il Giappone Scopre L'Occidente, Une Missione Diplomatica 1871-1873', Istituto Giapponese di Cultura, Roma in 1994.

Research

Our research is mainly concerned with two aspects:
(1) archival evaluation and classification of the manuscripts and old prints.
Some examples of the materials, which have been evaluated and classified up to the present, are shown below.
(2) historical studies on Kume Kunitake and his works.
Some of the reference materials for these purposes, most of which are available at the Museum, are listed in 6. below.

Library Services

The classical books and manuscripts are available for consultation, provided that the request is registered beforehand.

OUTLINE OF THE ARCHIVAL MATERIAL

General Classification

A.	Books/Japanese binding	350 titles, ca. 1200 vols.
B.	Books/modern binding	ca. 300 vols.
C.	Mss ca. 3000 items.	
D.	Magazines	ca. 1000 numbers
E.	Newspapers	ca. 100 items.
F.	Photographs/Albums	ca. 50 items.
G.	Miscellaneous (maps, certificates, rubbed copies etc.)	

Thematic Classification

① *Bei-ō Kairan Jikki*

B. 1st edition (1878), hard cover and paper back.

C. Mss. on Japanese paper, 10 versions or more.
Notebooks, memoranda and fragments.

G. Travel guides, maps, timetables etc.
Appleton's *Illustrated European Guide Book* (5th ed., 1872).
Philadelphia and its Environment.
New York Illustrated.
Frank Leslie's *Illustrated Newspaper* (1872).
Maps of the Central Pacific Railroad and its Connections.
The Central Pacific Railroad Timetable.

② Works of the Shūshikan (National Office for History Compilation) Period

B. *The Itinerary of the Emperor Meiji's Tour in the Tōkai and Tōsan Areas*, 1880.
The History of Japan in view of the Regime Changes, 1890.

C. *The Itinerary of the Emperor Meiji's Tour in the Tōkai and Tōsan Areas.*
The Authentic Japanese Chronology in Chinese Composition.
A Report of the Search for Historical Materials in the Chinzei Area.
The History of Japan in view of the Regime Changes.

③ Treatises on Japanese History

C. and/or D.

'The hero is the slave of the public', *Shigaku-kai Zassi*, 1891-92.
'Taiheiki is not useful for historical science', *ibid.*, 1891.
'Shintōism is an outmoded custom of worshipping heaven', *ibid.*, 1891 (Reprinted in the magazine *Shikai* in 1892).
'A study of the Taika Reform', *Shigaku-kai Zassi*, 1892.
'Dōkyō, the Buddhist priest', *Shikai*, 1892.
'Why did the capital move to Heiankyō?', *Shigaku-kai Zassi*, 1892.
'The temperament of islanders', *Kokumin no Tomo* (The Nation's Friend), 1894.
'On the essentials of historical geography', *Rekishi-Chiri* (Journal of Historical Geography), 1901.
'The past and the future of Manchuria', *ibid.*, 1905.
'A study of Shintōism', *Tōa no Hikari* (East-Asian Light), 1908.

④ Lectures and Monographs in the Waseda University Period

B. and C.

'Lectures on the ancient history of Japan', part, 1902.
'Lectures on archival science', part, 1903.

'A study on Shōtoku-Taishi'. 1905.
'A biography of Nabeshima Naomasa', 1920.

⑤ Chinese and Japanese Classics in Kume's own possession (thematic examples)

Classics on cultural thoughts (mostly based on Confucianism), history, tactics, social systems, poetry, archives, politics and geography; either of China or of Japan.

⑥ Books on Natural Science and Technology in Kume's own possession (not listed)

RECENT PUBLICATIONS FOR REFERENCE PURPOSES – MOSTLY AVAILABLE AT THE MUSEUM

ⓐ Kume's own Books and Treatises

1. *Bei-ō Kairan Jikki* [The Iwakura Mission's Itinerary, orig., 1878], 5 vols., reprint, Munetaka Shobō, 1975.
2. *Bei-ō Kairan Jikki* [The Iwakura Mission's Itinerary], 5 vols., critically edited and annotated by A. Tanaka, Iwanami-Bunko, 1977-82.
3. *Selected Works of K. Kume*, 5vols. and 1 supplementary vol. [ⓒ1, below], Yoshikawa Kōbunkan, 1988-91.
   vol. 1 Studies on Shōtoku-Taishi.
   vol. 2 Studies in the ancient and Mediaeval History of Japan.
   vol. 3 Theory and Methodology of History.
   vol. 4 Archival Studies.
   vol. 5 Studies in the History of Japanese Cultures.
   supp. vol. [ⓒ1, below]
4. *Selected Writings of K. Kume*, 4 vols., Yoshikawa Kōbunkan, in preparation.
   vol. 1 The Itinerary of the Emperor Meiji's Tour in the Tōkai and Tōsan Areas, etc.
   vol. 2 Writings in the field of Science and Technology.
   vol. 3 Writings related to the Iwakura Mission.
   vol. 4 Historical Writings on the Orient, etc.
5. English Translation of 'Bei-ō Kairan Jikki', in progress.
   Supervisor: Prof. M. Jansen,
   Translators: Prof. M. Collcutt, Prof. G. Healey, Prof. E. Soviak.

ⓑ Kume's Reminiscences

The Reminiscences of Dr. K. Kume [orig., 1934-5], 2 vols., reprint, Munetaka Shobō, 1985.

ⓒ Studies on Kume's Life and Works

Studies on K. Kume, edited by T. Ōkubo, Yoshikawa Kōbunkan, 1991. [the supplementary vol. to ⓐ 3, above].

ⓓ Studies on 'Bei-ō Kairan Jikki' [The Iwakura Mission's Itinerary, orig., 1878]

1. A. Tanaka, *The Iwakura Mission*, Kōdansha, Gendai Sensho, 1977.

1'. op. cit. with slight amendment, Iwanami Shoten, Dōjidai Bunko, 1994.

2. Kume Museum of Art, ed., *The Copper Plates from 'Bei-ō Kairan Jikki'*, 1985, with Captions and Explanatory Notes.
3. A. Tanaka and S. Takata, eds., *Interdisciplinary Studies on 'Bei-ō Kairan Jikki'*, Hokkaido UP, 1993, with Abstracts in English.
4. N. Nishikawa and H. Matsumiya, eds., *Readings in 'Bei-ō Kairan Jikki' – the World and Japan in the Decade of the 1870s*, Hōritsu-Bunka-Sha, 1995.
5. S. Takata, *The Scientific Spirit in the Restoration Period – Industrial Technology as described in 'Bei-ō Kairan Jikki'*, Asahi Shinbun-Sha, Asahi Sensho, 1995.

ⓔ The Catalogues of the Museum

K. Kume, the Historian, 1997, including articles written by Japanese historians.

Acknowledgement: The authors express their gratitude to Ms Komori Kyoko, the archivist of the Museum, for her assistance in preparing this article.

ENDNOTES

INTRODUCTION

1. Okubo Toshiaki (ed.), *Iwakura shisetsu no kenkyu*, Tokyo: Munetaka Shobo, 1976, p. 53ff. Yasuoka Akio, 'Iwakura Tomomi no gaiko seiryaku' in *Hosei shigaku*, vol 21(1969), 1-23
2. The ages of senior members of the embassy were Iwakura 47; Kido 39; Okubo 42; Ito 31; Yamaguchi, 30
3. J.E. Hoare, 'Japan's Treaty Ports and Foreign Settlements, 1858-99' in Ian Nish (ed.), *Britain and Japan: Biographical Portraits*, vol I, Folkestone: Japan Library, 1994
4. *Japan Weekly Mail*, 28 Dec. 1872
5. Ian Nish (ed.), *British Documents on Foreign Affairs*, Part I, Series E, 1860-1914, vol.I, Washington: UPA, 1989
6. Ian Nish, 'The Iwakura Mission in Britain: The Issue of Treaty Revision' in The Japan Society (London), *Proceedings*, 122(1993), 52-64
7. For works on the Iwakura mission in the Netherlands, see the writings of Miyanaga Takeshi, Tokyo: Hosei, 1988
8. *Japan Weekly Mail*, 28 Dec. 1872. Among exhibits at the Kume Museum, Tokyo, is an admission ticket for the Vienna exhibition. It is marked: 'Nihonkan, Mitglied der ausserorderlichen Japanischen Botschaft' [Japan Pavilion, member of the extraordinary Japanese embassy].
9. Entry for 4 May 1873 in Sidney Devere Brown and Akiko Hirota (eds), *The Diary of Kido Takayoshi*, vol. II, 1871-4, Tokyo: University Press, 1985, p. 321
10. Nagashima Yoichi, 'Denmark ni okeru Iwakura shisetsudan' in Tanaka Akira and Takada Seiji (eds.), *'Bei-O kairan jikki' no gakusaiteki kenkyu*, Sapporo: Hokkaido University Press, 1993, 163-81; and *Meiji no gaikoku buki shonin*, Tokyo: Chuo korosha, 1995. Olof Lidin, 'Japanese-Danish Official Relations' in M. LaDerriere, *Danes in Japan, 1868-1940*, Copenhagen: Akademisk Forlag, 1984, pp. 65-6
11. *Japan Mail*, 23 April 1873
12. Okubo (ed.), *Iwakura shisetsu*, p. 71ff
13. *Japan Weekly Mail*

CHAPTER 1

1. Itinerary as per Tanaka Akira, *Iwakura Shisetsudan Beio Kairan Jikki*, Dojidai Raiburarii, 1994, pp. 218- 221. See also Nishikawa Nagao & Matsumiya Hideharu, *Beio Kairan Jikki wo Yomu*, Horitsu Bunka Sha, 1995, Chapter Eleven, regarding the Mission's consideration of Switzerland as a model for a neutral minor power.
2 Soviak, 'On the Nature of Western Progress: The Journal of the Iwakura Embassy' in *Tradition and Modernization in Japanese Culture*, D.H. Shively (Ed.), Princeton, 1971, pp. 7-9.

3 While not wishing to suggest that there is factual error in various general histories that cover the 'Japanese Enlightenment', the tendency to run the influences of Rousseau/ Locke and Smiles/Spencer together in more or less the same 'enlightenment' category does not take adequate account of the very significant differences within this actually rather diverse body of thought.

4 Lanman, *The Japanese in America*, in *Mori Arinori Zenshuu*, Vol. II, Okubo Toshiaki et al (Eds), Senbunshoten, 1972, p. 61 for Iwakura, pp. 38-39, 40-42 for Ito. Iwakura's diary and *Ito Hirobumi Den.*

5. Lanman, *The Japanese in America*, Ibid., pp. 42 & 44.

6. See Randall, J.G., & Donald, David, *The Civil War and Reconstruction*, D.C. Heath and Co., 1965, pp. 652-677, regarding the Grant administration and contemporary developments.

7 Hall, *Mori Arinori*, Harvard, 1973, pp. 140-143.

8 Lewis, C.S., *Studies in Words*, Cambridge, 1960, pp. 6-8.

9 Gellner, Ernest, *Nations and Nationalism*, Basil Blackwell, 1983, pp. 19-38.

10 This definition of conservative enlightenment is based on Pocock, J. G. A., 'Conservative Enlightenment and Democratic Revolutions: The American and French Cases in British Perspective', the text of the Government and Opposition/Leonard Schapiro Lecture delivered at the London School of Economics, 19 October 1988. Published in *Government and Opposition*, Weidenfeld and Nicolson, 1989, Vol. 24, No. 1, pp. 81-105.

11 Pocock, Ibid., pp. 81-83.

12 Gellner, Op. Cit., pp. 18-24.

13 Soviak, Op. Cit., pp. 28-29.

14 See Briggs, Asa, *The Age of Improvement*, Longmans, 1959, Chapter Nine on Victorianism, esp. pp. 446- 454.

15 See Braisted, W. R., *Meiroku Zasshi: Journal of the Japanese Enlightenment*, University of Tokyo, 1976, pp. xxiii-xxxiii of the introduction regarding the background of various Meiroku Society members. See also Gluck, Carol, *Japan's Modern Myths*, Princeton, 1985, pp. 51-52 regarding Mori's apolitical stance.

16 Marlene Mayo, 'A Catechism of Diplomacy: The Japanese and Hamilton Fish, 1872', in *The Journal of Asian Studies*, Vol. XXVI, No. 3, Association for Asian Studies, 1967, pp. 389-390.

17 See Hall, Op. Cit., pp. 155-174 for a general account of Mori's entré into American diplomatic circles. Also Lanman, Op. Cit., pp. 50-51 & 67-69.

18 Mayo, Loc.Cit., p. 397.

19 Mayo, Ibid., pp. 397-402.

20 Hall, Op. Cit., pp. 156-157. Mayo, Ibid., p. 400.

21 Mayo, Ibid., p. 408.

22 Mayo, Ibid., p. 402-3.

23 Mayo, Ibid., pp. 403-404; it is hard to accept Mayo's blame of the failure in communication with Fish to Mori. C.f. Payson J Treat on p. 407.

24 For an insight into the anxieties and jealousies afflicting the Mission at the time see Hall, Op. Cit., pp. 216-228 and Mayo, Ibid., p. 405.

25 Richie, Donald, *The Honorable Visitors*, Charles Tuttle & Co., 1994, pp. 48-63.

26 Soviak, Op. Cit., p. 7.

27 Soviak, Ibid., pp. 15-18.

28 Soviak, Ibid., pp. 20-25.

29 Soviak, Ibid., pp. 28 -29 & 32-33.

30 Hall, Op. Cit., pp. 218-219.

31 Lanman, Op. Cit., p. 54.

32 Mori, *Religious Freedom in Japan*, in *Mori Arinori Zenshuu*, Okubo Toshiaki et al (Eds), Senbunshoten, 1972, Vol. I, pp. 22-23.

33 Mori, *Life and Resources in America*, in *Mori Arinori Zenshuu*, Okubu Toshiaki et al (Eds), Senbunshoten, 1972, Vol. III, pp. 6-7.

34 Mori, *Life and Resources in America*, Ibid., p. 6.

35 Mori, Ibid., pp. 6-7.

36 Mori, *Religious Freedom in Japan*, Op. Cit., pp. 16-17.
37 Mori , Ibid., pp. 20-21. Note the parallel with the thought in Kume Kunitake as quoted in Soviak, Op. Cit., p. 26.
38 Kume Kunitake, *Beio Kairan Jikki*, Tokyo, 1878, Vol. I, pp. 21-22. Translation as per Soviak, Ibid., p. 18
39 Kume, Ibid., Vol. V, p. 245. Translation as per Soviak, p. 19
40 Translation as per Soviak, p. III, 315
41 Kume, Ibid., Vol. V, p. 306. Translation as per Soviak, Ibid., p. 16.
42 Kume, *Beio Kairan Jikki*, Tanaka Akira (Ed.), Iwanami Shoten, 1994, Vol. I, p. 70-71.
43 Kume as quoted in Soviak, Op. Cit., pp. (Vol. II, pp. 111-112)
44 Kume as quoted in Soviak, Ibid., pp. (Vol. III, p. 55)
45 'The benefits of forcing the people to abandon ancient practices are extremely few. The disadvantages of injuring their traditional sentiments and producing discontent are numerous.' Kume as quoted in Soviak, Ibid., pp. (Vol. IV, p. 218)
46 'The white race are avid in their desires and zealous in their religion, and they lack the power of self control. . . . The yellow race have weaker desires and are strong in subduing their natures. . . . Consequently, the main purpose of their political institutions are also different. In the West there is protective [of self-interest] government; in the East there is benevolent government.' Kume as quoted in Soviak, Ibid., pp. (Vol. V, p. 148)
47 Kume as quoted in Soviak, Ibid., pp. (Vol. I, p. 208).
48 Kume, *Beio Kairan Jikki*, Tanaka Akira (Ed.), Op. Cit., Vol. I, p. 208-209.
49 Kume, Ibid., Vol. I, p. 209. See also Tanaka, Op. Cit., pp. 81-83 re the evils of [excessive] freedom.

CHAPTER 2 [BRITAIN 1]

1. *The Times*,19 August 1872
2. R. H. Brunton, *Rebuilding Japan 1868-1876*,(Folkestone, 1991), p.118
3. Kume Kunitake, *Kume Hakushi Kujūnen Kaikoroku*, (Tokyo, 1934), vol.2, p.298
4. R. Tsunoda et al., *Sources of Japanese Tradition*, (New York, 1959), vol.2, p.137
5. C. Lanman, *Leaders of the Meiji Restoration in America*, (Tokyo, 1931), p.29
6. Nihon Shiseki Kyokai, *Kido Takayoshi Nikki*, vol.2 (Tokyo, 1933), p.157
7. *Kaikoroku*, pp.421
8. *Ibid.*, p.299
9. 'Sugiura Kōzō Memo', *Kagoshima Kenritsu Tanki Daigaku Chiiki Kenkyūsho Nenpō*, No.8, 1990, pp.45-7
10. Shunpō-kō Tsuisho-kai, *Itō Hirobumi Den*, (Tokyo, 1943), vol.1, p.675
11. *Kaikoroku*, p.303
12. *Ibid.*, pp.321, 323-8. Inuzuka Takaaki, *Wakaki Mori Arinori*, (Tokyo, 1983), p.242
13. S. Devere Brown and A. Hirota (trans.), *The Diary of Kido Takayoshi*, vol.2 (Tokyo, 1985), pp.201-2, 248
14. Ozaki Saburō, *Ozaki Saburō Jijo Ryakuden*, (Tokyo, 1980), vol.1, p.121
15. *The Diary of Kido Takayoshi*, pp.201-2, 248
16. Moritani Hideaki, 'Kōtokuin Go-Ryakureki: Minami Teisuke Jiden', *Shinkyū Jidai*, vol.3, no.9, October 1927, pp.31-2
17. Ibid., p.32
18. Tanaka Akira (ed.), Kume Kunitake, *Tokumei Zenken Taishi Bei-Ō Kairan Jikki*, (Tokyo, 1985), vol.2, p.394. Yamaguchi's given name is often pronounced Naoyoshi, but in his native Hizen he is known as Yamaguchi Masuka, and it was under this name that he was presented to Queen Victoria. *The Times*, 7 December 1872
19. Hayashi Tadasu, *Ato wa Mukashi no Ki*, (Tokyo, 1970), pp.182-3
20. *Ibid.*
21. *Kaikoroku*, pp.377, 379-80
22. Nihon Shiseki Kyōkai, *Ōkubo Toshimichi Monjo*, vol.4 (1928), pp.448-9
23. *Kaikoroku*, p.312
24. *The Times*, 13 September 1872
25. *Kaikoroku*, pp.306, 312

26. *Ibid.*, p.309
27. *Ibid.*, p.312, 383
28. *ŌkuboToshimichi Monjo*, p.468
29. *Kairan Jikki*, p.68
30. *Kaikoroku*, pp.314-5
31. *Kairan Jikki*, pp.119. 158. 191. A *shaku* is just under one foot in length.
32. *Kaikoroku*, pp.336, 340-1, 344. *Kairan Jikki*, p.238
33. *Kaikoroku*, pp.340-1. *Kairan Jikki*, p.242
34. *Kairan Jikki*, pp.67-8
35. *Kairan Jikki*, p.312. *Kaikoroku*, p.403
36. *Kairan Jikki*, pp.66-9
37. *Kairan Jikki*, p.295. *Kaikoroku*, pp.376, 394
38. *Kaikoroku*, pp.318, 393-4
39. *Ibid.*
40. *Ozaki Saburō Jijo Ryakuden*, p.124
41. *The Diary of KidoTakayoshi*, p.248. *Ozaki Saburō Jijo Ryakuden*, pp.124, 130. *Ōkubo Toshimichi Monjo*, p.459. Even Iwakura may have lost some money. Ozaki claimed that both he and Kido escaped by handing their allowances over to Tanaka Mitsuaki of the Treasury Department, but Kido admitted losing a deposit, and Hayashi suggested that Iwakura too was involved. *Ato wa Mukashi no Ki*, p.183
42. *The Diary of KidoTakayoshi*, p.249. *Kaikoroku*, p.436. *Ato wa Mukashi no Ki*, p.183. *Ozaki Saburō Jijo Ryakuden*, p.131. Kido thought Kume had lost £100, but Hayashi, Ozaki and Kume himself put the figure at £150. The studious Kume had a reputation as something of a sage, and one verse coined in the wake of the Minami affair jested: 'The Sage of Kume could not bring himself to gaze on a woman's white thighs, but was toppled by £150'. (There was a holy man by the name of Kume who was famous for falling out of a tree after catching sight of a woman's legs as she washed in a river). On Shioda's loss, another verse ran: 'Tears filled the Devil's eyes when he saw his bank collapse'.
43. *Ozaki Saburō Jijo Ryakuden*, p.129
44. *ŌkuboToshimichi Monjo*, pp.461-2
45. *Ozaki Saburō Jijo Ryakuden*, p.130
46. *Kairan Jikki*, p.406. *KidoTakayoshi Nikki*, p.249
47. *The Diary of Kido Takayoshi*, p.214
48. *Ibid.*, pp.261-2. *Kaikoroku*, p.420-1
49. *Kairan Jikki*, p.40

CHAPTER 2 [BRITAIN 2]

1. Soviak, 1971, p. 9
2. Imai, 1994, p. 106. The second of five volumes is entirely devoted to Britain.
3. Checkland, 1991, p.109; Beasley, 1995, p. 157
4. See Mayo, 1973, for details of Kume's intellectual background. Iwakura deliberately chose someone well-versed in Confucian studies. He was searching for a theory or rationale of reform to persuade himself and others that what the government was doing was right. Mayo notes (p. 6) 'A Confucian scholar with some flexibility of mind and moderation of language seemed best suited to speak to a broad segment of the public.' Kume Kunitake succeeded brilliantly as an observer of Western life.

Kume grew up in Saga, the capital of Hizen, where there was an active interest in Dutch learning, and considerable awareness of Western technology.

Checkland (p. 115) notes that one member of the mission, Yasukawa, concentrated upon the work of the Houses of Parliament, paying some twenty visits to the Commons and nearly twenty visits to the Lords.

5. Altman, 1966. Discussing the significance of Verbeck's paper, Altman states: 'The basic motivations for the Embassy came from the Japanese. The Meiji leaders required no Verbeck to inspire dissatisfaction with the treaties and Japan's international status. Neither did they need him to instruct them to desire reform of their institutions, and that, along Western lines. Nor did he instil in the Meiji leaders a fear of revision negotia-

tions, or a wish to escape from them. While Verbeck did none of these, his letter did serve the oligarchs as a guide. Drafted with consummate skill, tact, and an appreciation of the Japanese point of view, it provided them with a manual laying down the procedure to follow to solve the problems they faced. The plan was comprehensive and written with a knowledge of Western institutions and diplomacy which they still lacked. . . . Verbeck's paper, therefore, offered the Meiji leaders a design which they adapted to their ends, not his. Such selectivity was to be repeated more than once in the history of Japan's modernization.' (p. 57)

6. Foreign Office to Parkes, 28 May 1872, in F.O. 46/150
7. See G. Daniels, *Sir Harry Parkes: British Representative in Japan* pp. 134-5
8. See W.G. Beasley, *Japan Encounters the Barbarian* p. 167
9. See Fox, 1969, Chapter X, pp. 250-273 for a detailed description of British influence on the Japanese navy.
10. Manchester City Council Proceedings, reproduced in Kume Bijutsukan museum pamphlet, *Rekishika Kume Kunitake*, 1997 p. 58
11. M. J. Mayo, 'The Western Education of Kume Kunitake, 1871-6', p. 30, quoted by Checkland, 1989, p. 113.
12. Yokohama Archives of History, 1991, *R.H. Brunton*, p. 94. See also Checkland, 1989, pp. 45-48, and Chapter 28 of Brunton's memoirs for his account of the mission: 'Home Again – With the Japanese in England'. (William Elliott Griffis papers, Rutgers University Library, New Jersey, USA.)
13. Checkland, 1989, p. 114
14. Fox, 1969, p. 500
15. The above is an extended version of the text of a paper delivered at the 8th Conference of the European Association for Japanese Studies in Budapest, 27-30 August 1997. I was able to attend the conference through the generosity of the Meisenkai alumni association of Kyushu Institute of Technology to which I extend my sincere gratitude.

CHAPTER 3

1. If one can judge from the letters of Ito Hirobumi and Okubo Toshimichi and the diary of Kido Takayoshi, they were also constantly concerned with, and possibly sometimes distracted by, news of what was happening in Japan. See Shumpo Ko Tsuishokai (ed.), *Ito Hirobumi Den* (3 vols., Tokyo, 1940), I, 682-703; Nihon Shiseki Kyokai (ed.), *Okubo Toshimichi Bunsho* (10 vols., Tokyo, 1927-29), IV, 475-498; and S. D. Brown & A. Hirota (trans.), *The Diary of Kido Takayoshi* (3 vols., Tokyo, 1983-86), II, 263-87.
2. The latter meeting is mistakenly implied to have occurred on 24 December. The report on 27 December of the official encounter of the previous day states that the ambassadors all wore blue dress coats (*habits*) braided with gold, opera-style hats (*chapeau à claque*) like those worn by Second Empire senators, some with white plumes, others with black-and-white trousers with gold bands. At the general diplomatic reception on New Year's Day they apparently wore simple black dress coats, in contrast to the members of the visiting Burmese embassy, who were attired in national costume.
3. The one feature which does seem to have attracted some public attention was Iwakura's disproportionately large head. Phrenologists apparently made their curiosity known, and even Thiers commented on it. See *Ito Hirobumi Den*, I, 694.
4. It is worth noting that in 1873 Japan was the main focus of the first Congress of Orientalists, which was organized by Léon de Rosny and held in Paris. See Ellen P. Conant, 'The French Connection: Emile Guimet's Mission to Japan, a Cultural Context for *Japonisme*', in H. Conroy et al (ed.), *Japan in Transition* (London & Toronto, 1984), 119-121.
5. Some of the students had acquired useful contacts or experience of which mission members took advantage. A notable case was the young Saionji Kimmochi's invitation of Kido and others to a masked ball which lasted all night and which Kido described as 'one of the most interesting spectacles of either America or Europe' (*The Diary of Kido Takayoshi*, II, 287).
6. Not Rue de Berri or Place Berri, as S. D. Brown read the katakana rendering in Kido's diary, (*op. cit.*, 264,287).

7. *Le Temps*, 28 December 1872. It also noted that according to the Agence Havas the emissaries were 'men of absolutely superior intelligence and very serious character, the most important personages in their country'. See also *Le Monde Illustré*'s reference (22 February 1873) to Iwakura's 'rare intelligence'.
8. *Le Temps*, 28 December 1872.
9. Like tourists they bought souvenirs, including in Ito's case, photographs of the ex-emperor Napoleon III, who died during their visit (*Ito Hirobumi Den*, I, 697).
10. *Tokumei Zenken Taishi Bei-O Kairan Jikki*, III, 140-3.
11. *Ibid.*, 69-76.
12. *Ibid.*, 91-8. Kido found Versailles unequalled in its splendour.
13. *Ibid.*, 51-79.
14. *Ibid.*, 91-111.
15. *Ibid.*, 117-57.
16. See the commentary by Tanaka Akira in his Iwanami edition of Kume's *Bei-O Kairan Jikki* (Tokyo, 1979), III, 375-6.
17. *Tokumei Zenken Taishi Bei-O Kairan Jikki*, III, 92-3, iii.
18. *Ibid.*, 61.
19. *Ibid.*, 41, 78.
20. *Ibid.*, 14.
21. *Ibid.*, 120.
22. *Ibid.*, 37-9.
23. *Ibid.*, 36.
24. *Ibid.*, 51.
25. According to Marlene Mayo, 'The Western Education of Kume Kunitake, 1871-1876', *Monumenta Nipponica* XXVIII (Spring 1973), 59, being in Paris was like entering paradise to Kume.
26. *Okubo Toshimichi Bunsho*, IV, 477.
27. *Ibid.*, 481.
28. *Ibid.*, 484.
29. *Tokumei Zenken Taishi Bei-O Kairan Jikki*, III, 137-9.
30. Quai d'Orsay archives, Correspondance Politique, Japon, XIX, 2 October 1869, Outrey to Quai d'Orsay. The characteristics of French diplomacy are examined in detail in my *French Policy towards the Bakufu and Meiji Japan, 1854-1895*, (Japan Library, 1998).
31. *Ibid.*, XXI, 28 September 1871, Rémusat to Outrey.
32. *Ibid.*, XXI, 23 December 1872, Turenne to Quai d'Orsay.
33. Quai d'Orsay archives, Mémoires et Documents, Japon, II, compte-rendu of conference of 24 January 1873.
34. *Ibid.*
35. Correspondance Politique, Japon, XXI, 17 July 1872, Turenne to Quai d'Orsay.
36. Enclosure in *Ibid.*
37. *Ibid.*, 17 December 1872.
38. *Ibid.*, XXII, 27 July 1873.
39. *Les Missions Catholiques*, V, 31 January 1873.
40. Correspondance Politique, Japon, XIX, 22 January 1870, Outrey to Quai d'Orsay.
41. Correspondance Politique, Japon, XXI, 8 & 23 January, 19 February, 8 May, 28 August, 23 December 1872, all Turenne to Quai d'Orsay.
42. The speech was published in the *Journal Officiel de la République Francaise* of 8 December 1872. It was reprinted in *Les Missions Catholiques* of 20 December and later in F. Marnas, *La Religion de Jesus Resuscitée au Japon* (Clermont Ferrand, 1897), 241-3.
43. *Ibid.*
44. Correspondance Politique, Japon, XXI, 20 December 1872, Rémusat to Turenne.
45. Mémoires et Documents, Japon, II.
46. *Ibid.*, 25 March 1873.
47. Correspondance Politique, Japon, XXII, 24 February 1873.
48. Ibid., 7 August 1873, Broglie to Berthemy.
49. Ibid., XXIII, 1 December 1873, Decazes to Berthemy.

50. By Dr. John Breen (SOAS) in a symposium at the London School of Economics, December 1997.
51. Correspondance Politique, Japon, XXIII, 22 September 1873. Berthemy had, however, to acknowledge in this dispatch to Paris that the Japanese government was closing its eyes to breaches of the ban and that it would 'not open them as long as the Christians do not cause it any embarrassment'.
52. One account which makes this assumption is Abe Yoshiya, 'From Prohibition to Toleration', *Japanese Journal of Religious Studies*, 5/2-3 (1978).
53. See Sims, *op. cit.*, chapter IV.
54. Correspondance Politique, Japon, XXIII, 9 November 1873, Berthemy to Quai d'Orsay.
55. *Le Monde Illustré*, 22 February 1873.
56. Mémoires et Documents, Japon, II, 24 January 1873.

CHAPTER 4

1 See Willy Vande Walle, 'Count de Montblanc and the 1865 Satsuma Mission to Europe', in *Orientalia Lovaniensia Periodica* 27 (1996), pp. 151-76.
2 At least not in terms of international law, for the Ryūkyū Islands were not recognized as an independent state, nor did the envoys carry any official credentials from the daimyō of Satsuma.
3 Isomi Tatsunori, Kurosawa Fumitaka, Sakurai Ryōju, *Nihon Berugī Kankeishi*, (Tokyo: Hakusuisha, 1989), p. 79.
4 Aoyama Hideyuki, 'Ryūgakusei to Iwakura shisetsudan', in Tanaka Akira and Takata Seiji eds, *Bei-Ō kairan jikki no gakusaiteki kenkyū* (Sapporo: Hokkaidō daigaku tosho kankōkai, 1993) p. 355ff.
5 *Ibid.*, p. 12.
6 Bart Pluymers m.m.v. Suzy Pasleau, 'Het kleine België: een grote industriële mogendheid', in: *Nijver België*, onder redactie van Bart Van der Herten, Michel Oris en Jan Rogiers (Brussels: Gemeentekrediet, 1995), p. 33.
7 *Ibid.*
8 Kume Kunitake, *Bei-Ō kairan jikki* (Tokyo, 1878; reprint ed. by Tanaka Akira, Tokyo: Iwanami shoten, 1978-82), p. 167.
9 Ishizaka Akio, 'Iwakura shisetsudan to Berugī: 1873nen no senshin jūkōgyōkoku Berugī', in Tanaka Akira and Takata Seiji eds, op. cit., p. 122.
10 Adolphe Demeur, *Les sociétés anonymes de Belgique en 1857, collection complète des statuts* (Bruxelles: chez l'éditeur, 1859), p. v. There existed however a few companies during the Austrian period, which were founded by imperial charter.
11 *Ibid.*
12 Cfr. infra.
13 See Takata Seiji, '*Bei-Ō kairan jikki* to Kume shukō Butsurigaku', in Tanaka Akira and Takata Seiji (eds.), *op. cit.*, p. 265.
14 *Ibid.*, p. 267.
15 Kume, *op. cit.*, p. 188.
16 Ishizaka, *op. cit.*, p. 122; also Hervé Hasquin (ed.), *La Wallonie, le pays et les hommes: histoire, économies, sociétés* (Bruxelles: la Renaissance du Livre, 1975-76), t. 2, pp. 75-92.
17 Kume, *op. cit.*, p. 170-172.
18 Ishizaka, *op. cit.*, p. 122.
19 *Ibid.*, p. 129, note 4.
20 *Ibid.*, p. 123.
21 *Ibid.*
22 Memorandum d'une conférence officielle qui a eu lieu, le 23 février 1873, au Ministère des Affaires étrangères à Bruxelles, entre le Baron Lambermont, Envoyé extraordinaire et Ministre plénipotentiaire, Secrétaire-Général de ce Département (M. Ministre des affaires étrangères étant empêché par l'état de sa santé): Archives of the Ministry of Foreign Affairs, Brussels, Nr. 2865. There is a Japanese translation in Isomi, *op. cit.*, p. 86-94. Ishizaka, *op. cit.*, p. 123, notes that Kume erroneously states that Iwakura met Minister

of Finance Jules Malou. In *Ibid.*, p. 129, note 7, he points out that Kume also mistakes the Prime Minister, for he mentions Baron Jules d'Anethan, whereas the latter had resigned after a clash with the king in December 1871 and had been succeeded by Meylandt, Comte de Theux, of the same Catholic Party.

23 Ishizaka, *op. cit.*, p. 124.

24 Letter from Lambermont to Saville Lumley, British Minister in Brussels, dated, Brux., 21-1-1873 (Archives of the Ministry of Foreign Affairs, Brussels, Sheaf 2865, document A. Nr. 4332), asking Lumley to convey his gratitude to Sir Henry Barron and to Lord Granville for the copies.

25 The memoranda date from 22 November, 27 November and 6 December, 1872.

26 Isomi, *op. cit.*, p. 82-3.

27 Kume, *op. cit.*, p. 165.

28 Ishizaka, *op. cit.*, p. 129, note 6.

29 Godai Tomoatsu, 'Kaikoku nikki', in Nihon keiei-shi kenkyūjo ed., *Godai Tomoatsu denki shiryō*, vol.4 (Tokyo:, 1974), p. 33.

30 Kume, *op. cit.*, p. 187.

31 *Ibid.*, p. 167.

32 Ishizaka, *op. cit.*, p. 122 overstates the democratic character but qualifies his statement in note 1.

33 See Joseph Jennes, *A History of the Catholic Church in Japan* (Tokyo: Oriens Institute for Religious Research, 1973), p. 225.

34 *Ibid.*, p. 226.

35 *Ibid.*, pp. 227 and 229. In Urakami alone, by the time the persecution was halted, 3404 Catholics had been deported.

36 *Ibid.*, p. 228.

37 *Ibid.* p. 228.

38 Francisque Marnas, *La 'Religion de Jésus' (Iaso ja-kyō) ressuscitée au Japon* (Paris, Lyon: Delhomme et Briguet, 1896), vol. 2, p. 240-245.

39 About the so-called Urakami question, see Richard Sims, *French Policy towards the Bakufu and Meiji Japan, 1854-95* (Richmond: Japan Library, 1998), p. 82 ff.

40 Marnas, *op. cit.* vol. 2, p. 240; also: Sims, *op. cit.*, p. 90.

41 Marnas, *op. cit.*, p 255.

42 Marnas, *op. cit.* p. 257.

43 *Journal d'Anvers*, lundi 24 février 1873, p. 2, Chronique locale; reproduced by *Le Bien Public*, mercredi 26 fév., p. 2, Faits divers.

44 Ishizaka, *op. cit.*, p. 124 says that it was King Willem I who sold the palace of the former Prince Bishop of Liège at a give-away price in 1817.

45 Laureyssens Julienne, *Industriële naamloze vennootschappen in België* 1819-1857, Interuniversitair centrum voor hedendaagse geschiedenis Bijdragen Nr. 78 (Leuven-Louvain, Paris: Editions Nauwelaerts,1975), p. 261.

46 *Ibid.*, p. 261 says there were seven, while Ishizaka, *op. cit.*, p. 124 mentions two mines within its own premises.

47 Marinette Bruwier, 'De dynamische relatie tussen de industriële vooruitgang en de machinebouw', in *Nijver België*, p. 133.

48 Laureyssens, *op. cit.*, p. 262.

49 *Ibid.*, p. 264.

50 Ishizaka, *op. cit.*, 125.

51 Antoon Soete, 'Van Cockerill tot Bessemer: de zware metaalnijverheid', in *Nijver België*, onder redactie van Bart Van der Herten, Michel Oris en Jan Rogiers (Brussel: Gemeentekrediet, 1995), p. 155.

52 Kume, *op. cit.* , p. 195 ff. Ishizaka, *op. cit.*, p. 125, referring to *110ème Anniversaire de la Fondation des Usines Cockerill 1817-1927*, Seraing, 1927 pp. 34-35.

53 Ishizaka, *op. cit.*, p. 124 mistakenly gives the date 1866.

54 Kume, *op. cit.*, pp.196-200.

55 *Ibid.*, pp. 192 ff.

56 *Ibid.*, p. 194 features an arresting picture of this oven.

57 Takahashi Kunitarō, *Hana no Pari e shōnen shisetsu; Keiō sannen Pari bankokuhaku funtōki* (Tokyo: Sanshūsha, 1979), p. 47-48.
58 Laureyssens, *op. cit.*, p. 247.
59 Ishizaka, *op. cit.*, p. 126.
60 *Ibid.*
61 Kume, *op. cit.*, p.201.
62 *Ibid.*, p. 186, erroneously thinks that the nurseries belonged to De Hemptinne. See the memorandum of the interview between Lambermont and Iwakura, where the former refers to Linden.
63 Peter Scholliers,'Van de proto-industrie tot de Industriële Revolutie: de katoen- en linnennijverheid', in *Nijver België*, p. 69.
64 *Ibid.*, p. 61.

CHAPTER 5

1 *Bei-O kairan jikki*. Vol. I-V.
(a) Facsimile edition: Tokyo, Munataka Shobō 1975
(b) Reprint (Tōyō Kanji): Edited by Akira Tanaka, Tokyo, Iwanami, 1977
Citations '*Kairan jikki*' after the Iwanami-Edition
2 *Kairan jikki* I, p.9ff
3 Tanaka, A. and Takada, S. (Ed): *Interdisciplinary Studies on Bei-O Kairan Jikki* (text mostly Japanese) Hokkaido daigaku tosho kankô kai, 1993, ISBN 4-8329-5571-3
4 *Kölnische Volkszeitung*, 7 March 1873
5 *Spenersche Ztg.*, 8 March 1873
6 *Kairan jikki* III, p.301
7 e.g. *Neue Preussische Ztg.*, 11 March 1873
8 Brown, S. and Hirota, A. (Transl.): *The Diary of Kido Takayoshi*, Univ. of Tokyo Press, 1983, Vol II, p.298
9 Verhandlungen des Reichstags, 12 March 1873
10 *Spenersche Ztg.*, 13 and 14 March 1873
11 *Neue Preussische Ztg.*, 28 March 1873
12 *Vossische Ztg.*, 16 March 1873
13 *Kairan jikki*, III, p.329
14 Bismarck. *Die gesammelten Werke*. Band 8 – Gespräche, p.64-5 Berlin 1925 (2nd. Edition)
15 *Neue Preussische Ztg.*, 26 March 1873
16 *Kairan jikki*, III, p.340
17 Wattenberg, U.,'Die Iwakura-Mission in Berlin'. in: Japanisch-Deutsches Zentrum Berlin (ed): *Berlin-Tokyo*. Springer 1997, pp. 61-70
18 *Neue Preussische Ztg.*, 25 March 1873
19 *Kairan jikki* III, p. 285
20 *Neue Preussische Ztg.*, 28 March 1873
21 *Die Gartenlaube*, 1873, p. 586
22 *Kairan jikki*, III, p.347
23 *Neue Preussische Ztg.*, 29 March 1873

CHAPTER 6

1. General works on this topic are: *Nichi Ro gaikoshi*, Tokyo: Gaimusho (for departmental use); *Nihon gaiko bunsho*, 6-nen, Tokyo: Gaimusho, 1956. Scholarly discussions are to be found in Togawa Tsuguo,'Iwakura shisetsudan to Rossiya'and Nakamura Kennosuke, 'Peterburg no Iwakura shisetsudan kankei shimbun kiji' in Tanaka Akira and Takada Seiichi (eds), *Bei-O kairan jikki no gakusaiteki kenkyu*, Hokkaido University, 1993, pp. 131-61; and Okubo Toshiaki (ed.), *Iwakura Shisetsu no kenkyu*, Tokyo: Munetaka Shobo, 1976. The most recent English-language account is in W.G. Beasley, *Japan Encounters the Barbarians*, London: Yale, 1995, chs. 9-11
2. W.G. Aston 'Russian Descents in Saghalien and Itorup in 1806-7', a lecture given on 7 June 1873, in *Transactions of the Asiatic Society of Japan*, first series, vol I(1882), 78-86. Useful

information is to be found in A. I. Alekseyev, *Osvoenie russkimi lyudmi dalnevo vostoka*, Moscow: NAUK, 1982, pp. 58-62. E. Y. Fainberg, 'Yapontsi v Rossii v period samoizolyatsii Yaponii, 1697-1852' in *Yaponiya: Vöprosi istorii*, Moscow: Izdatelstvo vostochnoi literaturi, 1959

3. George A Lensen, *The Russian Push toward Japan, 1697-1875*, Princeton: University Press, 1959; John Stephan, *Sakhalin*, Oxford: University Press, 1971.

4. On Vladivostok, Andrew Malozemoff, *Russian Far Eastern Policy, 1881-1904*, Berkeley, University of California Press, 1958, pp. 5-6. Also Ian Nish (ed.), *British Documents on Foreign Affairs*, Part I, Series E, 1860-1914, vol. I, Washington: UPA, 1989, pp. 383-95

5. Sakane Yoshihisa(ed.), *Aoki Shuzo jiden*, Tokyo: Heibonsha, 1970, chs 3-7; Sidney Devere Brown and Akiko Hirota (eds), *The Diary of Kido Takayoshi,* vol II, 1871-4, Tokyo: University Press, 1985, 19 Aug. 1872, p. 199 [hereafter 'Kido, *Diary*']

6. Sakamoto Tatsunosuke, *Danshaku Nishi Tokujiro den*, Tokyo 1933

7. *Ito Hirobumi den*, I, Tokyo, 1943, p. 714; Kido, *Diary*, 26 March 1873, p. 303

8. Kido, *Diary*, 29 March 1873, p. 304

9. Kido, *Diary*, 30 March 1873, pp. 304-5

10. *St Petersburg Gazette*; (Lord) Augustus Loftus, *Diplomatic Reminiscences*, 2 vols, vol. II, 1862-79, London: Cassell, 1894

11. Kume Kunitake, *Tokumei zenken taishi Bei-O kairan jikki*, vol. 62

12. Kume, op. cit., vol. 65. Also *Bei-O kairan jikki, Dohan gashu (Picture collection)*, Tokyo, 1986

13. *St Petersburg Gazette;* Kido, *Diary*, 10 April 1873, p. 313

14. Kume, *Kairan jikki,* vol. 65

15. A. Meller, Ob Osnovanii Uchilisha Gluhonemih v S. Peterburg, Moscow, 26 April 1872 [by courtesy of the Kume Museum, Meguro, Tokyo]; Kido, *Diary*, 9 April 1873, pp. 311-12

16. Kajima Morinosuke (ed.), *Nihon gaikoshi*, vol. 2, 'Joyaku kaisei mondai', Tokyo: Kajima Shuppankai, 1970, pp. 211-14

17. Orr to Fish, 2 May 1873 in *Foreign Relations of the United States 1873*, Part II

18. *Nishi-den*

19. Ian Nish, *Origins of the Russo-Japanese war*, London: Longmans, 1985, p.4. Yamanashi Gakuin Daigaku, *Otsu jiken kankeishi ryoshu*, vol. I, Tokyo: Seibundo, 1995, passim

20. Nakamura Kennosuke, 'Five News Reports on the Iwakura Mission in St Petersburg' in Tanaka, op. cit., pp. 157-61

21. E. M. Zhukov(ed.), *Mezhdunarodnie otnosheniya na dalnem vostoke, 1840-1949,* Moscow, 1956, pp. 52-4; *Diplomati entsiklopediya*, p. 808; Fainberg, op. cit., pp. 258-60

22. Brown, Introduction, in Kido, *Diary*, p. xxxiv

23. *Joyaku kaisei keika gaiyo (Nihon gaiko bunsho bekkan)*, Tokyo: Gaimusho, 1950, pp. 124-5. Lensen, op. cit., p. 437ff

24. *Japan Mail,* 23 Jan. 1874

25. *Nihon gaiko nempyo narabini shuyo bunsho*

CHAPTER 7

1 Fritz von Dardel, *Dagboksanteckningar 1873-1876* (Diary notes, 1873-1876). Stockholm 1916, p. 16.

2 Peter Duus, 'Introduction', in Peter Duus, ed., *Cambridge History of Japan*, vol. 5. Cambridge: Cambridge University Press, 1988, p. 26.

3 J. E. Thomas, *Modern Japan: A Social History since 1868*. London and New York: Longman, 1996, p. 60.

4 Einar Hedin, 'Sverige-Norges utrikespolitik i början av Oskar II:s regering' (Swedish-Norwegian foreign policy in the beginning of Oskar II's reign), *Historisk Tidskrift* (1946), p. 236.

5 Folke Lindberg, *Kunglig utrikespolitik: Studier i svensk utrikespolitik under Oskar II och fram till borggårdskrisen* (Royal foreign policy: Studies in Swedish foreign policy during Oskar II and until the courtyard crisis). Stockholm 1966, p. 9.

6 Tanaka Akira and Takata Seiji, eds, *Bei-Ō kairan jikki no gakusaiteki kenkyū* (Interdis-

ciplinary Studies on Bei-O Kairan Jikki). Sapporo: Hokkaidō daigaku tosho kankōkai, 1993.

7 Okuda Tamaki, 'Iwakura shisetsudan ga mita Sūeden – 'Bei-Ō kairan jikki' dai 68/ dai 69 ken 'Sudenkoku no ki jo/ge' o yomu' (The Iwakura embassy's view on Sweden – examining the Swedish part of *Bei-Ō Kairan Jikki*), *Kawamura gakuen joshi daigaku kenkyū kiyō*, vol. 6, no. 1 (1995), pp. 29-67. Okuda has published another contribution on the Bei-Ō kairan jikki, 'Meiji seifu no Sūeden hōmon – Iwakura shisetsudan to 'Bei-Ō kairan jikki'' (The Swedish visit of the Meiji government-the Iwakura mission and Bei-O kairan jikki), *Hoku-Ō shi kenkyū*, vol. 6, no. 13 (1996), p. 146-52. This article is based on her earlier publication but contains some new information.

8 The visit is briefly described in Tanaka Akira, *'Datsu-A' no Meiji ishin: Iwakura shisetsudan o ou tabi kara*. Tokyo: Nihon hōsō shuppan kyōkai, 1984; Tanaka Akira, Iwakura shisetsudan *Bei-Ō kairan jikki*. Tokyo: Iwanami shoten, 1994; Izumi Saburō, *'Bei-Ō kairan' hyakunijūnen no tabi: Iwakura shisetsudan no ashiato ōtte*. Tokyo: Tosho shuppansha, 1993; Tominaga Shigeki, 'Hoku-Ō de mita koto, Nan-Ō ni tsuite kīta koto', in Nishikawa Nagao and Matsumiya Hideharu, eds, *'Bei-Ō kairan jikki' o yomu-1870 nendai no sekai to Nihon*. Tokyo: Hōritsu bunkasha, 1995, pp. 321-38.

9 Kume Kunitake, *Tokumei zenken taishi Bei-Ō kairan jikki* (A true account of the tour in America and Europe of the Special Embassy). 5 vols. Tokyo 1878. I have used a reprinted edition by Tanaka Akira. Tokyo: Iwanami shoten, 1978-82.

10 Marlene J. Mayo, 'The Western Education of Kume Kunitake, 1871-6', *Monumenta Nipponica*, vol. 28, no. 1 (Spring 1973), p. 12.

11 Ōkubo Toshiaki, 'Iwakura shisetsu haken no kenkyū' (Research on the dispatch of the Iwakura mission), in *Ōkubo Toshiaki rekishi chōsakushū*, 2. Tokyo: Yoshikawa kōbunkan, 1986, p. 132.

12 Mayo, 'The Western Education of Kume Kunitake', p. 13.

13 Ōkubo, 'Iwakura shisetsu haken no kenkyū', p. 132.

14 Tanaka Akira, *Kaikoku* (The opening of the country). Nihon kindai shisō taikei, vol. 1. Tokyo: Iwanami shoten, 1991, p. 492.

15 Hirakawa Sukehiro, 'Japan's turn to the West', in Duus, ed., *Cambridge History of Japan*, Vol. 5, p. 465.

16 Personal communication, Professor Takata Seiji, 12 July 1995.

17 Riksarkivet, Kabinettet, UD, Huvudarkivet [henceforth RA] E2D:460, Kabinettet för utrikes brevväxlingen, Depescher från beskickningen i London, 1872. Letter from Steenbock to Adlercreutz, 21 August 1872.

18 RA E2D:460, Kabinettet för utrikes brevväxlingen, Depescher från beskickningen i London, 1872. Letter from Hochschild to von Platen, 4 December 1872.

19 RA E2D:460, Kabinettet för utrikes brevväxlingen, Depescher från beskickningen i London, 1872. Letter from Hochschild to von Platen, 9 December 1872.

20 W. G. Beasley, *Japan Encounters the Barbarians: Japanese Travellers in America and Europe*. New Haven and London: Yale University Press, 1995, pp. 168f.

21 RA E2D:184, Kabinettet för utrikes brevväxlingen, Depescher från beskickningen i Haag och Bryssel, 1873-1874. Letter from Burenstam to Björnstjerna, 20 February 1872 (sic!).

22 Sweden had two prime minister posts until 1876, the prime minister for foreign affairs [utrikesstatsministern] and the prime minister for justice [justitiestatsministern]. See e.g. *Nils Herlitz, Grunddragen i det svenska statsskickets historia* (The main outlines of the history of the Swedish form of government). 6th ed. Stockholm 1967, p. 255. There was actually also a third one, the Norwegian prime minister; until 1905, Sweden and Norway formed a union.

23 RA E2D:184, Kabinettet för utrikes brevväxlingen, Depescher från beskickningen i Haag och Bryssel, 1873-1874. Letter from Burenstam till Björnstjerna, 28 February 1873.

24 RA E2D:184, Kabinettet för utrikes brevväxlingen, Depescher från beskickningen i Haag och Bryssel, 1873-1874. Letter from Burenstam to Björnstjerna, 2 March 1873.

25 RA BiB:615, Kabinettet för utrikes brevväxlingen, Koncept, 1873, Svenska beskickningar: Aten-Köpenhamn. Telegram from Björnstjerna to Burenstam, 3 March 1873.

26 RA E2D:184, Kabinettet för utrikes brevväxlingen, Depescher från beskickningen i Haag och Bryssel, 1873-1874. Letter from Burenstam till Björnstjerna, 7 March 1873.
27 RA E2D:86, Kabinettet för utrikes brevväxlingen, Depescher från beskickningen i Berlin, 1873. Letter from Due to Björnstjerna, 23 March 1873.
28 RA E2D:747, Kabinettet för utrikes brevväxlingen, Depescher från beskickningen i Petersburg, 1873-1874. Telegram from Reuterskiöld to Björnstjerna, 11 April 1873.
29 I have been unable to trace this telegram.
30 RA E2D:747, Kabinettet för utrikes brevväxlingen, Depescher från beskickningen i Petersburg, 1873-1874. Letter from Reuterskiöld to Björnstjerna, 13 April 1873.
31 Ibid.
32 I have been unable to trace this letter.
33 RA E2D:347, Kabinettet för utrikes brevväxlingen, Depescher från beskickningen i Köpenhamn, 1873. Telegram from Beck-Friis to Björnstjerna, 17 April 1873.
34 Riksarkivet, Björnstjernska familjearkivet, O.M.F. Björnstjernas arkiv [henceforth BA], Brev from kungliga, furstliga och enskilda. Letter from Beck-Friis to Björnstjerna, 17 April 1873.
35 RA BiB:615, Kabinettet för utrikes brevväxlingen, Koncept, 1873, Svenska beskickningar: Aten-Köpenhamn. Telegram from Björnstjerna to Beck-Friis, 19 April 1873.
36 RA E2D:347, Kabinettet för utrikes brevväxlingen, Depescher från beskickningen i Köpenhamn, 1873. Telegram from Beck-Friis to Björnstjerna, 20 April 1873.
37 *Dagens Nyheter* 21 April 1873.
38 RA BiB:615, Kabinettet för utrikes brevväxlingen, Koncept, 1873, Svenska beskickningar: Aten-Köpenhamn. Telegram from Essen to Beck-Friis, 21 April 1873.
39 BA, Brev from kungliga, furstliga och enskilda. Letter from Beck-Friis to Björnstjerna, 21 April 1873.
40 RA E2D:347, Kabinettet för utrikes brevväxlingen, Depescher från beskickningen i Köpenhamn, 1873. Telegram from Beck-Friis to Björnstjerna, 22 April 1873.
41 *Dagens Nyheter* 25 April 1873.
42 *Aftonbladet* 24 April 1873, *Stockholms Dagblad* 25 April 1873.
43 The uncertainty of when the mission would actually arrive had made the foreign ministry book the rooms from the 23rd as seen in the invoice from Hotel Rydberg found in RA G2 AB:2. Utrikesdep:ts kameralavdelning – personal och räkenskapsavdelning. Räkenskaper. Tredje huvudtiteln och norska diplom. anslagen. Koncepthuvudboken, 1870-1879, entry no. 486.
44 *Dagens Nyheter* 25 April 1873, *Nya Dagligt Allehanda* 25 April 1873.
45 *Dagens Nyheter* 25 April 1873.
46 'Väderleken' (The weather), *Stockholms Dagblad* 25 April 1873.
47 Kume, *Bei-Ō kairan jikki*, vol. 4, p. 172.
48 Christer Wijkström, Center for History of Science of the Royal Swedish Academy of Sciences has been unable to trace any documents relating to the visit. Personal communication, 22 July 1997.
49 Kume, *Bei-Ō kairan jikki*, vol. 4, pp. 172-74.
50 Mayo, 'The Western Education of Kume Kunitake', p. 46.
51 *Nya Dagligt Allehanda* 25 April 1873.
52 *Dagens Nyheter* 26 April 873.
53 RA C2CE:1, Kabinettet för utrikes brevväxlingen, Diarium för Notifikationsskivelser från utländska hov, 1840-1899, entry no. 9, 1873.
54 RA E2JA:23, Kabinettet för utrikes brevväxlingen, Notifikationer 1870-1874.
55 BA, Björnstjerna, *Dagbok 1839-1905* (Diary 1839-1905), 25 April 1873.
56 Slottsarkivet, Hovförtäringsräkenskaperna fr.o.m. Karl XIV Johans tid, Oscar II, 1873, ID:51, 'Diner de S. M. le Roi en le 25 Avril 1873'.
57 Slottsarkivet, Handlingar och räkenskaper avseende fester, vol. 8, 1872-1875, Middagar och Soupeer hos DD HH Konungen och Drottningen 1872 8/10-1875 12/1, 'Middag den 25 April 1873 kl. 5 Stor uniform, bandet utanpå'.
58 *Aftonbladet* 26 April 1873, *Stockholms Dagblad* 26 April 1873.
59 BA, Björnstjerna, *Dagbok 1839-1905*, 26 April 1873.

60 Ibid., 29 April 1873.
61 Ingemar Ottosson, 'Svensk frihandelsimperialism: Det ojämlika fördraget med Japan 1868-1896' (Swedish free-trade imperialism. The unequal treaty with Japan, 1868-1896), *Historisk tidskrift*, no. 2 (1997), p. 203.
62 Kume, *Bei-Ō kairanjikki*, vol. 4, p. 172. Kume specifies the time to two o'clock. This is obviously a mistake either for the 25th, when the mission presented its credentials to the king, or a later time on the 24th when they met Björnstjerna.
63 Ishii Takashi, *Meiji shoki no kokusai kankei* ('The international environment of early Meiji). Tokyo: Yoshikawa kōbunkan kankō, 1977, pp. 92f.
64 Ottosson, 'Svensk frihandelsimperialism', p. 215.
65 BA, Björnstjerna, *Dagbok* 1839-1905, 27 April 1873.
66 Ottoson's view is probably based on the fact that the first document in the file of the archives of the foreign ministry, which should normally have included relevant documents, dates from 1877. See Riksarkivet, Utrikesdepartementet, 1902 års dossiersystem, 103A2: 'Underhandl: om revision af 1868 års traktat med Japan 1871-87' (Negotiations concerning revision of the 1868 treaty with Japan, 1871-87). The starting year for this file, 1871, should be noted, since it indicates that negotiations took place earlier than 1877. Relevant documents may be found in other files. In his study of Swedish relations with China, in which relations with Japan figure quite substantially, Jan Larsson found that documents are widely dispersed and not always found where one would expect them to be. See Jan Larsson, *Diplomati och industriellt genombrott: Svenska exportsträvanden på Kina 1906-1916* (Diplomacy and Modern Industry: Sweden's Quest for a Chinese Market, 1906-1916). Diss. Studia Historica Upsaliensia 96. Uppsala 1977, p. 30.
67 Hugh Cortazzi, *The Japanese Achievement*. London: Sidgwick and Jackson; and New York: St. Martin's Press, 1990, p. 187. In Denmark the situation is same: the archives of the foreign ministry lack documents indicating that the Iwakura mission pursued negotiations with the Danes regarding the Danish-Japanese treaty. See Nagashima Yōichi, 'Denmāku ni okeru Iwakura shisetsudan' (The Iwakura mission in Denmark), in Tanaka and Takata, eds, *Bei-Ō kairanjikki no gakusaiteki kenkyū*, p. 175.
68 Kume, *Bei-Ō kairanjikki*, vol. 4, p. 184.
69 Personal communication, Margareta Östergren, Senior Archivist, Military Records Office, 13 August 1997.
70 Kume, *Bei-Ō kairanjikki*, vol. 4, pp. 177-8. For a detailed treatment of this musuem, see Okuda, 'Iwakura shisetsudan ga mita Sūeden', pp. 49f.
71 *Aftonbladet* 28 April 1873, *Stockholms Dagblad* 28 April 1873.
72 Kume, *Bei-Ō kairanjikki*, vol. 4, pp. 180-2.
73 Okuda, 'Iwakura shisetsudan ga mita Sūeden', p. 55. Christina Nilsson, curator of the archives of the Stockholm County Council which keeps the papers of the Conradsberg Hospital has been unable to trace any documents relating to a visit by the Japanese. Personal communication, 30 July 1997.
74 *Aftonbladet* 28 April 1873, *Stockholms Dagblad* 28 April 1873. 'Den stumma från Portici' was an opera in five acts by Eugene Scribe and Germain Delarigue. See G. Wingren, *Svensk dramatisk litteratur under åren 1840-1913* (Swedish dramatic literature 1840-1913). Uppsala 1914, p. 158.
75 'Krönika' (Chronicle), *Svalan, weckotidning för familiekretsar, utgifven af Lea*, no. 18, 2 May 1873.
76 *Aftonbladet* 28 April 1873.
77 Mayo, 'The Western Education of Kume Kunitake', p. 58.
78 *Aftonbladet* 29 April 1873. This report is reprinted in the *Nya Dagligt Allehanda* 30 April 1873 and the *Stockholms Dagblad* 30 April 1873. Unfortunately, neither the message of the Alliance nor the Japanese answer are found in the archives of the Evangelical Alliance. At a meeting with the board of the Alliance on 20 August 1873 it is reported that the Alliance had met a Japanese mission. See Stockholms stadsarkiv, Evangeliska Alliansens Svenska Avdelning, Protokoll. Huv. Serie 1854-1980: AI, 'Komité-sammanträde den 20 Augusti 1873 (hos Sekr.)'.
79 Okuda, 'Iwakura shisetsudan ga mita Sūeden', p. 57.

80 Kume, *Bei-Ō kairan jikki*, vol. 4, p. 185.
81 They were also exported to Japan. Anton Bæckström (1840-1899), a naval officer employed by the French, reported in a book published in 1871 that he found Swedish matches being sold on the streets of Nagasaki when he visited Japan for three months in 1868, while on an around-the-world trip. See Anton Bæckström, *Ett besök i Japan och Kina jemte bilder från vägen dit öfver Goda-Hoppsudden, Bourbon, Nya Kaledonien, Manilla och Kochinkina. Anteckningar och minnen från en treårig tjenstgöring i franska flottan* (A visit to Japan and China and pictures from along the way, via the Cape of Good Hope, Bourbon, New Caledonia, Manila and Kochin China. Notes and memories from three years in the service of the French navy). Stockholm 1871, p. 185.
82 See Okuda, 'Iwakura shisetsudan ga mita Sūeden', p. 61.
83 *Stockholms Dagblad* 30 April 1873, *Dagens Nyheter* 30 April 1873.
84 For a description, see Kume, *Bei-Ō kairan jikki*, vol. 4, pp. 188-90, and Okuda, 'Iwakura shisetsudan ga mita Sūeden', p. 59.
85 *Dagens Nyheter* 29 April 1873. 'Villars dragoner' was a comical operetta in three acts by J. P. Simon and P. E. Piestre. See Wingren, *Svensk dramatisk litteratur under åren 1840-1913*, p. 162.
86 Okuda, 'Iwakura shisetsudan ga mita Sūeden', p. 61.
87 *Nya Dagligt Allehanda* 28 April 1873, *Stockholms Dagblad* 30 April 1873.
88 *Stockholms Dagblad* 28 April 1873, *Nya Dagligt Allehanda* 28 April 1873.
89 *Dagens Nyheter* 30 April 1873.
90 Kume, *Bei-Ō kairan jikki*, vol. 4, pp. 190f.
91 See Okuda, 'Iwakura shisetsudan ga mita Sūeden', p. 61, Tanaka, *'Datsu-A' no Meiji ishin*, p. 151, and Tanaka, *Iwakura shisetsudan 'Bei-Ō kairan jikki'*, p. 175.
92 See Gudrun Spetze, *Stockholms folkskolor 1842-1882: Ambition och verklighet* (Elementary schools in Stockholm 1842-1882: Ambition and reality). Årsböcker i svensk undervisningshistoria, 72. Uppsala 1992, p. 194.
93 *Stockholms Dagblad* 25 April 1873.
94 The quote from *Nya Dagligt Allehanda* 24 April 1873; cf. *Aftonbladet* 24 April 1873 and *Dagens Nyheter* 25 April 1873.
95 'Ett japanskt drama' (A Japanese drama), *Samtiden, veckoskrift för politik och literatur*. Utgifven af C. F. Bergstedt, no. 20, 17 May 1873, pp. 312f.
96 Charles Lanman, *Leaders of the Meiji Restoration in America*. Re-edited by Y. Okamura. Tokyo 1931, p. vi. This report of the Iwakura mission's visit to the United States was issued first in 1872.
97 Mayo, 'The Western Education of Kume Kunitake', p. 53.
98 Kjell Emanuelson, *Den svensk-norska utrikesförvaltningen 1870-1905: Dess organisations- och verksamhetsförändring* (The Swedish-Norwegian foreign service 1870-1905: Changes in its organization and activity-field). Diss. Bibliotheca Historica Lundensis XLVIII. Lund: CWK Gleerups, 1980, pp. 36ff.
99 RA G2 AB:2. Utrikesdep:ts kameralavdelning – personal och räkenskapsavdelning. Räkenskaper. Tredje huvudtiteln och norska diplom. anslagen. Koncepthuvudboken, 1870-1879, entry no. 486.
100 Slottsarkivet, Hovet, Gratifikationer, 1838-1890, 'Utdelnings-Lista å de Gratificationer . . . hvilka äro gifne af D.D. E.E Japanesiske, Franske, Tyske, Österrikiske, Italienske och Ryska Ambassadörerne samt Holländske och Danske Envoyéerne'.
101 BA, Brev from kungliga, furstliga och enskilda.

CHAPTER 8

1 Iwakura Shōko (editor), *Il Giappone scopre l'Occidente. Una missione diplomatica, 1971-73*, Japanese Cultural Institute, Rome, 1994.
2 Iwakura Shōko (editor), *Iwakura shisetsudan to Itaria*, Kyoto, Kyoto daigaku gakujutsu shuppankai, 1997.
3 For the text in Japanese, *Itari jōyaku futsubun honyaku* (French translation of the treaty with Italy), Tokyo, Kokuritsu kōbunshokan, 2A 33-9, 1101.
4 For the problems arising during the *bakumatsu* on whether the Japanese Authority

that the western powers had to recognise was the Mikado or the Tycoon, see Adolfo Tamburello, 'I trattati internazionali delle potenze occidentali col Giappone. Considerazioni sulle strategie diplomatiche dello shogunato Tokugawa', *Il Giappone*, XXXI, 1993, pp. 177-190.

5 Francesco Ammannati, Silvio Calzolari, *Un viaggio ai confini del mondo 1865-1868. La crociera della pirocorvetta Magenta dai documenti dell'Istituto Geografico Militare*, Florence, published by Sansoni, 1985; Raoul Gueze, 'Fonti archivistiche per la storia delle relazioni italo-giapponesi. Elementi di ricerca', in *Lo stato liberale italiano e l'età Meiji*, Rome, 1987, pp. 191-218.

6 Romano Ugolini, 'La missione Iwakura in Italia: l'inizio del periodo aureo nelle relazioni italo-giapponesi (1873-1896)', in Iwakura Shōko (editor), *Il Giappone scopre l'Occidente. . . .*, *op. cit.*, pp. 25-39.

7 Laura Monaco, 'Relazioni di Sallier de La Tour, primo inviato in Giappone (9 giugno 1867-15 gennaio 1869)', *Il Giappone*, V, 1965, pp. 33-43.

8 Italian companies such as Dell'Oro & Co. (by Isidoro Dell'Oro from Milan) were already established in Yokohama in 1868. See: Yokohama kaikō shiryōkan (ed.), *Yokohama gaikokujin kyoryūchi*, Yokohama, Yūrindō, 1998, p. 82.

9 Claudio Zanier, 'La seta ed i rapporti commerciali italo-giapponesi ai tempi della missione Iwakura', in Iwakura Shōko (editor), *Il Giappone scopre l'Occidente. . . .*, *op. cit.*, pp. 67-74.

10 Telesforo Sarti, *Il parlamento italiano nel cinquantenario dello statuto*, 1898, p. 252.

11 Rossana Prestini, 'Alessandro Fè d'Ostiani e le origini della collezione dei dipinti orientali dei Musei civici d'arte e storia di Brescia. Regesto', in *Dipinti giapponesi a Brescia*, Brescia, Grafo publications, 1995, pp. 169-178.

12 Iwakura Shōko, 'Il Conte Alessandro Fè d'Ostiani e la missione Iwakura', in *Dipinti giappo*, *op. cit.*, p. 39.

13 ASDMAE, *cit.*, env. 1288, no.1, 3.11.1870.

14 ASDMAE, *cit.*, env. 1288, no. 2, 11.11.1870.

15 Various authors, 'La Missione Iwakura', in Iwakura Shōko (editor), *Il Giappone scopre l'Occidente. . . .*, *op. cit.*, pp. 11-16.

16 ASDMAE, *cit.*, env. 1288, no. 17, 22.11.1871.

17 ASDMAE, *cit.*, env. 1288, no. 18, 30.11.1871.

18 ASDMAE. *cit.*, env. 1288, no. 44, 29 January 1873. Quoted in Romano Ugolini, 'Corrispondenza anteriore all'arrivo della missione Iwakura in Italia', in *Prima e dopo la missione Iwakura. Testimonianze inedite*, Japanese Cultural Institute, Rome, 1994, p. 21. We should point out here that, as mentioned in carefully researched studies, Gottfried Wagener (1831-92), one of the *oyatoi gaikokujin* taken on by the Meiji government had been placed in charge of the Japanese representation at the Great Exhibition in Vienna. See Takata Seiji, *Ishin no kagaku seishin. Beio kairan jikki no mita sangyō gijutsu*, Tōkyō, Asahi shinbunsha, 1995, p. 135 onwards. Furthermore, in May 1881, upon the advice of the very same Wagener, the *Tōkyō shokkō gakkō*, Tōkyō School for Workmen (the modern day *Tōkyō kōgyō daidaku*) was founded whose fortunes were to be different from those of the *kōbu bijutsu gakkō*, School of Fine Art – which will be dealt with further on – set up following the suggestion of Count Fè d'Ostiani.

19 ASDMAE, *cit.*, env. 1288, no. 46, 2.3.1873. Quoted in Romano Ugolini, 'Corrispondenza . . .', *op. cit.*, pp. 22-25.

20 Our research was carried out under the supervision of Prof. Iwakura Tomotada and Prof. Iwakura Shōko in the following libraries: (in Rome) the Emanuele II National Central Library and the Modern and Contemporary History Library; (in Naples) the Vittorio Emanuele III National Library, the Lucchesi Palli Library, the Central Library of Naples University Federico II and the newspaper and periodical section of the V. Tucci Library; (in Milan) the Braidense National Library.

21 *Omnibus*, 12th May 1873, p. 175.

22 *Il Giornale di Napoli*, 13th April 1873, p. 2. It should be pointed out that during the Iwakura mission the statesmen who stayed behind in Japan replaced the traditional Japanese calender with the Gregorian calender.

23 *La Gazzetta di Venezia*, 15th April 1873.
24 *L'Osservatore Romano*, 14th May 1873, p. 3.
25 Iwakura Shōko, 'Itariajin no mita Iwakura shisetsudan – Venezia no baai, in *Shūjitsu ronsō*, XXIII, 1993, pp. 75-96.
26 *Il Secolo*, 26th May 1873, p. 2.
27 Kume Kunitake, *Tokumei zenken taishi Beiō kairan jikki*, Tōkyō, Iwanami shoten, 1992, IV.
28 *Ibidem*, pp. 355-6.
29 This issue is dealt with in: Eugene Soviak, 'On the Nature of Western Progress: The Journal of the Iwakura Embassy', in *Tradition and Modernisation in Japanese Culture*, edited by Donald H. Shively, Princeton University Press, 1971, pp. 7-34.
30 See Isabella L. Bird's description of her journey through Japan in 1878. Isabella Bird (translated by Takanashi Kenkichi), *Nihon okuchi kikō* (original title: *Unbeaten Tracks in Japan*), Tokyo, Heibonsha, 1987 (XII ed.) *passim*.
31 Kume Kunitake, *op. cit.*, IV, p. 338.
32 Silvana De Maio, 'La missione Iwakura e la tecnologia occidentale, in Iwakura Shōko (editor), *Il Giappone scopre l'Occidente. . . .*, *op. cit.*, p. 65.
33 Iwakura Shōko, 'Iwakura shisetsudan no Itaria ni okeru kōtei' (Itinerary of the Iwakura mission in Italy), in *The Research Bulletin of Shūjitsu Women's University and Shūjitsu Junior College*, XXII, 1992, pp. 273-288.
34 Tanaka Akira, 'Iwakura shisetsudan to *Beiō kairan jikki*, in Tanaka Akira and Takata Seiji (editors), *Beiō kairan jikki no gakusaitaki kenkyū*, Sapporo, Hokkaidō daigaku tosho kankō kai, p. 34.
35 Kume Kunitake, *op. cit.*, IV, p. 275.
36 Kume Kunitake, *op. cit.*, IV, p. 276 and comment by Donald Keene in *Modern Japanese Diaries. The Japanese at Home and Abroad as Revealed Through Their Diaries*, New York, 1995, p. 104.
37 Iwakura Shōko, 'La Missione Iwakura e l'arte italiana', in *Il Giappone scopre l'Occidente. . .*, *op. cit.*, pp. 75-82.
38 Kotani Toshiji, 'Iwakura shisetsudan no Itaria taiken', in *Beio kairan jikki wo yomu. 1870 nendai no sekai to Nihon*, Kyōto, Hōritsu bunkasha, 1995, pp. 303-310.
39 'The Times' 14 May 1873, in Kokusai nyūsu jiten shuppan iinkai (ed.), *G*, Tōkyō, 1989, p. 604.
40 Kume Kunitake, *op. cit.*, IV, pp. 305-306.
41 Kume Kunitake, *op. cit.*, IV, p. 307 onwards.
42 Kume Kunitake, *op. cit.*, IV, pp. 322-323.
43 This Roman city completely submerged by vulcanic ash and lapilli during an eruption of Mount Vesuvius in 79 AD lay hidden and forgotten about until the mid-1700s when archaeological digs were finally undertaken.
44 During the eruption of Mount Vesuvius in 79 AD Herculaneum was buried by flows of lava and mud, and at the time of the mission only a small part of the underground town had been unearthed by archaeologists and this was only visible by candlelight.
45 Kume Kunitake, *op. cit.*, IV, pp. 330-335.
46 Kume Kunitake, *op. cit.*, IV, p. 348.
47 Adriana Boscaro, 'I primi giapponesi in Italia', in Iwakura Shōko (editor), *Il Giappone scopre l'Occidente. . .*, *op. cit.*, pp. 59-62.
48 Kume Kunitake, *op. cit.*, IV, pp. 351-352.
49 *La Sentinella Bresciana*, 30 May 1873.
50 Adolfo Tamburello, 'La Missione Iwakura nella prima internazionalità del Giappone', in Iwakura Shōko (editor), *Il Giappone scopre l'Occidente. . . .*, *op. cit.*, pp. 56-57.
51 Ōkurashō insatsukyoku kinenkan (ed.), *Oyatoi gaikokujin Chiossone botsugo 100nen ten. – Sono gyōseki to Meiji no insatsu bunka -*, Tokyo, 1997.
52 Tokyo to rekishi bunka zaidan (ed.), *Fontanesi to Nihon no kindai bijutsu*, Tokyo, 1997.
53 Regarding the construction of the school and its organisation, see *Bijutsu (Kōbushō)*, Tokyo, Kokuritsu kōbunshokan, 2A 33-5, 126.
54 Translated from: Silvana De Maio, 'La missione Iwakura nella stampa italiana', in-

Prima e dopo. . ., *op. cit.*, pp. 91-122.

CHAPTER 9

1 Yoshikawa Hiroyuki, 'The Second Henry Dyer Symposium', in *The Henry Dyer Symposium*, Tokyo, 1997, pp. 6-7.
2 Kawanabe Kasumi *et al.* (edited by), *Rokumeikan no kenchikuka Josiah Conder ten zuroku*, Tokyo, 1997.
3 Ian Nish, *Japanese Foreign Policy 1869-1942}*, London, Routledge & Kegan Paul, 1977, p. 18.
4 Istituto Giapponese di Cultura di Roma (edited by), *Il Giappone scopre l'Occidente. Una missione diplomatica, 1871-1873*, Roma, 1994, pp. 11-12.
5 Guido Verbeck, *Brief Sketch*, in Albert Altman, 'Guido Verbeck and the Iwakura Embassy', *Japan Quarterly*, XIII, (1966), p. 61.
6 Ian Nish, *op. cit.*, 1977, p. 19.
7 Ishii Kendō, *Meiji jibutsu kigen* (reprint) 3, Tokyo: Chikuma gakugei bunko, 1997, p. 152.
8 W. G. Beasley, 'The Iwakura Mission in Britain, 1872', in *History Today*, XXXI (1981), p. 31.
9 Iida Ken'ichi, *Nihon kindai shisō taikei. 14: kagaku to gijutsu*, Tokyo: Iwanami shoten, 1989, p. 462.
10 Miyoshi Nobuhiro, *Nihon kōgyō kyōiku seiritsushi no kenky*, Tokyo: Kazama shobō, p. 379.
11 Yaguchi Hajime, *History of Industrial Education in Japan*, Japanese National Commission for Unesco, 1969, p. 2.
12 Henry Dyer, *Japan in World Politics*, London, 1909, pp. 310-12.
13 W.H. Brock, 'The Japanese Connexion: Engineering in Tokyo, London, and Glasgow at the end of the nineteenth century', *The British Journal for the History of Science*, XIV (1981), pp. 227-43.
14 Olive Checkland, *Britain's Encounter with Meiji Japan, 1868-1912*, London, Macmillan Press, 1989. See also Japanese translation: Sugiyama Chūhei and Tamaki Norio (translators), Olive Checkland, *Meiji Nihon to Igirisu. Deai, gijutsu iten, netto wāku no keisei*, Tokyo: Hōsei daigaku shuppankyoku, 1996.
15 Olive Checkland, '"Working at their Profession": Japanese Engineers in Britain before 1914', in Ian Nish (edited by), *Britain & Japan. Biographical Portraits*, Vol. I Folkestone: Japan Library, 1994, p. 45.
16 Miyoshi Nobuhiro, *op. cit.*, 1979; Miyoshi Nobuhiro, *Dyer no Nihon*, Tokyo: Fukumura shuppan, 1989.
17 Kita Masami, *Kokusai Nihon wo hiraita hitobito: Nihon to Sukottorando no kizuna*, Tokyo: Dōbunkan, 1984.
18 Olive and Sydney Checkland, 'British and Japanese Economic Interaction under the Early Meiji: the Takashima Coal Mine 1868-88', in *Business History*, XXVI (July 1984), p. 151.
19 J.K. Fairbank *et al.*, 'The Influence of Modern Western Science and Technology on Japan and China', in *Explorations in Entrepreneurial History*, VII, 1955, p. 189.
20 Recently the mathematics notebooks of Tatsumi Hajime, student in Yokosuka's *Kōsha* have been found out and new attention is paid to the education system in that institution. I wish here to thank Prof. Hashimoto Takehiko of Tokyo University who has provided me a still unpublished list of the notebooks. See also: Sasaki Chikara, 'Tatsumi Hajime bunsho no sūgakushiteki igi', *Sūgaku seminā*, Feb. 1998, pp. 2-5.
21 Hayashi Takeshi, *Kindai Nihon no gijutsu to gijutsu seisaku*, Tokyo: Kokusai rengō daigaku, 1986, p. 171.
22 Tomita Hitoshi, Nishibori Akira, *Yokosuka seitetsujo no hitobito*, Tokyo: Yūrindō, 1983, p. 141.
23 *Ibid*, p. 145.
24 *Ibid*, p. 149.
25 *Ibid*, p. 151.

26 Due to the necessity of monitoring earthquakes for the construction of lighthouses, Japanese asked Italian Professor Palmieri, director of the Vesuvius Observatory, to reproduce his seismograph that would have been used in Japan. See: Silvana De Maio, 'La missione Iwakura e la tecnologia occidentale', *Il Giappone scopre l'Occidente. Una missione diplomatica 1871-73*, Istituto Giapponese di Cultura di Roma, 1994, p. 65; Izumi Yokoyama & Antonio Nazzaro, 'History of the Italian-Japanese Cooperation in Volcano Geophysics', *The Safe City*, Napoli, 1996, p. 24.
27 Silvana De Maio, 'Gli *oyatoi gaikokujin* e l'introduzione dell'ingegneria civile in Giappone. Richard Henry Brunton: ingegnere 'figlio del suo tempo'. I parte', *Il Giappone*, XXXI, Roma, 1993, pp. 209-236.
28 Hugh Cortazzi, 'The Pestilently Active Minister: Dr. Willis's Comments on Sir Harry Parkes', in *Monumenta Nipponica*, XXXIX, (1984), p. 147.
29 Richard Henry Brunton, *Building Japan 1868-1876*, Folkestone: Japan Library, 1991, pp. 55-6.
30 Miyoshi Nobuhiro, *op. cit.*, 1979, p. 229.
31 Kaijō hoanchō tōdaibu (edited by), *Nihon tōdaishi*, Tokyo: Tōkōkai, 1969, pp. 131-2.
32 Tessa Morris-Suzuki, *The Technological Transformation of Japan. From the Seventeenth to the Twenty-first Century*, Cambridge University Press, 1994, pp. 81-2.
33 W. Innes Addison (compiled by), *A Roll of the Graduates of the University of Glasgow from December 1727 to December 1897*, Glasgow, 1898, p. 174.
34 Muramatsu Teijirō, *Westerners in the Modernization of Japan*, Tokyo, 1995, pp. 194-200.
35 Kyūkōbu daigakkō hensankai, *Kyūkōbu daigakkō shiryō*, Tokyo, 1978, p. 3.
36 For the role played by the Chōshū group in the early Meiji government, see e.g.: Hiromi Naoki, *Nihon kanryōshi*, Tokyo, Daiyamondo-sha, 1997, tables pp. 21 and 23.
37 Muramatsu Teijirō *et al.*, *High-tech Nippon tanjō ten. Meiji no kindaika isan*, Tokyo, Kokuritsu kagaku hakubutsukan, 1997, p. 84.
38 Kita Masami, 'Kōbu daigakkō token Henry Dyer', in Shimada Tadashi *et al.* (ed.), *The Yatoi. Oyatoi gaikokujin no sōgōteki kenkyū*, Kyōto, 1990, pp. 292-313.
39 Anon., 'Kōgakukai ichigatsu no tsūjō kai to shinnen enkai', in *Kōgakukaishi*, CX, 1891, p. 105.
40 Ishii Kendō, *Meiji jibutsu kigen* (reprint) 4, Tokyo: Chikuma gakugei bunko, 1997, p. 146.
41 Endō Kazuo, 'Iwakura shisetsudan to seiyō gijutsu', in Tanaka Akira and Takata Seiji (edited by), *Beiō kairan jikki no gakusaiteki kenkyū*, Hokkaidō Daigaku tosho hakkōkai, 1993, p. 255. See also: Miyoshi Nobuhiro, *op. cit.*, 1989, pp. 33-41.
42 Henry Dyer, *Dai Nippon. The Britain of the East. A study in national evolution*, London, 1905, pp. 1-2. Ujihashi T., 'Enjiniaringu kyōiku, kotohajime. Meiji shoki no Eikoku to no kakawari', *Tōkyō kuronikuru*, n. 301, 1996, p. 7.
43 Ishiyama Hiroshi, 'Meiji kagaku no onjintachi (13). Henry Dyer', *Kagaku gijutsu bunken sābisu*, n. 35, 1973, p. 38. However not all the professors arrived in Japan with the same ship. See Katō Shōji, 'Henry Dyer no kekkon', in *UP* (Tokyo Daigaku Shuppankai), n. 304, 1998, pp. 16-20.
44 Usami Tatsuo (transl. by), *Meiji Nihon wo sasaeta Eikokujin. Jishingakusha Mirun den*, Tokyo: Nihon hōsō shuppan kyōkai, 1982.
45 Dallas Finn, *Meiji Revisited. The Sites of Victorian Japan*, New York: Weatherhill, 1995, p. 18. Hatakeyama Kenji, *Rokumeikan wo tsukutta otoko. Oyatoi kenchikuka Josiah Conder no shōgai*, Tokyo: Kawade shobō, 1998.
46 The Engineering College building, planned by Charles Alfred Chastel de Boinville, was sometimes used by the government for official functions like the visit of General Grant on 8 July 1879. Richard T. Chang, 'General Grant's 1879 Visit to Japan', *Monumenta Nipponica*, XXIV, 4, 1969, pp. 386-387. Chastel de Boinville arrived from Paris to Glasgow in 1871 and one year later left for Japan. See: Campbell Douglas, 'The Late Charles Alfred Chastel de Boinville', *Journal of the Royal Institute of British Architects*, 4, 1896-97, pp. 359-360.
47 Imperial College of Engineering, Tokei, *Calendar. Session MDCCCLXXVI-LXXVII*, Tokyo, 1876, pp. 39-55.
48 *The Japan Weekly Mail*, 18 Sept. 1875, pp. 810-16.

49 *The Japan Weekly Mail*, 25 Sept. 1875, pp. 853-5. See also Brunton's reply: *The Japan Weekly Mail*, 2 Oct. 1875, pp. 872-3.
50 Here I would like to thank Prof. Janet Hunter of London School of Economics who has kindly allowed me to read her BA dissertation, presented at the University of Sheffield in 1971 titled: *The Development of Technical Education in Japan – Foreign Teachers at the Imperial College of Engineering 1872-1885*, p. 15. See also: Janet Hunter, 'British Training for Japanese Engineers: the Case of Kikuchi Kyōzō (1859-1942)', in Hugh Cortazzi and Gordon Daniels (ed. by), *Britain and Japan 1859-1991. Themes and Personalities*, London, Routledge, 1991, pp. 137-146.
51 Henry Dyer, *op. cit.*, 1909, pp. 4-5.
52 Herbert Passin, *Society and Education in Japan*, Columbia University, 1965, p. 95.
53 Imperial College of Engineering, Tokei, *op. cit.*, 1876, p. 15.
54 W.H. Brock, *op. cit.*, 1981, p. 232. Nakayama Shigeru, 'Kōbu daigaku no genryū – Suisu renpō kōka gakuin ni tsuite', *Butsurigakushi kenkyū*, III (1966), pp. 1-5.
55 Albert Altman, 'Guido Verbeck and the Iwakura Embassy', in *Japan Quarterly*, XIII, (1966), p. 58.
56 Henry Dyer, *op. cit.*, 1909, p. 121.
57 *Ibid*, pp. 310-12.
58 Henry Dyer, *op. cit.*, 1905, p. 90.
59 Ian Nish, *op. cit.*, 1977, p. 22.
60 Olive Checkland, *op. cit.*, 1989, p. 87.
61 See for example: Miyoshi Shinrokurō, *Locomotive Engines*, 1879, Imperial College of Engineering, Tokyo (unpublished thesis):

PART I History of Locomotives and Tables of Locomotives in Our Country.

PART II General Theory of Engine together with Constructions and Descriptions of the details of Engine.

PART III General Theory of Locomotive Boilers together with Construction and Descriptions of Details of the Boiler.

PART IV General Theory of the Carriage together with Constructions and Descriptions of Details of Carriage

PART V Theory of Stability of the Locomotive and Way of Designing of Locomotive

62 Ichikawa Kōji, *Marine Engines*, 1879, Imperial College of Engineering, Tokyo (unpublished thesis).
63 Harry D. Harootunian, 'The Economic Rehabilitation of the Samurai in the Early Meiji Period', in *Journal of Asian Studies*, XIX, (1960), p. 435.
64 (. . .) Boys here have not had fathers, and uncles, and brothers, and so on, who have been and are engineers. They have not been able yet to live, so to speak, in a natural atmosphere of engineering from the time of their birth. Then, again, the educated engineer here has not yet grasped the fact that to soil his hands with manual labour, with the object of mastering the practical part of his training, does not necessarily lower his dignity. It is only of late years that the better class Japanese have descended to trade, or adopted a profession other than that of arms (. . .).' Anon., 'Modern Japan. – Industrial and Scientific. XIII. The Training of Engineers', *The Engineer*, 10 Dec. 1897, pp. 567-8.

CHAPTER 10

1 This paper has been translated by Malcolm Hicks. Minatomachi. *Yokohama no toshi no keiseishi* (Yokohama 1981), p. 15.
2 Pat Barr, *The Coming of the Barbarians. A Story of the Western Settlement in Japan 1853-1870* (London 1967), p. 186; Pat Barr, *The Deer Cry Pavilion. A Story of Westerners in Japan 1868-1905* (Bristol) 1968, pp. 59, 101, 109; Minatomachi, p. 31. There were over 30,000 Japanese in Yokohama by 1872. Paul C. Blum, Yokohama in 1872 (Tokyo 1983), p. 1.
3 William Elliot Griffis, *The Mikado's Empire* (New York 1976), p. 350.
4 Barr, 1868-1905, p. 57; Blum, p. 32.
5 Barr, 1868-1905, p. 57; Blum, pp. 4, 47-51; Harold S. Williams, *Foreigners in Mikadoland* (Tokyo 1972), pp. 89-91.

6 Barr, 1868-1905, pp. 185-186; Williams, pp. 109, 229-243.
7 Barr, 1868-1905, p. 58.
8 Barr, 1868-1905, pp. 155; John R. Black, *Young Japan. Yokohama and Yedo 1858-79*, Volume One (With an Introduction by Grace Fox. New York 1883. Tokyo 1868), pp. 379-380; Blum, pp. 8-9; Griffis, p. 331.
9 Griffis, pp. 341-342. See Hugh Cortazzi, *Victorians in Japan. In and around the Treaty ports* (London), passim; Grace Fox, *Britain and Japan 1858-1883* (Oxford 1969), passim; Olavi K. Fält, *The Clash of Interests. The transformation of Japan in 1861-1881 in the eyes of the local Anglo-Saxon press* (Studia Historica Septentrionalia 18. Jyväskylä 1990), passim; *Britain & Japan. Biographical Portraits.* edited by Ian Nish (Japan Library 1994). passim; M. Paske-Smith, C.B.E., *Western Barbarians in Japan and Formosa in Tokugawa Days 1603-1868* (Second Edition. New York 1968), passim.
10 Blum, p. 28.
11 Griffis, p. 340-341; Barr, 1868-1905, pp. 63-64, 109, 111; Blum, pp. 35-36.
12 *Hong List and Directory* for 1875, pp. 7-10.
13 Ibid.
14 Yokohama Abstinence Society, *The Japan Weekly Mail* 24.10.1874; Barr, 1868-1905, p. 71.
15 *Hong List and Directory* for 1876, pp. 15-17.
16 *Japan Herald Directory* 1872, p. 4.
17 Carlton J.H. Hayes, *A Generation of Materialism 1871-1900* (New York 1963), p. 331; Eugen Weber, 'Pierre de Coubertin and the Introduction of Organised Sport in France' (*Journal of Contemporary History*, Vol 5 Number 2 1970), pp. 6-7.
18 Stella Margetson, *Leisure and Pleasure in the Nineteenth Century* (London 1969), pp. 52-61; W. J. Reader, *Life in Victorian England* (Third Impression. London 1967), pp. 31-32, 108, 134, 148-149.
19 *Hong List and Directory* for 1875, pp. 7-10; *Hong List and Directory* for 1876, pp. 15-17.
20 *The Japan Weekly Mail* 1874 passim.
21 *The Japan Weekly Mail* 1874 passim.
22 *The Japan Weekly Mail* 1874 passim.
23 *The Japan Weekly Mail* 1874 passim.
24 *The Japan Weekly Mail* 1874 passim; *The Japan Daily Herald* passim.
25 *The Japan Weekly Mail* 1874 passim; *The Japan Daily Herald* 1874 passim.
26 Barr, 1868-1905, pp. 113-114, 240-243.
27 Barr, 1868-1905, p. 114.
28 Griffis, p. 352.
29 The Bluff Gardens, *The Japan Weekly Mail* 7.3.1874.
30 Yokohama Rifle Association, *The Japan Weekly Mail* 28.11.1874; Yokohama Rifle Association, *The Japan Daily Herald* 24.11.1874.

CHAPTER 11

1 Miyachi 1979.
2 Tanaka 1991 p.368.
3 Tanaka 1991 pp.372-374
4 Okubo 1988, p. 92.
5 Kume 1911.
6 Shigeno 1880.
7 Shigeno 1890.
8 Kume 1893.
9 Kurasawa 1975 pp.667-669, Shigeno 1880.
10 Tanaka and Miyachi 1991 pp.260-272.
11 Rieß 1890.
12 Imai 1939.

AFTERMATH AND ASSESSMENT

1. James L. Huffman, *Politics of the Meiji Press: The life of Fukuchi Genichiro*, Honolulu: Uni-

versity Press of Hawaii, 1980, pp. 70-2. I am grateful for this reference to Professor Benami Shillony of the Hebrew University, Jerusalem, himself a participant at the conference. Sidney D. Brown and Akiko Hirota, *The Diary of Kido Takayoshi*, vol. 2, Tokyo: University Press, 1985, pp. 349-50. *Japan Mail*, 10 Feb. 1874

2. Kido, *Diary*, p. 382, entry for 18 Oct. 1873 in which he admits to being 'terribly distressed to think that matters have reached such a state.' On the tensions within the Meiji leadership, see Okubo Toshiaki (ed.), *Iwakura shisetsu no kenkyu* Tokyo: Munetaka Shobo, 1976, pp. 15-26, 53-87

3. *Japan Mail*, 23 Jan. 1874. Haga Toru, 'Western Cities as observed by the Iwakura Mission' in *Japan Foundation Newsletter*, 18(1990), 1-9

4. *Japan Mail*, 23 Jan. 1874

5. R.H. Brunton, *Building Japan, 1868-76*, Folkestone: Japan Library, 1991, p. 134

6. *Japan Mail*, 23 Jan. 1874

7. Note on an interview between Granville and Iwakura, 22 Nov. 1872 in Ian Nish (ed.), *British Documents on Foreign Affairs*, Part I, Series E: Asia, 1860-1914, vol. 1, Washington: UPA, 1989, doc. 260. [Hereafter 'BDOFA'] See also Ian Nish, 'Iwakura Mission in Britain' in *Proceedings of the Japan Society*, 122(1993), 52-64

8. *Japan Weekly Mail*, 14 Dec. 1872

9. Samuel Mossman, *New Japan: The Land of the Rising Sun*, London: John Murray, 1873, p. 433. Cf Yokoyama Toshio, *Japan in the Victorian Mind*, London: Macmillan, 1987, pp. 110-12, 115-24

10. *Japan Weekly Mail*, 16 Nov. 1872

11. Shoko Iwakura, *Iwakura shisetsudan to Itariya*, Kyoto: University Press, 1997, pp. 174-5

12. United Presbyterian Church to Granville, 16 Nov. 1872 in *BDOFA*, vol I, doc. 270

13. Akiko Ohta, 'The Iwakura Mission in Britain: their observations on education and Victorian society' in *International Studies* (STICERD, LSE), IS/98/349, 17-35

INDEX

I have omitted from this index the following members of the Iwakura mission whose names recur on practically every page: Iwakura Tomomi, Kido Takayoshi, Okubo Toshimichi, Ito Hirobumi, Yamaguchi Naoyoshi and Kume Kunitake. I have not included countries to which chapters are devoted.